SUCCESS STORIES

Dear Jyl,

First I want to commend you on your latest book. I feel I've died and gone to Heaven. You really have a winner! I went on a so-called new way of eating (I can't call it a diet). I just cut out the fat. Then after a struggle of menus I discovered your book. What a blessing. G-d bless you Jyl, you are a doll. Your devoted and new-found friend and lover of your books. Keep up the good work.

Shirley Kent

Dear Jyl,

I just purchased all of your cookbooks after reading *Ladies Home Journal* - GREAT ARTICLE! GREAT COOKBOOKS! DELICIOUS RECIPES! One of our favorites are Garlic Scallops and Angel Hair Pasta. Everyone loves it! "Thanx" a bunch!

Jennifer Koslock

Dear Jyl,

I have two reasons our family is changing to a nonfat lifestyle. One, I've gained too much weight over the last couple of years and now that the big "40" is getting close it's not been easy to lose it. The second, is because my husband ended up in the hospital two weeks ago with chest pressure. He had a Heart Cath, which ended up to be good news of clean arteries, but he has high cholesterol that is genetic and the Cardiologist warned that if we didn't make some lifestyle changes of diet and exercise he would be quite certain to see us in the future with a different result.

We've both talked about changing things for a while but never really made a commitment. We are now working at changing old habits but the wonderful thing is I've found delicious recipes, so we don't miss the bad stuff. We look forward to trying all your recipes.

Cheryl Eggert

Dear Jyl,

Your book on breads will complete my collection of your books. Thank you for your contribution to fat-free everywhere!

Patricia Morrison

Dear Jyl,

Thanks so much for your newest cookbook, "The FAT FREE Living SUPER COOKBOOK". I've lost another 10 pounds since I last wrote you (60 pounds so far). I really like how you have listed the food exchanges for each serving size. I love all the recipes that I've tried from your other four books. Thanks for being so caring and supportive to help everyone live healthier and fat-free lives!

Gloria Blankschien

Dear Jyl,

I want to THANK YOU for your four FAT FREE COOKBOOKS. About three years ago I was turned on to FAT FREE LIVING after having read Dr. Dean Ornich's book, "Eat More, Weigh Less", and embraced the concept that damage done physically could be reversed with healthy eating. Shortly thereafter, I came across your first book because I wanted something to simplify meal preparation and still be appetizing. As a result of following this regimen I shed 95 pounds and have not gained back one since. I have been intrigued, each new offering through book number four has been a delectable adventure.

Keep up the splendid work and again, I say THANK YOU!

Fred Moore

Dear Jyl,

I have the great privilege of owning <u>Recipes for FAT FREE Living Cookbook 2</u>. I received it as a birthday gift, I use it regularly. It has helped me greatly, as I am on a mission of losing weight. I have already lost 108 pounds in less than one year. This is the mission of a lifetime. I exercise daily, and watch what I eat. Thank you!

Maryelizabeth DaPonte

Dear Jyl,

As a person who has heart disease as well as diabetes, I not only eat fat-free but also sugar-free. I have all of your books and have purchased them as gifts for family members and friends. Thanks to you for helping all of us have a healthier life-style.

Peggy Breadon

Dear Jyl,

I have recently purchased your FAT FREE Living SUPER COOKBOOK. We are impressed with the results of your recipes, menus and suggestions. We do appreciate your efforts to help us have a healthy lifestyle.

I had an angioplasty three years ago that resulted in a heart attack. There is heart disease in my family. Anyway, I am always on the lookout for new ideas and ways to prepare tasty meals. We are in our late sixties and semi-retired. I'd love to order all four of the other cookbooks. Yours very truly,

Mrs. John W. Raine

Dear Mrs. Steinback,

I purchased your FAT FREE Living SUPER COOKBOOK after seeing you on the CBS Morning Show last week. We are on an extremely low-fat diet since my husband's quintuple by-pass surgery (at age 47) two years ago. Needless to say, I had to learn how to cook all over again. I just love your cookbook! Thanks for the great work! It's so disappointing to see a "low-fat" recipe, then they say "only 28 grams of fat" or something like that! I really appreciate your delicious, truly fat-free recipes!!!

Jane Pogorzelski

Dear Jyl,

I just love your books! I have all your books! These are a must in our home and never leave my kitchen. Keep up the great work!

Tonya Bailey

Dear Jyl,

My husband had a heart attack in February. He's 55 years old. I love your books. It's the only books I have to use. His cholesterol went from 267 to 180 in two months.

Judith A. Brazeal

Dear Jyl,

Your books are a blessing indeed. This FAT FREE life we are living is really paying dividends...we are eating probably more than ever before but our bodies are getting better every day. It all started just after Christmas when one night I experienced what we thought might be a heart attack. It was pretty frightening at the time and I was admitted to the hospital for observation overnight and the next day they did a catherization along with a bunch of other tests. My heart was o.k. but they found my gallbladder was full of stones. So out it came and I returned home full of resolutions to lose weight and get healthy!

We drove down to our local bookstore and I searched for help in the diet section and found your books. You have been my guiding light ever since. I went right through my cupboards and threw out (or gave away) everything that had fat in it and then we went and spent hours in the supermarkets searching for fat-free foods.

My son came home from Atlanta last week and he said I look like a different person. I've lost 28 pounds so far and am very excited. It's as though after all these years of struggling to lose weight. I've been given the key to the door. Kindest Regards,

Jackie Forman

Jyl,

I was given the cookbook for Christmas. We love it - my boyfriend made me my favorite dish of FAT FREE Fettuccine Alfredo for Valentines Day and it tasted better than any I have had at restaurants! I am hooked and now learning to cook NO FAT meals. Your book was a blessing to me because I am losing weight without starving. Thanks!

Molly Britton

Jyl,

I watch every fat gram! I have gone from 207 to 132 pounds from watching the fat. Thank you for your help! Keep up the good work!

P.S. My husband even loves the meals I've fixed from FAT FREE LIVING!

Cheryl L. White

Dear Jyl,

I want to let you know I LOVE YOUR COOKBOOKS! We recently celebrated a birthday at the office, and I made the blueberry muffins and everyone loved them. I made sure to let everyone know that they were from the FAT FREE LIVING Cookbook. It is definitely a recipe I will make again and again. I really like how fat free the recipes are, and they are also so very easy. It takes hardly any time to prepare the recipes, being a single mom of two, I really like and need that!

Thank you again for your motivation, inspiration and lessons on FAT FREE LIVING!

Colleen Jammer

Dear Jyl,

Thank you very much for the beautiful and delicious recipes for the FAT FREE Breads. They have been a huge success at our weight watcher group. Now I need all of your other cookbooks.

Many thanks!

Paulette Pucker

Dear Jyl,

My mother brought home your books, FAT FREE Living Cookbooks just the other day. Let me tell you, I am so excited! I have a million cookbooks that are low fat and light recipes, but they don't cut it! I have already tried some of your recipes and I am very happy with these books. They are NONFAT, not light or low fat only! But FAT FREE! Thank you!

Sincerely, a very faithful FAT FREE eater and your fan!

Romina Mazlumian

The FAT FREE LIVING FAMILY COOKBOOK

* * *

Jyl Steinback

FAT FREE LIVING, INC.

The FAT FREE LIVING FAMILY COOKBOOK

Please consult your doctor with any personal questions about yourself and this book. Jyl Steinback and Fat Free Living, Inc. disclaim all liability in connection with the use of this book.

Fat Free Living, Inc. 15202 N. 50th Place, Scottsdale, AZ 85254
(602) 996-6300; Fax (602) 996-9897; E-Mail fatfree@dancris.com
Visit our Web Site at www.fatfreeliving.com

 Fat Free Living, Inc.

Printed in the United States of America

ISBN 0-9636876-9-7

First Printing: January 1998

Cover photos by Elliot Lincis, Camel Studios
Cover design by Jim Nissen, JNA Design
    and Michael Swaine, Michael Swaine Design

The recipes in this book were analyzed using the Nutrients III and IV nutrient analysis program. Products not listed on the original data base were added using the nutrition facts section of the product label. All nutrients were rounded to the nearest whole number.

Debra Kohl, MS.RD

ATTENTION SCHOOLS AND CORPORATIONS
Fat Free Living Cookbooks are available
at quantity discounts with bulk purchase
for educational, business, or sales
promotional use. For information write to:
    Fat Free Living, Inc.
    15202 N. 50th Place
    Scottsdale, Arizona 85254
    (602) 996-6300

ACKNOWLEDGMENTS

The FAT FREE LIVING FAMILY COOKBOOK is HERE! Today, thousands of families are discovering the benefits of healthy living. Everywhere you look, families are out walking, biking, swimming and doing some fun activity. In the home, healthier foods have hit the cabinets, refrigerators and dinner tables. For most of us, the first priority in our lives is our family. Because life is too short, we need to get the most out of it while we're here. To do that requires health. So, thank you all for buying the FAT FREE LIVING FAMILY COOKBOOK…it is definitely a step in the healthy direction.

Gary, we are a lucky pair! We dream big, aim high, expect the BEST, laugh often, believe in each other, and family always comes first. Thank you for always walking next to me and being my very "bestest" friend. I love you with all of my heart.

Jamie and Scott, you are growing up way too fast for me! You're such a blessing in my life. I know the phone is glued to my ear sometimes but you both are glued to my heart 24 hours a day. You are both #1 and I think you are SENSATIONAL! I love you more than life! Thank you!

Mom and Dad, Betty and Bill Levy, it's been a lucky year for all of us this year and we are very blessed for our good fortune of health and family. As you always tell me, "keep those cards and letters coming." I love you both very much and I thank our lucky stars for all the love that we share.

Jacie, thanks for all of your wonderful support and love.

Jeff, Diane, Alex and Casey, I wish you lots of success with JOURNEY HOME. What a wonderful way to help people live healthier lives. You are a gift as a family and to everyone you touch.

Snooky and Harlan Steinback (my mother and father-in-law), you're great! I love you lots and I love my fat-free bagels. Thanks for always going the extra for making our lives so special.

I am extremely thankful for the opportunity to work with each and every-one of you. You have been a gift in my life and I thank you all for helping make this book possible.

Mikki Eveloff, you are one in a million! I am thankful for you! For your time, positive energy, persistence, motivation, dedication, and very special friendship. Thank you for everything!

Debbie Kohl, as you know, I am not a night person, but you still don't give up on me! Thank you for all of your help and wonderful support! Debra Kohl is a Registered Dietitian with a master's degree in Nutrition and Dietetics and you can reach her services at (602) 266-0324.

INTRODUCTION

Watch the sugar, watch the fat...A little of this and none of that. This is "good" and those are "bad"...It drives you crazy, makes you mad. Forget the diet, numbers too...A very simple thing to do. Follow some of these great tips...whittle inches from those hips. Healthy living here and now...simple tips to show you how. From the kitchen, foods and tools...shopping tips but never rules. Superfoods and Snacks for you...Substitutes and options too. Dining in or eating out...Healthy choices, there's no doubt! Training tips and exercise...Keeps you healthy, keeps you wise. Fight the cravings, fight the urge...Tips for when you want to splurge. Getting fit and healthy too...Now's the time, it's up to you!

1. Your body is 70% water. Eat your "water" foods first. They are low in calories and high in nutrients.
   - fruits
   - vegetables
   - water (drinking 6-8 glasses a day). Try sparkling water, water with lemon, 1/2 juice and 1/2 water, and enjoy!
2. Eat plenty of whole grain products (breads, cereal, pasta, rice, provide B-vitamins and complex carbohydrates).
3. Choose lean sources of protein (fat-free chicken, seafood and fish, egg whites, or egg substitutes, low-fat dairy products, beans and legumes).
4. Keep a close watch on fat and sugar intake. Stay away from fried foods, margarine or butter, cream, salad dressing, oils, sugar, soft drinks, rich desserts, candy, cookies.
5. Add more fiber to your diet. It fills you up and it's healthy. The more fiber-rich a diet the healthier you are going to be. You need about 25 grams a day. (The average person has about 10-15 grams a day.)
6. Exercise! DO IT! No matter how little time you spend, it is <u>always</u> better than doing nothing. MOVE YOUR BODY! Exercise improves long-term health, fights stress, increases your energy and metabolism, decreases cholesterol, and helps disease (heart, diabetes, arthritis, cancer, etc.).
7. Take ACTION TODAY!

ALL YOU NEED TO FURNISH A FAT-FREE KITCHEN!

* Nonstick cookware - worth the investment! Include saucepans, Dutch oven or soup pot, small and large skillets, and assorted lids. Aluminum, cast iron and stainless steel cookware are the best choices. Food cooks more evenly in heavier pans due to heat distribution.
* Plastic or wooden utensils - won't scratch the coating on nonstick cookware.
* Skewers - great for grilling or broiling poultry, fish, seafood or vegetables.
* Nonstick baking sheets, muffin pans, cake pans.
* Glass baking dishes: 9"x13", 8"x8", 12"x8".
* Microwave - the ultimate appliance for quick and healthy cooking!
* Hot-air corn popper - make your own and season with butter-flavored granules, spices or fat-free cheese ("lite" microwave popcorn packages can contain 3-4 grams of fat per serving).
* Blender - make great smoothies, soups and fat-free sauces!
* Food processor - cut, chop, grate, slice, blend, purée in a snap.
* Wok - simple quick stir-fries, omelets, soups, and more, can be prepared in this versatile appliance!
* Breadmaker - for breads, pizzas, muffins, and more.
* Sharp, high-quality knives for peeling, cutting, trimming.

FAT FREE LIVING MADE SIMPLE

When you can't find a fat free food, here are toll-free numbers that you can call and find where their product is in your area or you can order direct.

* Buttermilk Blend: 1 800 373-7226
* Foster Farms: Fat Free Chicken: 1 800 227-0811
* Delightful Farms: Fat Free Chicken: 1 800 447-2670
* Lighter Bake: 1 800 447-5218
  substitution = 1/2 apple butter and 1/2 "baby prunes"
* Fat Free Green Giant Harvest Burgers: 1 800 998-9996
  Distributed by Pillsbury Co., Minneapolis, MN
* Fat Free Morningstar Farms Ground Meatless: 1 800 243-1810
  Distrubuted by Worthington Foods, Inc., Worthington, Ohio

BEST FAT-FREE
COOKING TECHNIQUES

It's not always what you eat but how you prepare it! Invest in a high-quality set of nonstick cookware and you'll never need to use oil again. You will save 120 calories and 14 grams of fat for each tablespoon of oil you DON'T use!

*Dry-Frying: Heat nonstick skillet over medium-high heat. Lightly spray chicken, turkey or fish with nonfat cooking spray; place in hot skillet. This method will sear the meat on the outside but keep it moist and tender throughout.

*Stir-Frying: Lightly spray nonstick skillet or wok with nonfat cooking spray and heat over medium-high heat. Cut vegetables and meat into small pieces and add to hot skillet. For best results, cook in small batches.

*Oven-Frying: Coat poultry, fish, seafood or vegetables with egg whites or egg substitute and roll in seasoned fat-free bread crumbs or Cornflake Crumbs until well coated. Place on baking sheet lined with foil and lightly sprayed with nonfat cooking spray and bake according to recipe directions. Tastes like fried, without the fat!

*Caramelizing: Use onions, garlic, shallots or leeks with poultry, fish or vegetables. Lightly "dry-fry" onions and garlic in nonstick pan just until soft. Add remaining ingredients and cook over low to medium heat, uncovered; stir frequently during cooking.

DRY-HEAT COOKING:

*Broiling: Broiling vegetables, meat, poultry and seafood seals in the juices while quickly browning the outside; works like a grill inside without the smoky flavor. Line broiler pan with foil and lightly spray with nonfat cooking spray for quick clean-up. For added flavor, marinate foods before broiling, or baste while cooking. Watch foods carefully to prevent burning.

*Grilling: Foods are seared on the outside and kept juicy and moist on the inside. For quick clean-up, lightly spray grill, cooking rack, or grill pan with nonfat cooking spray beforehand. For added flavor, marinate or baste as you would when broiling.

*Roasting: Simple method of cooking for vegetables, poultry, fish and seafood. Lightly spray roasting pan with nonfat cooking spray before adding food. Use variety of seasonings and marinades for added flavor. Cover the food for part of the cooking time to keep it moist and tender.

*Microwaving: Healthy cooking method that keeps food moist without adding calories or fat. Great for vegetables, chicken, fish and egg white omelets. Lightly spray pans with nonfat cooking spray beforehand and follow recipe directions for covering pans. Frozen vegetables can be cooked with or without added liquid; for a fresh steamed flavor, microwave without liquid.

MOIST-HEAT COOKING:
*Steaming: Speedy healthy method of cooking - most vegetables and fish steam in under 10 minutes while retaining their flavors, vitamins, minerals, colors and shapes. Seafood, poultry and vegetables can be steamed in steaming baskets, on the grill, in the oven, or wrapped in packets and seasoned with broth, wine or water.

*Poaching: Seafood, poultry and vegetables are cooked in simmering seasoned liquid (water, broth, wine, or juice). When poaching foods, cook at a low simmer, not a boil. Add flavor to the poaching liquid with herbs and spices and serve as a broth after the food is removed.

*Braising: Foods are prepared in a tightly covered pan or baking dish with a small amount of liquid (water, wine, broth). Dry-frying the poultry or fish before braising will enhance the flavor of the dish.

*Sweating: Cook poultry, fish and vegetables in a tightly-covered pan over very low heat. The foods cook in their own juices; foods soften but do not brown with this cooking method.

BEST SUBSTITUTES FOR BAKING IDEAS:
You really can have your cookies, cakes, pies and other delicious dessert treats - but the best part is you can EAT THEM TOO! Baking without fat is simple with the right substitutions but it may take a bit of patience and experimentation. Follow these tips the next time you want to bake that favorite dessert - just cut some of the calories, all of the fat, but none of the flavor!

When you think about baking cookies or cakes, the first ingredient that comes to mind is butter, margarine or oil. These bind the ingredients together while giving the baked goods a moist texture. There are a variety of fat-free products that can be used in place of these high-fat ingredients.

*Puréed fruit (apple butter or baby prunes) works well in muffins, breads and chocolate recipes. You may want to reduce the amount by 2 to 4 tablespoons and adjust after you have added the dry ingredients.

*Applesauce or mashed bananas make delicious substitutes in muffins, cakes, cookies, and sweet breads. Try out some of the new applesauce flavors in your favorite recipes: cranberry, strawberry, mixed berry, cinnamon, and apple-cherry. (Try cranberry bread with cranberry applesauce and dried cranberries. Great for the holidays! One simple substitution will cut 80 calories and 9 grams of fat!)

*Crushed pineapple adds wonderful flavor to muffins, carrot bread or zucchini bread.

*Substitute egg whites or fat-free egg substitute for whole eggs - saves 30 calories, 4 grams of fat and 181 milligrams of cholesterol.

*Fat-free dairy products (milk, sour cream, yogurt, evaporated skim milk, cottage cheese, etc.) keep baked goods moist and flavorful. Try fat-free flavored yogurts for a burst of fruity flavor!

*Frost cakes with marshmallow creme or sprinkle with powdered sugar.
*Cut out the nuts but keep the crunch! Try Grape-Nuts, fat-free granola, or dried fruits in place of nuts - you'll save 30 calories and 5 grams of fat per tablespoon (most recipes call for about 1/2 cup of nuts which adds 438 calories and 40 grams of fat!).
*Create a pie crust with crushed fat-free granola, Cornflake Crumbs, or crushed fat-free cookies. Mix with just enough fat-free yogurt, preserves, or liquid Butter Buds to moisten and press into pie plate.
*Use canned pie fillings for flavorful muffins and breads. Replace half the butter or oil called for with applesauce and the remainder with pie filling. If batter seems too thin, add flour 1 tablespoon at a time.

SHOPPING TIPS AND MORE; tips to make shopping your first step to healthy living. Filling a fat-free kitchen begins with a healthy shopping list and smart shopping strategies. Steer your shopping cart around the perimeter of the store; begin in the produce department (get the most for your money - vitamins, minerals and fiber), cruise through meats, fish and poultry, dash through the center aisles and head straight for the dairy and grain section.
*Make a shopping list and STICK WITH IT! You will save fat, calories, money and time. Challenge yourself not to purchase one item off the list - if you stick with it, pick up your favorite magazine as a reward!
*Browse through low-fat cookbooks and design a menu for the week. Make a list of all ingredients required and make this your master list. Make copies; post it on the refrigerator or bulletin board. As you run out of particular items, circle them on the list. Add any extra items from new recipes to the list as needed.
*Try to outline your grocery list with the store design in mind. This is a sure way to save calories, fat and TIME!
*Eat something before you go to the grocery store so you don't have to battle impulse buying. Shopping while hungry will only increase your food bill!
*Steer clear of food samples, marketing displays, and tempting food aisles. Stick to the perimeter of the store as much as possible. Fresh fruit and vegetables; meat, fish and poultry; dairy products; and breads are usually located in the outer aisles.
*Try to shop alone - kids have a harder time resisting those temptations placed at the end of aisles. If you kids do go with you let each one pick out one special healthy treat.
*Give yourself enough time to shop. Pay attention to food labels and healthy choices; don't be distracted by fancy packaging or advertising.

As you stroll through aisles, keep these tips in mind and make the healthiest choices.

*Go for fresh fruits and vegetables. Purchase four different colors of vegetables (orange, dark green, red and yellow) for a variety of healthy vitamins and minerals. Since fresh produce is perishable, buy only what you need for the week. Try to stick with seasonal fruits and vegetables for variety, freshness and flavor.

*Steer clear of avocados and coconuts - their fat content far outweighs their nutrient value.

*If you purchase canned fruits and vegetables, stick with those packed in water or juice, not syrup or oil. Stick with canned products without added sugar, salt or fat. Canned vegetables are usually higher in sodium than fresh or frozen, but simply rinse away the salt with water before eating them.

*Take advantage of packaged precut or shredded vegetables for quick salad or stir-fry preparation.

*Pick up perfect portions at the supermarket salad bar (prewashed, precut); stick with fruits and vegetables and stay away from the extras (i.e. bacon bits, croutons, cheese).

*Explore the condiment aisle and take your pick of fat-free salad dressing or flavored vinegar. Read labels carefully - 98% fat-free can still contain A LOT of fat! A 2-tablespoon serving of low-fat salad dressing with 2 grams of fat and 35 calories per serving is actually over 50% fat! Even salad dressings that claim to be "fat-free" can contain partially hydrogenated oil. Your best bet is to stick with dressing that is labeled "oil free". Stir in Dijon, spicy or flavored fat-free mustard to fat-free dressings for added flavor.

*Choose mustard and ketchup for low-calorie, fat-free flavor additions to sandwiches and vegetables.

*Choose fat-free varieties of dairy products. Dairy products provide calcium, protein and vitamins, but whole milk, cottage cheese, sour cream and yogurts also contain a substantial amount of saturated fat. Skim milk, fat-free cottage cheese, fat-free sliced or shredded cheese, fat-free sour cream, fat-free plain or flavored yogurt can all be substituted for whole varieties in your favorite recipes. For those who are lactose-intolerant, try some of the fat-free nonlactose dairy products available, or select fat-free rice products (i.e. Rice Dream - plain or vanilla flavored). Don't be fooled by "low fat" or "no cholesterol" labels. Look at the serving size, fat and calorie content, and overall nutritional value for the most accurate comparisons.

*If you aren't getting enough calcium in your food plan, try calcium-enriched orange juice!

*Save fat, cholesterol and calories by choosing fat-free egg substitutes in place of whole eggs.

*Try Harvest Burger beef crumbles** or Morningstar Farms in place of ground beef - great for casseroles, Mexican dishes, chili and pasta sauce.

Discover new fat-free Gardenburgers or Veggie burgers in the freezer section.

Choose fat-free poultry; breasts, tenders and cutlets can be baked, broiled, grilled, microwaved, dry-fried or stir-fried.

Watch out for ground turkey products! Be sure to read labels carefully. Although some ground turkey is fat-free, other types can contain up to 11 grams of fat per serving.

Best fish and seafood choices: haddock, flounder, halibut, cod, sea bass, monkfish, shrimp, scallops, crab, and fat-free canned tuna.

Steer away from packaged breaded fish; the breading adds extra calories and fat and usually recommends deep-frying for best results.

Choose several of the fat-free poultry, fish or seafood bottled-marinades available (usually located in the meat and fish section).

Buy a variety of frozen vegetables but keep them plain and simple. Stay away from any vegetables in cream or cheese sauce.

Choose fat-free popsicles, frozen fruit bars, sorbet, or fat-free yogurt for dessert treats. Watch the portion sizes and caloric content.

Stick with whole-grain varieties for all types of bread.

Choose breads with at least 2 grams of fiber per serving.

Beware of cereal advertising lures - FAT FREE - LOW IN SUGAR - LOW IN CHOLESTEROL! - read labels to find out what's really inside the box. Go for cereals high in fiber, low in sugar, and fat-free. Sugary cereals are usually placed on middle shelves, right at "little one's" eye level! Compare the total carbohydrate content against the sugars; if the numbers are close, those carbohydrates are mostly sugar calories. Remember: the items are listed in the order of highest quantity so look for sugar at the end of the list! Watch out for "healthy granola" cereal; granola is usually loaded with nuts, seeds, coconut, and oil!

Check serving sizes on cereal packages. If you end up doubling or tripling the serving size to fill your bowl, you are also doubling or tripling the calories, sugar, and fat!

Best choices in the snack aisle include: melba toast, matzo, rice cakes, fat-free pretzels, air-popped popcorn. Watch sodium content and serving size!

Aisle by Aisle Fill a Healthy Cart to Guarantee a Healthy Heart! Your Very Best Bets!

Refrigerator/Freezer Must Haves
fat-free cheese varieties (Cheddar, Parmesan,
   Swiss, mozzarella, American, cream)
skim milk
fat-free yogurt or sour cream
egg substitute
fat-free pita pocket/tortillas
fat-free popsicles
fresh fruits/vegetables
frozen fruits/vegetables
frozen fat-free bread dough
fat-free chicken (breasts, tenders, ground)

Pantry Staples
fat-free barbecue sauce
fat-free tuna
fat-free salsa
nonfat dry milk
fat-free rice (white and brown)
fat-free pretzels
pasta
canned tomatoes
fat-free bread, pitas
canned beans (kidney, white Northern, pinto, etc.)
fat-free cooking spray
plain popcorn
fat-free broth (chicken, beef, vegetable)
fat-free mustard (variety of flavors)
fat-free pasta sauce
low-sodium soy sauce
fat-free salad dressing
low-fat hot cereal (multi-grain oatmeal, cream of wheat, cream of rice)
high-fiber, low-fat, low-sugar cereal
variety of grains (i.e. couscous, barley, wheat berries)
raisins (or other dried fruit)
flavored rice cakes
fat-free mayonnaise
unsweetened cocoa powder
unsweetened applesauce

Sure-bet Seasonings
basil, bay leaves, celery flakes,
chili powder, cinnamon, cumin,
garlic powder, ginger, nutmeg,
onion flakes, onion powder,
oregano, parsley, pepper,
rosemary, sage, tarragon, thyme

CONTENTS

RECIPES FOR

Fat Free Living®
Wok Cookbook

by Jyl Steinback

- Stirfry
- Chili/Soups
- Seafood Specialties

TIPS FOR THE WOK

The wok is such a versatile appliance for all types of cooking and creates wonderful stir-fried or steamed fat-free dishes. The wok is not limited to Oriental foods, but can be used for many types of international dishes. Wok cooking is not only fun, but saves time and energy. All you really need for wok cooking is a long-handled spatula and a metal or bamboo rack for steaming. Here are a few simple tips for successful wok cooking:

- **Stir-frying:** Foods are cooked quickly by tossing them in hot liquid (oil is usually used, but for fat-free cooking, substitute fat-free broths). This quick cooking method seals in the flavor and juices and keeps vegetables tender-crisp.
  - read recipe through; prepare and assemble all ingredients
  - cut up all foods in advance
    - keep cut-up foods relatively small and uniform
    - chicken cooks best when cut in 2x1/4" strips
    - line up seasonings near wok
  - prepare any sauces in advance; **always** restir before adding to wok because the cornstarch will settle in the bottom of the bowl
  - spray the wok with cooking spray **before** heating
  - heat the wok on medium-high or high heat before adding liquid; pour liquid into hot wok and tilt the wok to coat on all sides
    - for **FAT-FREE STIR FRY**, you will use a variety of fat-free broths (chicken, beef, oriental, vegetable) and a light spray of nonfat cooking spray
  - work **quickly**, tossing foods and coating with any liquid or sauce being used
  - toss seasonings with hot liquid before adding meat or vegetables in most recipes
    - some recipes will call for the meat or vegetables to be sprinkled with a variety of seasonings and then quickly stir-fried
  - never add more than 1 pound of meat at a time; do not overload the wok as the food will not cook evenly
    - do not cook more than 5 cups of cut-up vegetables in a 12- to 14-inch wok; cook in batches if necessary
  - remove cooked meat and add more liquid to wok; when liquid is hot, add vegetables, starting with those that take the longest to cook
  - if necessary, add additional broth or water to vegetables while cooking; cook just until tender-crisp
  - return all meat and vegetables to wok and cook with sauce recommended in the recipe until sauce boils and thickens

1

-think of the cooking times recommended in the recipes as a guide; cooking time will vary according to the type of wok or heating element that is being used.

-stir-fried dishes are best if served immediately

• **Steaming:** Steaming in the wok requires a ring stand, a lid, and a metal rack for the most efficient cooking. Stacking bamboo baskets with lids can be used in place of the ring stand and work well when you are cooking more than one food at a time.

-place the wok in a ring stand over heat

-pour in 2 inches of hot water and set the rack in place

-food that is arranged on the rack should be just above the hot water, but not touching it

-cover the wok and bring the water to a boil before placing the food on the rack or in the steaming basket

-do not cover the holes in the rack

-always cover the wok when steaming so water continues to boil

-add water as needed so wok does not get dried out

A WELL-STOCKED WOK KITCHEN WILL INCLUDE MOST OF THE FOLLOWING INGREDIENTS FOR SIMPLE STIR-FRY:

-angel hair pasta (or other thin noodles); great for mixing with stir-fried vegetables, chicken or seafood

-cornstarch - used for thickening sauces

-couscous - finely ground semolina that is quick-cooking and a wonderful addition to most stir-fried dishes; can be used the same as rice or pasta in most recipes

-fat-free broths - chicken, beef, oriental or vegetable - used in place of oil for fat-free stir-fry

-garlic - whole, fresh garlic; garlic powder; minced garlic; or garlic purée

-ginger - gingerroot can be peeled with a vegetable peeler and grated or minced; many of the recipes call for ginger powder which works well for quick stir-fry

-hoisin sauce - a sweet and spicy sauce used in a variety of stir-fry dishes

-nonfat cooking spray - essential to **fat-free** stir-fry - spray the wok lightly with spray; a little spray goes a very long way. Remove wok from heat if you need to respray and then heat several seconds before adding foods

-oyster sauce - a thick, brown sauce used in a variety of stir-fry dishes

-rice - use a variety of quick-cooking, long-grain or short-grain rice; toss with stir-fried vegetables, chicken or seafood

-soy sauce - used in most stir-fry recipes; look for low-sodium varieties as soy sauce has a very high sodium content

-stir-fry sauce - a variety of fat-free stir-fry sauces are available which can be used for quick stir-fries

CHICKEN WON TONS

AVERAGE - DO AHEAD - FREEZE

ingredients:
1 1/2 cups fat-free chicken tenders, cooked and minced
2 tbsp. chopped celery
2 tbsp. water chestnuts, chopped fine
2 tbsp. chili sauce
1 tbsp. sherry
2 cups fat-free chicken broth
24 frozen won ton wrappers, thawed
3/4 cup sweet and sour sauce, optional

directions:
Combine chicken, celery, water chestnuts, chili sauce and sherry in a medium bowl and mix well. Lay won ton skins on work surface. Spoon 1 teaspoon filling onto won ton; fold corners into center and lightly moisten to seal.

Fill bottom of wok with water and heat over medium-high heat. Pour chicken broth into shallow baking dish; arrange won tons, seam-side down, in a single layer (do not crowd).

Place baking dish on a rack over the simmering water. Cover wok and steam won tons 30 35 minutes. Remove won tons from broth and keep warm. Repeat with remaining won tons and filling.

Serve hot or at room temperature with sweet and sour sauce.

Serves: 6

Nutrition per Serving		Exchanges
Calories	183	2 meat
Carbohydrate	28 grams	1 starch
Cholesterol	28 milligrams	1/2 fruit
Dietary Fiber	0 grams	
Fat	< 1 gram	
Protein	16 grams	
Sodium	505 milligrams	

Shopping List: 1 pound fat-free chicken tenders, 16 ounces fat-free chicken broth, 6 ounces sweet and sour sauce (optional), won ton wrappers, water chestnuts, chili sauce, sherry, celery.

MEAT BALLS WITH PLUM SAUCE

EASY

ingredients:
1 lb. fat-free beef crumbles (Morningstar Farms)
3/4 cup canned, sliced water chestnuts, chopped fine
1 tbsp. onion powder
2 tbsp. low-sodium soy sauce
1/2 cup egg substitute
3/4 cup fat-free bread crumbs
3 tbsp. fat-free beef broth, divided
1 cup plum sauce

directions:
In a medium bowl, combine beef crumbles, water chestnuts, onion powder, soy sauce, egg substitute and bread crumbs and mix until ingredients are moistened and hold together.
Shape beef mixture into 1-inch balls and set aside.
Lightly spray wok with nonfat cooking spray; pour 1 tablespoon beef broth into wok and heat over medium-high heat.
Add meat balls to wok and cook 10 minutes, stirring frequently, until meat balls are browned and cooked through.
Remove cooked meat balls, set aside; repeat with remaining meat balls.
Pour plum sauce into center of wok and cook until heated through.
Add meat balls to sauce and simmer over low heat 8-10 minutes.

Serves: 6

Nutrition per Serving		Exchanges
Calories	188	1 starch
Carbohydrate	28 grams	1 fruit
Cholesterol	0 milligrams	1 1/2 meat
Dietary Fiber	3 grams	
Fat	< 1 gram	
Protein	16 grams	
Sodium	1084 milligrams	

Shopping List: 1 pound fat-free beef crumbles (Morningstar Farms); canned, sliced water chestnuts; 4 ounces egg substitute, low-sodium soy sauce, fat-free bread crumbs, fat-free beef broth, 8 ounces plum sauce, onion powder.

MU SHU VEGETABLE ROLLS

AVERAGE

ingredients:
6 fat-free flour tortillas
1 tbsp. vegetable broth
1 cup shredded carrots
3 cups shredded cabbage
1 cup shredded zucchini
1 1/2 tsp. garlic powder
1/2 tsp. ginger
2 cups bean sprouts
1 1/2 cups sliced mushrooms
1 cup sliced green onions
1/4 cup fat-free stir-fry sauce
1/3 cup fat-free hoisin sauce

directions:
Preheat oven to 350 degrees. Wrap tortillas in foil and heat 10 minutes; keep warm.

Lightly spray wok with nonfat cooking spray; pour vegetable broth into wok and heat over medium-high heat.

Add carrots, cabbage and zucchini to wok and sprinkle with garlic powder and ginger; stir-fry 1-2 minutes.

Add bean sprouts, mushrooms and green onions and stir-fry 1-2 minutes, until all vegetables are tender-crisp; push vegetables to the side of wok.

Pour stir-fry sauce into wok and heat until bubbly; stir vegetables into sauce and cook 2-3 minutes, until well coated and heated through.

Brush 1 side of tortillas with hoisin sauce; top with vegetable mixture. Fold tortilla up over mixture, secure with toothpicks and serve with additional hoisin sauce, if desired.

Serves: 6

Nutrition per Serving		Exchanges
Calories	224	2 starch
Carbohydrate	46 grams	3 vegetable
Cholesterol	0 milligrams	
Dietary Fiber	5 grams	
Fat	< 1 gram	
Protein	8 grams	
Sodium	699 milligrams	

Shopping List: Fat-free flour tortillas, 2 ounces fat-free stir-fry sauce, fat-free hoisin sauce, 8-ounce package shredded carrots, 1 zucchini, 12-ounce package shredded cabbage, 1/2 pound bean sprouts, 6 ounces sliced mushrooms, green onions, vegetable broth, garlic powder.

SEAFOOD LETTUCE WRAPS

AVERAGE

ingredients:
1 1/2 lb. iceberg lettuce, separate leaves
1 1/2 tbsp. oriental broth
1 1/2 tbsp. minced garlic
2 tsp. ginger
1/2 cup chopped green onions
1 cup chopped red bell pepper
1 cup chopped green bell pepper
1 cup chopped celery
3/4 lb. large fat-free, shrimp
1 tbsp. fat-free stir-fry sauce
1/2 cup fat-free hoisin sauce

directions:
Wash, dry and separate lettuce leaves; set aside. Peel and devein the shrimp.

Lightly spray wok with nonfat cooking spray; pour oriental broth into wok and heat over medium-high heat.

Add garlic, ginger and onions to wok and stir-fry 45 seconds. Add red and green bell peppers and celery to wok; stir-fry 3-4 minutes until tender-crisp.

Add shrimp and stir-fry sauce and cook, stirring frequently 2-3 minutes, until shrimp turn pink.

Spoon shrimp mixture into serving bowl; arrange lettuce leaves on platter.

To serve, wrap shrimp mixture in lettuce and dip in hoisin sauce.

Serves: 6

Nutrition per Serving

Calories	122
Carbohydrate	21 grams
Cholesterol	7 milligrams
Dietary Fiber	2 grams
Fat	< 1 gram
Protein	8 grams
Sodium	650 milligrams

Exchanges
4 vegetable
1/2 meat

Shopping List: 1 1/2 pounds iceberg lettuce, 3/4 pound large shrimp, 1 red bell pepper, 1 green bell pepper, 3/4 pound celery, green onions, oriental broth, fat-free stir-fry sauce, 4 ounces fat-free hoisin sauce, minced garlic, ginger.

BLACK BEAN CHILI

EASY

ingredients:
1 1/2 tbsp. vegetable broth
1 1/2 cups chopped green bell pepper
1 1/2 cups chopped red bell pepper
1 1/2 tsp. garlic powder
1 1/2 tbsp. onion powder
2 1/2 cups zucchini, chopped fine
2 1/2 cups frozen corn kernels, thawed
2 1/4 tsp. chili powder
2 cups canned, chopped tomatoes
1 16-ounce can black beans, drained
1 cup tomato sauce
1 1/2 tbsp. chopped green chilies
3 cups couscous, cooked

directions:
Lightly spray wok with nonfat cooking spray; pour vegetable broth into wok and heat over medium-high heat.
Add green pepper, red pepper, garlic powder and onion powder; stir-fry 2-3 minutes until tender. Remove from wok and set aside.
Add zucchini and corn to wok and stir-fry 2-3 minutes; sprinkle with chili powder and cook 1-2 minutes until tender.
Return peppers to wok; add tomatoes, beans, tomato sauce and chopped green chilies; mix well. Cook, stirring frequently, 5-6 minutes until heated through.
Serve over cooked couscous.

Serves: 6

Nutrition per Serving

Calories	283
Carbohydrate	60 grams
Cholesterol	0 milligrams
Dietary Fiber	12 grams
Fat	< 1 gram
Protein	13 grams
Sodium	434 milligrams

Exchanges
2 vegetable
3 starch

Shopping List: 1 large green bell pepper, 1 large red bell pepper, 2 medium zucchini, 10 ounces frozen corn kernels, 28-ounce can chopped tomatoes, 16-ounce can fat-free black beans, 4-ounce can chopped green chilies, 8 ounces tomato sauce, couscous, vegetable broth, garlic powder, onion powder, chili powder.

HOT AND SOUR ORIENTAL SOUP

AVERAGE - DO AHEAD

ingredients:
2 14 1/2-ounce cans fat-free oriental broth
1 1/2 cups sliced mushrooms
1/4 tsp. ginger
1/2 lb. fat-free chicken tenders, sliced thin
1/2 cup bamboo shoots, sliced
3 tbsp. rice vinegar
3 tbsp. low-sodium soy sauce
1/2 tsp. crushed red pepper
1 large egg white, lightly beaten
1/2 cup frozen pea pods, thawed
1/4 cup chopped green onions
1 tbsp. cornstarch
1/4 cup water

directions:
Pour oriental broth into wok; add mushrooms, ginger and chicken to broth and bring to a boil over high heat. Reduce heat to medium-low and simmer 10 minutes. Add bamboo shoots and cook 5-6 minutes. Pour rice vinegar and soy sauce into soup; sprinkle with red pepper and bring to a boil over high heat. Gradually pour beaten egg white into boiling soup and mix lightly so egg breaks into thin pieces. Add green onions and pea pods; cook over medium-high heat until vegetables are tender. In a small bowl, combine cornstarch and water; mix until blended smooth. Stir mixture into soup and bring to a boil over high heat; cook, stirring constantly, until soup slightly thickens and mixture is blended.

Serves: 6

Nutrition per Serving		Exchanges
Calories	76	1 vegetable
Carbohydrate	6 grams	1 1/2 meat
Cholesterol	24 milligrams	
Dietary Fiber	1 gram	
Fat	< 1 gram	
Protein	11 grams	
Sodium	852 milligrams	

Shopping List: 2 - 14 1/2-ounce cans fat-free oriental broth, 1/2 pound mushrooms, 1/2 pound fat-free chicken tenders, 6 ounces bamboo shoots, 6 ounces frozen pea pods, 3-4 green onions, egg, rice vinegar, low-sodium soy sauce, ground ginger, crushed red pepper, cornstarch.

STIR-FRY TACO SALAD

EASY - DO AHEAD

ingredients:
1 1/4 cups Mexican stewed tomatoes
1 cup corn kernels, drained
3 cups fat-free frozen Harvest Burger beef crumbles
1 tbsp. onion powder
1 tsp. garlic powder
1 tbsp. chili powder
1/8 tsp. pepper
3 oz. low-fat tortilla chips
1 1/2 cups fat-free shredded cheddar cheese
3 cups shredded lettuce
1 1/2 cups fat-free garden-style salsa

directions:
Lightly spray wok with nonfat cooking spray and heat over medium-high heat.
Add tomatoes, corn, beef, onion powder, garlic powder, chili powder and pepper to wok and cook, stirring constantly, until mixture comes to a boil.
Reduce heat to low, cover, and simmer 10-15 minutes until heated through. Break tortilla chips into small pieces (not crushed); add chips and cheese to wok.
Cook over medium heat, stirring constantly, until cheese is slightly melted.
Place shredded lettuce in bowl; top with taco mixture. Serve with salsa.

Serves: 6

Nutrition per Serving

			Exchanges
Calories	216		1 starch
Carbohydrate	31 grams		3 vegetable
Cholesterol	0 milligrams		2 meat
Dietary Fiber	4 grams		
Fat	< 1 gram		
Protein	22 grams		
Sodium	1102 milligrams		

Shopping List: 10 ounces fat-free frozen Harvest Burger beef crumbles, 16 ounces Mexican stewed tomatoes, 8-ounce can corn kernels, 6 ounces fat-free shredded cheddar cheese, 12 ounces fat-free garden-style salsa, 2 packages shredded lettuce (or 2 heads lettuce), low-fat tortilla chips, onion powder, garlic powder, chili powder.

CHICKEN AND RICE WITH HOISIN SAUCE

EASY - DO AHEAD

ingredients:
3/4 cup fat-free hoisin sauce
1/4 cup + 2 tbsp. water
1 1/2 tsp. minced garlic
1 1/2 lb. fat-free chicken tenders, cut in strips
1 tsp. onion powder
1 tsp. garlic powder
1 tbsp. fat-free chicken broth
1 red bell pepper, cut in 1-inch pieces
1 large onion, cut in 1-inch pieces
1 cup sliced mushrooms
1 zucchini, sliced 1/4-inch thick
3 cups fat-free cooked rice

directions:
Combine hoisin sauce, water and garlic in a small bowl and mix until blended; pour half the sauce into a small cup and set aside.

Place chicken in a shallow baking dish and sprinkle with onion and garlic powder. Pour remaining sauce over chicken; cover and marinate in refrigerator 1 hour. Discard chicken marinade.

Lightly spray wok with nonfat cooking spray; pour chicken broth into wok and heat over high heat.

Reduce heat to medium-high; add bell pepper, onion, zucchini and mushrooms to wok and stir-fry 3-4 minutes until tender. Add chicken and reserved sauce to wok and cook, stirring frequently, 4-5 minutes, until chicken is cooked through and no longer pink.

Serve with hot rice.

Serves: 6

Nutrition per Serving		Exchanges
Calories	275	1 starch
Carbohydrate	35 grams	4 vegetable
Cholesterol	56 milligrams	3 meat
Dietary Fiber	2 grams	
Fat	< 1 gram	
Protein	30 grams	
Sodium	578 milligrams	

Shopping List: 1 1/2 pounds fat-free chicken tenders, 6 ounces fat-free hoisin sauce, 1 red bell pepper, 1 onion, 8-10 mushrooms, 1 medium zucchini, fat-free rice, fat-free chicken broth, minced garlic, garlic powder, onion powder.

CHICKEN-ASPARAGUS STIR-FRY

EASY - DO AHEAD

ingredients:
1/2 cup water
2 tbsp. cornstarch
1 tsp. dry mustard
1 tsp. ground ginger
1/2 tsp. crushed red pepper
1/2 cup low-sodium soy sauce
1 1/2 lb. fat-free chicken tenders, cut in half
1 20-ounce package frozen pepper-onion stir-fry, thawed
16 ounces frozen cut asparagus

directions:
Combine water, cornstarch, mustard, ginger, red pepper and soy sauce in a small bowl and mix well; set aside.
Lightly spray wok with nonfat cooking spray and heat over medium-high heat. Add chicken to wok and cook until browned on all sides, about 4-5 minutes. Add pepper-onion stir-fry and asparagus and mix lightly; pour sauce over top and cook, stirring frequently, 6-8 minutes, until vegetables are tender-crisp and sauce thickens.
Serve over fat-free cooked rice, if desired.

Serves: 6

Nutrition per Serving		Exchanges
Calories	191	3 meat
Carbohydrate	16 grams	3 1/2 vegetable
Cholesterol	56 milligrams	
Dietary Fiber	2 grams	
Fat	< 1 gram	
Protein	31 grams	
Sodium	1041 milligrams	

Shopping List: 1 1/2 pounds fat-free chicken tenders, 20 ounces frozen pepper stir-fry, 16 ounces frozen cut asparagus, 4 ounces low-sodium soy sauce, cornstarch, dry mustard, ground ginger, crushed red pepper.

CHICKEN CHOW MEIN

AVERAGE

ingredients: 1 1/2 cups + 1 tbsp. fat-free chicken broth, divided
3/8 cup low-sodium soy sauce
1/4 cup cornstarch
1 1/2 tsp. ground ginger
1 1/2 lb. fat-free chicken tenders, cut in strips
1/2 tsp. onion powder
1 tsp. garlic powder
1 1/2 cups shredded carrots
1 1/2 cups sliced celery
1 1/2 cups chopped onions
1 1/2 cups shredded cabbage
1 1/2 cups frozen chopped spinach,
    thawed and drained

directions: Combine 1 1/2 cups chicken broth, soy sauce, cornstarch and ginger in a small bowl and mix until blended ; set aside.
Lightly spray wok with nonfat cooking spray; pour remaining chicken broth into wok and heat over medium-high heat.
Add chicken; sprinkle with onion and garlic powder. Stir-fry chicken 4-5 minutes. Add carrots, celery, onions, cabbage and spinach to wok and stir-fry 3-5 minutes, until vegetables are tender-crisp and chicken is no longer pink.
Pour broth mixture over chicken; cover and cook 3-5 minutes until heated through.

Serves: 6

Nutrition per Serving		**Exchanges**
Calories	197	3 meat
Carbohydrate	19 grams	4 vegetable
Cholesterol	56 milligrams	
Dietary Fiber	4 grams	
Fat	< 1 gram	
Protein	30 grams	
Sodium	1074 milligrams	

Shopping List: 1 1/2 pounds fat-free chicken tenders, 15 ounces fat-free chicken broth, 8-ounce package shredded carrots, 1 small onion, celery, 8-ounce package shredded cabbage, 10 ounces frozen chopped spinach, low-sodium soy sauce, cornstarch, ground ginger, garlic powder, onion powder.

CHICKEN FAJITAS

AVERAGE

ingredients:
1/4 cup lime juice
3 tbsp. fat-free chicken broth
3/4 tsp. ground cumin
1/4 tsp. ground red pepper
1 lb. fat-free chicken tenders, cut in half
1 large onion, thinly sliced
1 green bell pepper, thinly sliced
1 red bell pepper, thinly sliced
1 yellow bell pepper, thinly sliced
1 tsp. garlic powder
6 fat-free flour tortillas

directions:
Combine lime juice, chicken broth, cumin and red pepper in a shallow baking dish and mix well. Add chicken tenders and toss until well coated. Cover with plastic wrap and refrigerate 1-2 hours. Lightly spray wok with nonfat cooking spray and heat over medium-high heat.
Add chicken with sauce, onion and bell peppers; sprinkle with garlic powder and toss lightly.
Cook over medium-high heat 4-5 minutes, until chicken is no longer pink and vegetables are tender-crisp.
Wrap tortillas in foil and heat in 450 degree oven 3-5 minutes until heated through.
Wrap chicken mixture in tortillas and serve immediately.

Serves: 6

Nutrition per Serving		Exchanges
Calories	203	1 1/2 meat
Carbohydrate	30 grams	3 vegetable
Cholesterol	47 milligrams	1 starch
Dietary Fiber	3 grams	
Fat	< 1 gram	
Protein	20 grams	
Sodium	521 milligrams	

Shopping List: 1 pound fat-free chicken tenders, 2 ounces lime juice, 1 onion, 1 green bell pepper, 1 red bell pepper, 1 yellow bell pepper, fat-free chicken broth, fat-free flour tortillas, ground cumin, ground red pepper, garlic powder.

ORANGE-APRICOT CHICKEN TENDERS

EASY

ingredients:
2 tsp. fat-free chicken broth
2 lb. fat-free chicken tenders
2 tsp. onion powder
1/2 cup apricot preserves
1/3 cup orange juice
1 tbsp. fresh cilantro, minced
2 tsp. garlic powder
1/4 tsp. cinnamon
1/8 tsp. cloves
1/4 tsp. nutmeg
1/8 tsp. pepper

directions:
Lightly spray wok with nonfat cooking spray; add chicken broth and heat over medium-high heat. Add chicken tenders; sprinkle with onion powder. Cook chicken 6-8 minutes, stirring frequently, until no longer pink.
Remove chicken from wok; set aside and keep warm. Combine apricot preserves, orange juice, cilantro, garlic powder, cinnamon, cloves, nutmeg and pepper in wok and mix well; bring to a boil over high heat.
Remove wok from heat and stir in chicken tenders; toss until well coated.
Serve immediately over rice or couscous.

Serves: 6

Nutrition per Serving

Calories	235
Carbohydrate	22 grams
Cholesterol	74 milligrams
Dietary Fiber	< 1 gram
Fat	< 1 gram
Protein	35 grams
Sodium	306 milligrams

Exchanges
4 1/2 meat
1 1/3 fruit

Shopping List: 2 pounds fat-free chicken tenders, 4 ounces apricot preserves, orange juice, fat-free chicken broth, onion powder, garlic powder, fresh cilantro, cinnamon, cloves, nutmeg, pepper.

ORIENTAL CHICKEN WITH ANGEL HAIR PASTA

AVERAGE

ingredients:
1 1/2 lb. fat-free chicken tenders, cut in half
1 tsp. garlic powder
1 tsp. onion powder
1 cup frozen carrot slices, thawed and drained
1 large zucchini, sliced
1 tsp. minced garlic
1/2 tsp. ground ginger
1/2 tsp. crushed red pepper
8 oz. fat-free angel hair pasta, cooked and drained
3 tbsp. low-sodium soy sauce
1 tbsp. white wine vinegar
1/3 cup fat-free Parmesan cheese

directions:
Lightly spray wok with nonfat cooking spray and heat over medium-high heat.
Add chicken pieces and sprinkle with garlic and onion powder; stir-fry 5-6 minutes until browned on all sides and cooked through. Remove chicken from wok and set aside; remove wok from heat and respray with cooking spray.
Add carrots, zucchini, minced garlic, ginger and red pepper to wok and stir-fry 2-3 minutes over medium-high heat until vegetables are tender-crisp.
Add pasta, chicken, soy sauce and vinegar; cook 2-3 minutes until heated through.
Sprinkle with Parmesan cheese; cook 1 minute.
Serve immediately.

Serves: 6

Nutrition per Serving		Exchanges
Calories	250	3 meat
Carbohydrate	28 grams	3 vegetable
Cholesterol	56 milligrams	1 starch
Dietary Fiber	2 grams	
Fat	< 1 gram	
Protein	34 grams	
Sodium	591 milligrams	

Shopping List: 1 1/2 pounds fat-free chicken tenders, 10 ounces frozen carrot slices, 1 large zucchini, 8 ounces fat-free angel hair pasta, low-sodium soy sauce, white wine vinegar, fat-free Parmesan cheese, garlic powder, onion powder, minced garlic, ground ginger, crushed red pepper.

ZUCCHINI AND CHICKEN STIR-FRY
EASY - DO AHEAD

ingredients:
6 dried oriental mushrooms
1/2 cup black bean sauce
1 1/2 lb. fat-free chicken tenders, sliced
3 tbsp. fat-free chicken broth, divided
2 large zucchini, cut in chunks
1/2 cup canned bamboo shoots, drained
1 cup red bell peppers, cut in 1-inch pieces
1 cup fat-free stir-fry sauce

directions: Place mushrooms in small bowl and cover with warm water; let mushrooms soak 30 minutes; drain well. Cut off and discard stems; dry mushrooms and slice thin. Place chicken in baking dish; pour black bean sauce over chicken and turn to coat.
Cover and refrigerate 30-45 minutes.
Lightly spray wok with nonfat cooking spray; add 2 tablespoons chicken broth to wok and heat over medium-high heat. Add chicken mixture to wok and cook 4-5 minutes, until chicken is no longer pink and is cooked through. Remove chicken from wok and set aside.
Respray wok with cooking spray; pour remaining broth into wok and heat over medium-high heat. Add mushrooms, bamboo shoots, zucchini and peppers to wok and cook 2-3 minutes.
Pour 2 tablespoons water into wok, cover, and cook until vegetables are tender-crisp, about 2-3 minutes.
Push vegetables away from the center of wok.
Pour stir-fry sauce into wok and cook, stirring constantly, until thick and bubbly. Return chicken to wok.
Mix all ingredients with sauce and cook 1-2 minutes until heated through.

Serves: 4

Nutrition per Serving
Calories 254
Carbohydrate 17 grams
Cholesterol 86 milligrams
Dietary Fiber 2 grams
Fat < 1 gram
Protein 43 grams
Sodium 915 milligrams

Exchanges
5 meat
3 vegetable

Shopping List: 1 1/2 pounds fat-free chicken tenders, dried oriental mushrooms, 4 ounces black bean sauce, 8 ounces fat-free stir-fry sauce, 2 large zucchini, canned bamboo shoots, 1 red bell pepper, fat-free chicken broth.

GINGER STIR-FRY SHRIMP

EASY

ingredients:
2 tbsp. water
3 tbsp. brown sugar
1 tbsp. ground ginger
3/4 tsp. pepper
1 1/2 tsp. minced garlic
1 1/2 lb. fat-free shrimp (medium-large)
1 tbsp. dried basil
1 tsp. lemon juice

directions:
Lightly spray wok with nonfat cooking spray and heat over medium-high heat. Pour water into wok; add brown sugar, ginger, pepper and garlic to water and mix well.
Cook over high heat, stirring frequently, 3-4 minutes until mixture thickens.
Add shrimp and cook 3-4 minutes, stirring constantly, until shrimp turn pink.
Remove wok from heat; stir in basil and lemon juice; mix well.
Serve immediately over cooked fat-free rice or pasta.

Serves: 6

Nutrition per Serving		Exchanges
Calories	139	1 2/3 meat
Carbohydrate	23 grams	1 1/3 fruit
Cholesterol	13 milligrams	
Dietary Fiber	0 grams	
Fat	< 1 gram	
Protein	12 grams	
Sodium	750 milligrams	

Shopping List: 1 1/2 pounds fat-free shrimp, brown sugar, lemon juice, ground ginger, pepper, minced garlic, dried basil.

HONEY-ORANGE SHRIMP

AVERAGE

ingredients:
3/4 cup orange juice
3 tbsp. low-sodium soy sauce
1 1/2 tbsp. cornstarch
1 tbsp. honey
3 tbsp. oriental broth, divided
1 1/2 cups frozen broccoli flowerets, thawed
1 cup frozen carrot slices, thawed
1 cup frozen pea pods, thawed
1 large onion, cut in 1-inch pieces
3/4 tsp. ginger
1 1/2 lb. fat-free shrimp (medium-large)

directions:
In a small bowl, combine orange juice, soy sauce, cornstarch and honey; mix until blended; set aside. Lightly spray a wok with nonfat cooking spray; pour 1 1/2 tablespoons broth into wok and heat over medium-high heat. Add broccoli, carrots, pea pods and onion to wok and sprinkle with ginger. Stir-fry vegetables 3-4 minutes until tender-crisp. Remove vegetables from wok and keep warm. Pour remaining oriental broth into wok and heat over medium-high heat.
Add shrimp to wok and stir-fry 2-3 minutes until shrimp turn pink. Push shrimp to the side of wok and add orange sauce; cook, stirring frequently, until mixture comes to a boil and thickens.
Return vegetables to wok and heat with shrimp and sauce. Serve over rice, couscous, or thin, cooked noodles.

Serves: 6

Nutrition per Serving
Calories	178
Carbohydrate	30 grams
Cholesterol	13 milligrams
Dietary Fiber	2 grams
Fat	< 1 gram
Protein	15 grams
Sodium	1138 milligrams

Exchanges
1 meat
3 vegetable
1 fruit

Shopping List: 1 1/2 pounds fat-free shrimp (medium-large), 7 ounces orange juice, 10 ounces frozen broccoli flowerets, 6 ounces frozen carrot slices, 6 ounces frozen pea pods, 1 large onion, low-sodium soy sauce, cornstarch, honey, oriental broth, ginger.

LEMON-GARLIC SHRIMP

EASY

ingredients:
1 1/2 lb. fat-free shrimp
3 tbsp. flour
1/2 cup dry white wine
3 tbsp. lemon juice
1 1/2 tbsp. low-fat margarine
2 tsp. minced garlic
3 tbsp. chopped green onions
3 cups fat-free cooked rice

directions:
Place shrimp in a medium bowl; sprinkle flour over shrimp and toss to coat.

In a small bowl, combine wine and lemon juice; blend well.

Lightly spray wok with nonfat cooking spray and heat over medium-high heat. Add margarine to wok and cook until melted; add garlic and green onions to wok and stir-fry 1-2 minutes until green onions are tender.

Add shrimp to wok and stir-fry 2-4 minutes, until shrimp turn pink and are cooked through; remove from wok.

Pour wine-lemon sauce into wok and cook until bubbly; stir in shrimp and cook 1-2 minutes until heated through.

Serve over cooked rice.

Serves: 6

Nutrition per Serving		**Exchanges**
Calories	224	1 meat
Carbohydrate	36 grams	2 1/3 starch
Cholesterol	13 milligrams	
Dietary Fiber	1 gram	
Fat	< 1 gram	
Protein	14 grams	
Sodium	778 milligrams	

Shopping List: 1 1/2 pounds fat-free shrimp, 4 ounces dry white wine, green onions, lemon juice, low-fat margarine, fat-free rice, minced garlic, flour.

PASTA WITH SWEET AND SPICY SCALLOPS

AVERAGE

ingredients:
12 oz. fat-free angel hair pasta
1/3 cup chili sauce
1 1/2 tbsp. low-sodium soy sauce
4 tsp. oriental broth, divided
2 tsp. honey
1/2 tsp. ginger
1/4 tsp. crushed red pepper
1 tbsp. minced garlic
1 1/2 lb. fat-free scallops

directions:
Cook pasta according to package directions; rinse, drain and keep warm.

Combine chili sauce, soy sauce, 3 teaspoons oriental broth, honey, ginger and red pepper in a small bowl and mix until blended; set aside.

Lightly spray wok with nonfat cooking spray; pour remaining broth into wok and heat over medium-high heat.

Add garlic and stir-fry 2 minutes. Add scallops to wok and stir-fry 2 minutes.

Pour sauce over scallops and cook 3-4 minutes, stirring frequently, until scallops are opaque. Serve scallops over pasta.

Serves: 6

Nutrition per Serving

Calories	286
Carbohydrate	52 grams
Cholesterol	13 milligrams
Dietary Fiber	2 grams
Fat	< 1 gram
Protein	19 grams
Sodium	1100 milligrams

Exchanges
3 1/4 starch
1 meat

Shopping List: 12 ounces fat-free angel hair pasta, 1 1/2 pounds fat-free scallops, chili sauce, low-sodium soy sauce, oriental broth, honey, ginger, crushed red pepper, minced garlic.

SEAFOOD LO MEIN
AVERAGE

ingredients: 8 ounces fat-free angel hair pasta, cooked
and drained
1 1/2 tbsp. oriental broth
1 1/2 cups sliced celery
3/4 cup chopped onion
3 cups shredded cabbage
1 2 ounces frozen pea pods, thawed
3/4 cup shredded carrots
1 cup sliced water chestnuts
1 1/2 lb. fat-free shrimp
1/2 cup low-sodium teriyaki sauce

directions: Cook pasta according to package directions; drain
well and keep warm. Lightly spray wok with non-
fat cooking spray; pour broth into wok and heat
over medium-high heat. Add celery, onion, cabbage, pea pods, carrots and water chestnuts to wok
and stir-fry 3-5 minutes until vegetables are tender-crisp; remove vegetables from wok.
Respray wok with nonfat cooking spray; add
shrimp and stir-fry 2-3 minutes, until shrimp turn
pink and are cooked through.
Push shrimp to the side of the wok. Pour teriyaki
sauce into center of wok and heat until bubbly.
Add vegetable mixture, shrimp and cooked pasta
and stir-fry 3-4 minutes until all ingredients are
mixed, coated and heated through.
Serve immediately.

Serves: 6

Nutrition per Serving

		Exchanges
Calories	295	2 starch
Carbohydrate	54 grams	4 vegetable
Cholesterol	13 milligrams	1 meat
Dietary Fiber	5 grams	
Fat	< 1 gram	
Protein	20 grams	
Sodium	1238 milligrams	

Shopping List: 1 1/2 pounds fat-free shrimp, 4 ounces low-sodium teriyaki sauce, 2 6-ounce packages frozen
pea pods, celery, 1 large onion, 8 ounces packaged
shredded carrots, packaged shredded cabbage,
oriental broth, 8 ounces fat-free angel hair pasta,
8 ounces canned sliced water chestnuts.

SHRIMP WITH BROCCOLI
EASY - DO AHEAD

ingredients: 3 cups fat-free angel hair pasta, cooked and drained
3 tbsp. low-sodium soy sauce
3 tbsp. dry sherry
3/4 tsp. ginger
1 1/4 tsp. sugar
2 tbsp. oriental broth, divided
2 16-ounce packages frozen broccoli flowerets, thawed
1/2 cup chopped green bell pepper
1/2 cup chopped red bell pepper
1 tsp. garlic powder
1 1/2 lb. fat-free shrimp

directions: Cook pasta according to package directions; drain well and keep warm. Combine soy sauce, sherry, ginger and sugar in a small bowl and mix until blended.Place shrimp in a shallow baking dish; pour sauce over shrimp and turn to coat. Cover and refrigerate 30-45 minutes. Lightly spray wok with nonfat cooking spray; pour 1 tablespoon broth into wok and heat over medium-high heat. Add broccoli and peppers to wok; sprinkle with garlic powder. Stir-fry vegetables 3-4 minutes until tender-crisp. Remove vegetables from wok. Respray wok with nonfat cooking spray; pour remaining broth into wok and heat over medium-high heat. Add shrimp to wok (reserve marinade) and stir-fry 3-5 minutes, until shrimp turn pink and are cooked through. Push shrimp from the center of wok. Pour reserved marinade into center of wok and cook 1-2 minutes, stirring constantly, until sauce becomes bubbly. Return vegetable to wok; mix all ingredients with sauce and cook 1-2 minutes until heated through. Serve over cooked pasta.

Serves: 6

Nutrition per Serving
Calories	272
Carbohydrate	47 grams
Cholesterol	13 milligrams
Dietary Fiber	7 grams
Fat	< 1 gram
Protein	22 grams
Sodium	1108 milligrams

Exchanges
1 meat
2 starch
3 vegetable

Shopping List: 12 ounces fat-free angel hair pasta, 1 1/2 pounds shrimp, 2 16-ounce packages frozen broccoli flowerets, 1 small green bell pepper, 1 small red pepper, low-sodium soy sauce, dry sherry, oriental broth, sugar, garlic powder, ginger.

SEAFOOD WITH PEA PODS

EASY

ingredients:
2 tsp. cornstarch
1/2 tsp. ginger
1/4 cup low-sodium soy sauce
3 tbsp. dry sherry
1 cup fat-free chicken broth
1 1/2 tsp. minced garlic
3/4 lb. fat-free shrimp
3/4 lb. fat-free scallops
2 1/4 cups frozen pea pods, thawed
1 cup sliced water chestnuts
3 tbsp. sliced green onions
3/4 cup bamboo shoots, drained

directions:
Combine cornstarch, ginger, soy sauce, sherry and chicken broth in a medium bowl and blend until smooth; set aside.
Lightly spray wok with nonfat cooking spray and heat over medium-high heat.
Add garlic, shrimp and scallops to wok and stir-fry 1 minute.
Add pea pods and stir-fry 30-45 seconds.
Add water chestnuts, onions and bamboo shoots and stir-fry 1-2 minutes. Pour sauce over seafood mixture and cook over high heat until mixture boils and thickens; shrimp will turn pink and scallops will be opaque when done.

Serves: 6

Nutrition per Serving

		Exchanges
Calories	167	1 meat
Carbohydrate	25 grams	5 vegetable
Cholesterol	13 milligrams	
Dietary Fiber	2 grams	
Fat	< 1 gram	
Protein	15 grams	
Sodium	1303 milligrams	

Shopping List: 3/4 pound fat-free shrimp, 3/4 pound fat-free scallops, 2 6-ounce packages frozen Chinese pea pods, 8 ounces can sliced water chestnuts, 8-ounce can bamboo shoots, 8 ounces fat-free chicken broth, green onions, 2 ounces low-sodium soy sauce, dry sherry, minced garlic, cornstarch, ginger.

CHICKEN-FRIED RICE

AVERAGE - DO AHEAD

ingredients:
1/2 cup fat-free chicken broth
1/4 tbsp. low-sodium soy sauce
1 1/2 tsp. ginger
1 1/2 tbsp. hoisin sauce
1/2 tsp. crushed red pepper
1 1/2 cups fat-free chicken tenders, cubed
3/4 cup egg substitute
2 egg whites
10 oz. frozen pea pods, thawed
1 cup whole baby corn, drained
3/4 cup sliced water chestnuts
6 cups fat-free cooked rice
1 1/2 cups pineapple tidbits in juice, drained

directions: Combine chicken broth, soy sauce, ginger, hoisin sauce and red pepper in a small bowl and mix until blended. Lightly spray wok with nonfat cooking spray and heat over medium-high heat. Add chicken cubes to wok and cook 3-5 minutes, stirring frequently, until chicken is no longer pink; remove chicken and set aside. Respray wok and return to medium-high heat. In a small bowl, combine egg substitute and egg whites; mix until blended. Pour egg mixture into wok; cook until eggs are set, but still moist. Remove from wok and set aside. Remove wok from heat and respray with cooking spray; heat over medium-high heat. Add snow peas, corn and water chestnuts to wok and stir-fry 2-3 minutes until vegetables are tender-crisp. Push the vegetables to the side of the wok; add cooked rice and stir-fry 2-3 minutes until rice begins to brown. Add pineapple, chicken, egg mixture and vegetables; cook 5-6 minutes until heated through.

Serves: 6

Nutrition per Serving
Calories	326
Carbohydrate	57 grams
Cholesterol	28 milligrams
Dietary Fiber	4 grams
Fat	< 1 gram
Protein	22 grams
Sodium	325 milligrams

Exchanges
2 starch
1 meat
5 vegetable

Shopping List: 1 1/4 pounds fat-free chicken tenders, 16 ounces pineapple tidbits in juice, 6 ounces egg substitute, eggs, 10 ounces frozen pea pods, canned whole baby sweet corn, sliced water chestnuts, 4 ounces fat-free chicken broth, low-sodium soy sauce, hoisin sauce, ginger, crushed red pepper, fat-free rice.

COUSCOUS WITH VEGETABLE MEDLEY

AVERAGE

ingredients:
1 medium yellow squash, diced
2 medium zucchini, diced
1 1/2 cups sliced mushrooms
1/2 cup diced onions
1 1/2 cups diced red and green bell peppers
1/3 cup fat-free chicken broth, divided
3/4 cup + 3 tbsp. water
3/4 cup couscous, uncooked

directions:
Lightly spray a wok with nonfat cooking spray and heat over high heat.

Add squash, zucchini, mushrooms, onions and peppers to wok and stir-fry 3-4 minutes until tender-crisp.

Heat chicken broth in a saucepan or microwave until hot. Remove vegetables from wok and place in a medium bowl; pour 3 tablespoons chicken broth over vegetables.

Set aside, cover, and keep warm.

Combine remaining chicken broth and water in wok and bring to a boil over high heat.

Remove wok from heat and stir in couscous. Cover wok and let stand 5 minutes until liquid is absorbed.

Add couscous to vegetable mixture; toss and serve.

Serves: 6

Nutrition per Serving
Calories	118
Carbohydrate	25 grams
Cholesterol	0 milligrams
Dietary Fiber	6 grams
Fat	< 1 gram
Protein	5 grams
Sodium	51 milligrams

Exchanges
1 starch
2 vegetable

Shopping List: 1 yellow squash, 2 zucchini, 1 onion, 8-10 fresh mushrooms, 1 small red bell pepper, 1 small green bell pepper, fat-free chicken broth, couscous.

FRIED RICE

AVERAGE

ingredients:
1/4 cup egg substitute
2 large egg whites
1/3 cup shredded carrots
2 tbsp. chopped green onions
1/4 tsp. ginger
1 1/2 cups fat-free cooked rice
3/4 cup chopped Chinese cabbage
2 tbsp. low-sodium soy sauce
3/4 tsp. dry mustard

directions:
Combine egg substitute and egg whites in a small bowl and beat until blended.
Lightly spray wok with nonfat cooking spray and heat over medium-high heat.
Pour egg mixture into wok and cook, without stirring, until eggs begin to set.
Stir eggs and break into small pieces until cooked through; remove from wok and set aside.
Remove wok from heat and respray with cooking spray; heat over medium-high heat. Add carrots and green onions to wok; sprinkle with ginger and stir-fry 3 minutes until vegetables are tender.
Stir in rice, cabbage and cooked eggs. Pour soy sauce over mixture and sprinkle with mustard.
Carefully toss vegetables to coat and cook 4-5 minutes over medium heat until heated through.

Serves: 6

Nutrition per Serving		**Exchanges**
Calories	93	1 starch
Carbohydrate	19 grams	1 vegetable
Cholesterol	0 milligrams	
Dietary Fiber	< 1 gram	
Fat	< 1 gram	
Protein	4 grams	
Sodium	246 milligrams	

Shopping List: 2 ounces egg substitute, eggs, packaged shredded carrots, green onions, fat-free rice, 1/2 pound Chinese cabbage, low-sodium soy sauce, ground ginger, dry mustard.

SCRAMBLED EGGS WITH PEPPERS AND ONIONS

EASY

---

ingredients:
1/2 cup chopped green bell pepper
1/2 cup chopped red bell pepper
1 cup chopped red onion
1 tbsp. chopped green chilies
6 egg whites
2 cups egg substitute
1/2 cup fat-free sour cream
3/4 cup chopped tomatoes

directions:
Lightly spray wok with nonfat cooking spray and heat over medium-high heat. Add red and green peppers, onions and chilies to wok and stir-fry until vegetables become tender and soft.
Remove vegetables from wok and set aside.
Combine egg whites, egg substitute and sour cream in a large bowl and mix until frothy and blended. Add cooked vegetables and tomatoes to egg mixture and blend well.
Respray with cooking spray and heat over medium-high heat.
Pour egg mixture into wok and cook, stirring frequently, until eggs are cooked through.
Serve with fat-free salsa, if desired.

Serves: 6

Nutrition per Serving		Exchanges
Calories	87	2 vegetable
Carbohydrate	8 grams	1 meat
Cholesterol	0 milligrams	
Dietary Fiber	1 gram	
Fat	< 1 gram	
Protein	12 grams	
Sodium	242 milligrams	

Shopping List: 1 small green pepper, 1 small red bell pepper, 1 onion, canned green chilies, eggs, 16 ounces egg substitute, 4 ounces fat-free sour cream, 1 tomato.

SPICY COUSCOUS
EASY

ingredients: 2 1/4 cups couscous
3 cups fat-free chicken broth
1/2 tsp. pepper
1/4 tsp. cinnamon
1/8 tsp. ground cloves

directions: Lightly spray wok with nonfat cooking spray and heat over medium-high heat.
Add couscous and stir-fry 2-3 minutes.
Pour broth into wok; add pepper, cinnamon and cloves and mix well.
Cook over medium-high heat, stirring frequently, until liquid is completely absorbed.

Serves: 6

Nutrition per Serving   **Exchanges**
Calories   264   3 1/3 meat
Carbohydrate   54 grams
Cholesterol   0 milligrams
Dietary Fiber   11 grams
Fat   < 1 gram
Protein   9 grams
Sodium   457 milligrams

Shopping List: couscous, 16 ounces fat-free chicken broth, pepper, cinnamon, ground cloves.

SWEET AND SPICY APPLES

EASY

ingredients: 1 cup water
2 tbsp. sugar
2 tbsp. brown sugar
1/4 cup raisins
1/4 cup cranberry-apple juice
1 tsp. cinnamon
32 ounces canned apple slices

directions: Pour water into wok; stir in sugar, brown sugar, raisins, juice and cinnamon; bring to a boil over high heat, stirring frequently.
Add apple slices, cover and reduce heat to medium-low.
Cook apple mixture 8-10 minutes, until apples are tender and heated through.

Serves: 6

Nutrition per Serving		Exchanges
Calories	158	2 2/3 fruit
Carbohydrate	40 grams	
Cholesterol	0 milligrams	
Dietary Fiber	4 grams	
Fat	< 1 gram	
Protein	< 1 gram	
Sodium	8 milligrams	

Shopping List: 32 ounces canned apple slices, cranberry-apple juice, sugar, brown sugar, raisins, cinnamon.

CHINESE CABBAGE STIR-FRY

EASY

---

ingredients:
3/4 cup low-sodium teriyaki sauce
3 tsp. cornstarch
1/2 tsp. garlic powder
1/2 tsp. crushed red pepper
2 16-ounce packages frozen pepper-onion
    stir-fry mixture, thawed
4 cups Chinese cabbage, cut in thin strips

directions:
Combine teriyaki sauce, cornstarch, garlic powder and red pepper in a small bowl and mix until blended; set aside.
Lightly spray wok with nonfat cooking spray and heat over medium-high heat.
Add pepper stir-fry mix and cook 1-2 minutes until vegetables are tender.
Stir in cabbage and cook 2-3 minutes until cabbage is tender-crisp. Toss vegetables together and push to side of wok.
Pour sauce into center of wok and cook 1-2 minutes over medium heat, until sauce thickens.
Stir vegetables into sauce and mix well.
Serve immediately.

Serves: 6

Nutrition from Serving

Calories	90
Carbohydrate	20 grams
Cholesterol	0 milligrams
Dietary Fiber	3 grams
Fat	< 1 gram
Protein	3 grams
Sodium	650 milligrams

Exchanges

1 vegetable
1 fruit

Shopping List: 6 ounces low-sodium teriyaki sauce, 32 ounces frozen pepper-onion stir-fry mix, 3/4 pound Chinese cabbage, garlic powder, crushed red pepper, cornstarch.

FRESH SPINACH STIR-FRY

EASY

ingredients:
1 tsp. oriental broth
1 1/2 tbsp. minced garlic
3 lb. fresh spinach, torn into bite-size pieces
3 tbsp. lemon juice
1/4 tsp. pepper

directions:
Lightly spray wok with nonfat cooking spray; pour oriental broth into wok and heat over medium-high heat.
Add garlic and stir-fry 3-4 minutes until garlic becomes golden brown.
Add spinach and stir-fry 3-4 minutes, until spinach becomes wilted; reduce heat to medium.
Sprinkle lemon juice and pepper over spinach and cook, stirring frequently, 2-3 minutes.

Serves: 6

Nutrition per Serving		Exchanges
Calories	43	2 vegetable
Carbohydrate	7 grams	
Cholesterol	0 milligrams	
Dietary Fiber	1 gram	
Fat	< 1 gram	
Protein	5 grams	
Sodium	125 milligrams	

Shopping List: 3 pounds fresh spinach, minced garlic, lemon juice, fat-free oriental broth, pepper.

RED, WHITE AND GREEN STIR-FRY

EASY

ingredients: 1 1/2 tbsp. fat-free vegetable broth
1 small onion, cut into chunks
1/2 tsp. ground ginger
3/4 tsp. minced garlic
1 medium green bell pepper, cut into strips
1 medium red bell pepper, cut into strips
1/2 lb. jicama, cut in 2-inch strips
1/4 cup fat-free stir-fry sauce

directions: Lightly spray wok with nonfat cooking spray; pour broth into wok and heat over medium-high heat.
Add onion, ginger and garlic to wok and stir-fry 30 seconds.
Add peppers and jicama and stir-fry 2-3 minutes until vegetables are tender-crisp.
Pour stir-fry sauce over mixture and cook 1-2 minutes until heated through.

Serves: 6

Nutrition per Serving		Exchanges
Calories	51	2 vegetable
Carbohydrate	11 grams	
Cholesterol	0 milligrams	
Dietary Fiber	2 grams	
Fat	< 1 gram	
Protein	1 gram	
Sodium	70 milligrams	

Shopping List: fat-free vegetable broth, 2 ounces fat-free stir-fry sauce, 1 small onion, 1 green bell pepper, 1 red bell pepper, 1/2 pound jicama, ground ginger, minced garlic.

SWEET 'N SOUR CARROTS AND CAULIFLOWER

EASY

ingredients: 1/2 cup + 3 tbsp. fat-free chicken broth, divided
1/4 cup brown sugar
1/4 cup vinegar
2 tbsp. cornstarch
3 10-ounce packages frozen carrot slices
3 10-ounce packages frozen cauliflower
flowerets
1 large onion, cut in 1/4-inch slices

directions: Combine 1/2 cup chicken broth, brown sugar, vinegar and cornstarch in a medium bowl and blend well; set aside.
Lightly spray wok with nonfat cooking spray and heat over medium-high heat.
Add carrots, cauliflower and onion to wok and stir-fry 1-2 minutes.
Reduce heat to medium; pour remaining chicken broth over vegetables, cover, and cook 6-8 minutes until vegetables are tender-crisp.
Increase heat to high; pour reserved sauce into wok and cook, stirring constantly, until sauce becomes thick and bubbly.
Serve immediately.

Serves: 6

Nutrition per Serving
Calories	140
Carbohydrate	33 grams
Cholesterol	0 milligrams
Dietary Fiber	9 grams
Fat	< 1 gram
Protein	5 grams
Sodium	172 milligrams

Exchanges
3 vegetable
1 fruit

Shopping List: 6 ounces fat-free chicken broth, 3 10-ounce packages frozen carrot slices, 3 10-ounce packages frozen cauliflower flowerets, 1 large onion, brown sugar, 2 ounces vinegar, cornstarch.

VEGETABLE STIR-FRY

EASY - DO AHEAD

ingredients:
3/4 cup fat-free chicken broth
3 tbsp. orange juice
3 tbsp. low-sodium soy sauce
1 1/2 tbsp. cornstarch
1/2 tsp. ginger
1 tbsp. garlic powder
1/4 tsp. crushed red pepper
1 1/2 cups cauliflower flowerets
1 1/2 cups broccoli flowerets
1 1/2 cups sliced carrots
1 red bell pepper, sliced thin
1 zucchini, sliced 1/4-inch thick

directions:
Combine chicken broth, orange juice, soy sauce and cornstarch in a small bowl and mix until well blended; set aside.
In a small bowl, combine garlic powder, ginger and crushed red pepper; mix well (seasoning blend).
Lightly spray wok with nonfat cooking spray and heat over medium-high heat. Add cauliflower, broccoli, carrots, bell pepper and zucchini to wok; sprinkle with seasoning blend and stir-fry 3-5 minutes, until vegetables are tender-crisp.
Pour sauce into wok and mix well with vegetables. Reduce heat to medium, cover wok and cook 2-3 minutes, until sauce thickens and mixture is heated through.
Serve immediately.

Serves: 6

Nutrition per Serving
Calories   49
Carbohydrate   11 grams
Cholesterol   0 milligrams
Dietary Fiber   2 grams
Fat   < 1 gram
Protein   3 grams
Sodium   513 milligrams

Exchanges
2 vegetable

Shopping List: 6 ounces fat-free chicken broth, orange juice, low-sodium soy sauce, 1 pound cauliflower, 1 pound broccoli, 1/2 pound carrots, 1 red bell pepper, 1 zucchini, cornstarch, ginger, garlic powder, crushed red pepper.

BLACK BEAN SAUCE

EASY - DO AHEAD

ingredients:
1 tbsp. low-sodium soy sauce
1 tbsp. cornstarch
1 tbsp. dry sherry
1 tbsp. water
1/4 tsp. garlic powder
1/4 tsp. ginger
1 tbsp. black beans, chopped
1 1/2 tsp. fat-free chicken broth

directions:
Combine all ingredients in a bowl and mix until blended.
Cover with plastic wrap and refrigerate until ready to use in favorite stir-fry recipe.

Serves: 4

Nutrition per Serving		Exchanges
Calories	20	Free
Carbohydrate	13 grams	
Cholesterol	0 milligrams	
Dietary Fiber	< 1 gram	
Fat	< 1 gram	
Protein	1 gram	
Sodium	157 milligrams	

Shopping List: low-sodium soy sauce, cornstarch, dry sherry, garlic powder, ginger, black beans, fat-free chicken broth.

STIR-FRY SAUCE

EASY - DO AHEAD

ingredients:
1 1/2 cups water
3 tbsp. dry sherry
5 tbsp. low-sodium soy sauce
1 tsp. sugar
2 tsp. fat-free chicken broth
2 tbsp. cornstarch

directions:
Combine all ingredients and mix until blended smooth.
Add mixture according to recipe directions calling for stir-fry sauce.
Heat until sauce becomes thick and bubbly.

Serves: 8

Nutrition per Serving		Exchanges
Calories	23	Free
Carbohydrate	4 grams	
Cholesterol	0 milligrams	
Dietary Fiber	0 grams	
Fat	< 1 gram	
Protein	1 gram	
Sodium	381 milligrams	

Shopping List: dry sherry, low-sodium soy sauce, sugar, fat-free chicken broth, cornstarch.

ECIPES FOR

Fat Free Living
BLENDERS

by Jyl Steinback

- Drinks
- Desserts
- Dressings
- Spreads & Dips
- Soups

APPLE BERRY CREAM SMOOTHIE

EASY - DO AHEAD - FREEZE

ingredients: 1 cup apple juice
3/4 cup fat-free frozen vanilla yogurt
3/4 cup frozen strawberries (unsweetened)
4-5 ice cubes

directions: Combine all ingredients in the blender and process on high speed until creamy and smooth.

Serves: 2

Nutrition per Serving		Exchanges
Calories	143	2 fruit
Carbohydrate	32 grams	1/4 milk
Cholesterol	0 milligrams	
Dietary Fiber	2 grams	
Fat	< 1 gram	
Protein	3 grams	
Sodium	54 milligrams	

Shopping List: 8 ounces apple juice, 6 ounces fat-free vanilla yogurt, frozen strawberries (unsweetened).

BERRY-CRANBERRY SMOOTHIE

EASY - DO AHEAD - FREEZE

ingredients:
1 cup low-calorie cranberry juice
1/2 cup fat-free frozen vanilla yogurt
1/4 cup frozen raspberries (unsweetened)
1/4 cup frozen blueberries (unsweetened)
1/4 cup frozen strawberries (unsweetened)
5-6 ice cubes

directions:
Combine all ingredients in the blender and process on high speed until creamy and smooth.

Serves: 1

Nutrition per Serving		Exchanges
Calories	182	2 fruit
Carbohydrate	41 grams	2/3 milk
Cholesterol	0 milligrams	
Dietary Fiber	4 grams	
Fat	< 1 gram	
Protein	5 grams	
Sodium	71 milligrams	

Shopping List: 8 ounces low-calorie cranberry juice, 4 ounces fat-free frozen vanilla yogurt, frozen raspberries, frozen blueberries, frozen strawberries (unsweetened).

BLUEBERRY BREAKFAST SHAKE

EASY - DO AHEAD

ingredients: 1 cup fat-free blueberry yogurt
1/2 cup skim milk
1 small banana, cut in chunks
1/2 cup frozen blueberries (unsweetened)
1 1/2 tbsp. nonfat dry milk powder
1 tsp. honey
1 tsp. sugar

directions: Combine all ingredients in the blender and process on high speed until creamy and smooth.

Serves: 2

Nutrition per Serving		Exchanges
Calories	164	1 milk
Carbohydrate	33 grams	1 1/4 fruit
Cholesterol	4 milligrams	
Dietary Fiber	2 grams	
Fat	< 1 gram	
Protein	8 grams	
Sodium	120 milligrams	

Shopping List: 8 ounces fat-free blueberry yogurt, 4 ounces skim milk, 1 banana, unsweetened frozen blueberries, nonfat dry milk powder, honey, sugar.

COCA-MOCHA SHAKE

EASY

ingredients: 1 cup fat-free frozen coffee yogurt
1 cup skim milk
2 tbsp. lite chocolate syrup
1 tbsp. freeze-dried coffee

directions: Combine all ingredients in the blender and process until creamy and smooth.

Serves: 2

Nutrition per Serving		Exchanges
Calories	160	1 milk
Carbohydrate	31 grams	1 1/3 fruit
Cholesterol	2 milligrams	
Dietary Fiber	9 grams	
Fat	< 1 gram	
Protein	9 grams	
Sodium	130 milligrams	

Shopping List: 8 ounces fat-free frozen coffee yogurt, 8 ounces
skim milk, 1 ounce lite chocolate syrup, freeze-
dried coffee.

CRANBERRY-RASPBERRY FIZZ

EASY - DO AHEAD

ingredients: 1 1/2 cups cranberry-raspberry juice
1 cup fat-free raspberry sherbet
1/2 cup seltzer water

directions: Combine all ingredients in the blender and process on high speed until smooth.

Serves: 2

Nutrition per Serving		Exchanges
Calories	243	4 fruit
Carbohydrate	57 grams	
Cholesterol	7 milligrams	
Dietary Fiber	0 grams	
Fat	< 1 gram	
Protein	1 gram	
Sodium	52 milligrams	

Shopping List: 12 ounces cranberry-raspberry juice, 8 ounces fat-free raspberry sherbet, 4 ounces seltzer water.

ORANGE-BANANA FREEZE

EASY - DO AHEAD - FREEZE

ingredients: 1 cup orange juice
3/4 cup fat-free frozen vanilla yogurt
1 small banana
1/2 cup crushed ice

directions: Combine all ingredients in the blender and process on high speed until creamy and smooth.

Serves: 1

Nutrition per Serving		Exchanges
Calories	344	1 milk
Carbohydrate	78 grams	4 1/3 fruit
Cholesterol	0 milligrams	
Dietary Fiber	2 grams	
Fat	< 1 gram	
Protein	9 grams	
Sodium	96 milligrams	

Shopping List: 8 ounces orange juice, 6 ounces fat-free frozen vanilla yogurt, 1 banana.

PEACH MELBA SMOOTHIE

EASY - DO AHEAD - FREEZE

ingredients:
1 cup cranberry-raspberry juice
1/2 cup frozen peach slices (unsweetened)
1/4 cup frozen raspberries (unsweetened)
1/2 cup fat-free frozen vanilla yogurt
4-5 ice cubes

BOUNTIFUL BLENDER

directions:
Combine all ingredients in the blender and process on high speed until creamy and smooth.

Serves: 2

Nutrition per Serving		Exchanges
Calories	143	1/4 milk
Carbohydrate	34 grams	2 fruit
Cholesterol	0 milligrams	
Dietary Fiber	1 gram	
Fat	< 1 gram	
Protein	2 grams	
Sodium	35 milligrams	

Shopping List: 8 ounces cranberry-raspberry juice, frozen peach slices, frozen raspberries, 4 ounces fat-free frozen vanilla yogurt.

PINEAPPLE-MANGO CHILL

EASY - DO AHEAD

ingredients:
1/2 mango, peeled and cut into chunks
1/2 banana, peeled and sliced
2 cups pineapple chunks in juice, drained
1/2 cup pineapple juice
6 ice cubes

directions: Combine all ingredients in the blender and process on high speed until creamy and smooth.

Serves: 2

Nutrition per Serving		Exchanges
Calories	245	4 1/4 fruit
Carbohydrate	63 grams	
Cholesterol	0 milligrams	
Dietary Fiber	4 grams	
Fat	< 1 gram	
Protein	2 grams	
Sodium	6 milligrams	

Shopping List: Mango, banana, 16 ounces pineapple chunks in juice, 4 ounces pineapple juice.

PROTEIN POWER SHAKE

EASY - DO AHEAD

ingredients:
1 cup apple juice
1 large banana
1 cup fat-free strawberry-banana yogurt
3/4 oz. protein powder
5-6 ice cubes

directions: Combine all ingredients in the blender and process on high speed until creamy and smooth.

Serves: 2

Nutrition per Serving		Exchanges
Calories	207	1 2/3 milk
Carbohydrate	38 grams	1 fruit
Cholesterol	4 milligrams	
Dietary Fiber	1 gram	
Fat	< 1 gram	
Protein	14 grams	
Sodium	88 milligrams	

Shopping List: 8 ounces apple juice, 1 banana, 8 ounces fat-free strawberry-banana yogurt, fat-free protein powder (purchase at health food store).

PURELY FRUIT CREAM SMOOTHIE

EASY - DO AHEAD - FREEZE

ingredients: 1/2 cup fat-free strawberry yogurt
1 small banana, sliced
1/4 cup frozen raspberries
1/2 cup fresh, sliced strawberries
4-5 ice cubes

directions: Combine all ingredients in the blender and process on high speed until creamy and smooth.

Serves: 1

Nutrition per Serving

Calories	191	
Carbohydrate	44 grams	
Cholesterol	0 milligrams	
Dietary Fiber	5 grams	
Fat	< 1 gram	
Protein	6 grams	
Sodium	5 milligrams	

Exchanges
2/3 milk
2 1/3 fruit

Shopping List: 4 ounces fat-free frozen strawberry yogurt, 1 banana, frozen raspberries, 1/4 pint fresh strawberries.

RASPBERRY LEMONADE SLUSH

EASY - DO AHEAD - FREEZE

ingredients: 6 ounces lemonade frozen concentrate, thawed
2 cups water
2 cups ice cubes
3/4 cup frozen raspberries
1 tbsp. sugar

directions: Combine all ingredients in the blender and process on high speed until slushy and smooth.

Serves: 2

Nutrition per Serving

Calories	210
Carbohydrate	55 grams
Cholesterol	0 milligrams
Dietary Fiber	4 grams
Fat	< 1 gram
Protein	0 grams
Sodium	2 milligrams

Exchanges
3 2/3 fruit

Shopping List: 6 ounces lemonade frozen concentrate, 6 ounces frozen raspberries, sugar.

RED, WHITE AND BLUE SMOOTHIE

EASY - DO AHEAD - FREEZE

ingredients:
1 cup low-calorie cranberry juice
3/4 cup fat-free frozen vanilla yogurt
1/4 cup frozen cranberries
1/2 cup frozen blueberries
4-6 ice cubes

directions:
Combine all ingredients in the blender and process on high speed until creamy and smooth.

Serves: 1

Nutrition per Serving		Exchanges
Calories	232	1 milk
Carbohydrate	51 grams	2 2/3 fruit
Cholesterol	0 milligrams	
Dietary Fiber	2 grams	
Fat	< 1 gram	
Protein	7 grams	
Sodium	101 milligrams	

Shopping List: 8 ounces low-calorie cranberry juice, 6 ounces fat-free frozen vanilla yogurt, frozen cranberries, frozen blueberries.

STRAWBERRY BREAKFAST BLAST

EASY - DO AHEAD

ingredients: 1 cup orange juice
1 cup fat-free strawberry-banana yogurt
1 medium banana, sliced
3/4 cup strawberries, sliced
4-5 ice cubes

directions: Combine all ingredients in the blender and process on high speed until creamy and smooth.

Serves: 2

Nutrition per Serving		Exchanges
Calories	166	2/3 milk
Carbohydrate	37 grams	2 fruit
Cholesterol	3 milligrams	
Dietary Fiber	2 grams	
Fat	< 1 gram	
Protein	6 grams	
Sodium	74 milligrams	

Shopping List: 8 ounces orange juice, 8 ounces fat-free strawberry-banana yogurt, 1 banana, 1/2 pint strawberries.

SWEET AND SPICY BANANA SMOOTHIE

EASY - DO AHEAD

ingredients:
3/4 cup skim milk
1/2 cup fat-free banana yogurt
1 large banana, sliced
3/4 tsp. cinnamon
1/4 tsp. nutmeg
5-6 ice cubes

directions:
Combine all ingredients in the blender and process on high speed until creamy and smooth.

Serves: 2

Nutrition per Serving		Exchanges
Calories	124	2/3 milk
Carbohydrate	25 grams	1 fruit
Cholesterol	3 milligrams	
Dietary Fiber	1 gram	
Fat	< 1 gram	
Protein	6 grams	
Sodium	83 milligrams	

Shopping List: 6 ounces skim milk, 4 ounces fat-free banana yogurt, 1 banana, cinnamon, nutmeg.

TROPICAL FRUIT SMOOTHIE

EASY - DO AHEAD - FREEZE

ingredients: 1 cup frozen Tropical Fruit Medley
1/2 cup fat-free frozen vanilla yogurt or fat-
free pineapple sherbet
4-5 ice cubes

directions: Combine all ingredients in the blender and process on high speed until creamy and smooth.

Serves: 1

Nutrition per Serving

Calories	325
Carbohydrate	78 grams
Cholesterol	0 milligrams
Dietary Fiber	4 grams
Fat	< 1 gram
Protein	6 grams
Sodium	75 milligrams

Exchanges

4 2/3 fruit
2/3 milk

Shopping List: Frozen Tropical Fruit Medley, 4 ounces fat-free
frozen vanilla yogurt or 4 ounces fat-free pine-
apple sherbet.

CHOCOLATE SHERBET

AVERAGE - DO AHEAD - FREEZE

ingredients:
1/3 cup unsweetened cocoa powder
1/2 cup sugar
1/3 cup hot water
1 1/4 cups skim milk
3 tbsp. cold water

directions:
Combine cocoa and sugar in a small saucepan and cook over low heat.

Add hot water and cook, stirring constantly, 2-3 minutes until the sugar is dissolved.

Remove from heat and stir in milk; mix until blended.

Pour mixture into 9x13-inch baking dish, cover, and freeze 6-8 hours.

Remove from freezer and let stand at room temperature 5 minutes.

Break sherbet apart and place in blender with cold water.

Blend on high speed until creamy and smooth.

Pour into plastic container, cover, and freeze 4-6 hours until set.

Serves: 6

Nutrition per Serving		Exchanges
Calories	87	1/3 milk
Carbohydrate	21 grams	1 fruit
Cholesterol	1 milligram	
Dietary Fiber	0 grams	
Fat	< 1 gram	
Protein	3 grams	
Sodium	29 milligrams	

Shopping List: 10 ounces skim milk, unsweetened cocoa powder, sugar.

FROZEN FRUIT YOGURT POPS

EASY - DO AHEAD - FREEZE

ingredients: 2 cups fat-free strawberry-banana yogurt
1/2 cup crushed pineapple
6 ounces frozen pine-orange banana concentrate

directions: Combine all ingredients in the blender and process on high speed until creamy and smooth.
Pour mixture into paper cups or 8-inch baking dish and freeze 4-6 hours until firm.
If using paper cups, peel paper away and invert into bowl to serve.

Serves: 6

Nutrition per Serving		Exchanges
Calories	88	1/3 milk
Carbohydrate	19 grams	1 fruit
Cholesterol	2 milligrams	
Dietary Fiber	<1 gram	
Fat	< 1 gram	
Protein	3 grams	
Sodium	48 milligrams	

Shopping List: 16 ounces fat-free strawberry-banana yogurt, 4 ounces crushed pineapple, 6 ounces frozen pine-orange banana concentrate.

FRUIT ROLL-UPS

EASY - DO AHEAD

ingredients: 2 pints strawberries, sliced
2 3/4 tbsp. corn syrup

directions: Preheat oven to 140 degrees.
Line baking sheet with plastic wrap and lightly spray with nonfat cooking spray.
Combine strawberries and corn syrup in blender and blend on high speed until smooth.
Pour mixture onto baking sheet and spread until mixture is even.
Bake in preheated oven with door slightly ajar 3 hours, or until fruit is dry.
Cool completely at room temperature; roll in plastic wrap and store.

Serves: 4

Nutrition per Serving		Exchanges
Calories	86	1 1/3 fruit
Carbohydrate	21 grams	
Cholesterol	0 milligrams	
Dietary Fiber	4 grams	
Fat	< 1 gram	
Protein	1 gram	
Sodium	12 milligrams	

Shopping List: 2 pints strawberries, corn syrup.

RASPBERRY-LEMONADE SORBET

BOUNTIFUL BLENDER

ingredients: 12 oz. raspberry-lemonade frozen concentrate
1/4 cup honey
1 3/4 cups cold water
3/4 cup frozen raspberries

directions: Combine all ingredients in the blender and process on high speed until creamy and smooth.
Pour mixture into 8-inch square baking dish.
Cover with plastic wrap and freeze 4-6 hours until firm.
Stir mixture several times to keep smooth.
Just before serving, garnish with extra raspberries, if desired.

Serves: 6

Nutrition per Serving		Exchanges
Calories	177	3 fruit
Carbohydrate	45 grams	
Cholesterol	0 milligrams	
Dietary Fiber	1 gram	
Fat	< 1 gram	
Protein	<1 gram	
Sodium	1 milligram	

Shopping List: 12 ounces raspberry-lemonade frozen concentrate, frozen raspberries, honey.

STRAWBERRY APPLESAUCE YOGURT

EASY - DO AHEAD

ingredients: 1 cup fat-free strawberry yogurt
1 cup strawberry applesauce
1 tbsp. honey

directions: Combine all ingredients in the blender and process on medium speed until blended.
Pour into 4 small or 1 large bowl and refrigerate 1-2 hours before serving.

Serves: 4

Nutrition per Serving		Exchanges
Calories	119	2 fruit
Carbohydrate	30 grams	
Cholesterol	1 milligram	
Dietary Fiber	1 gram	
Fat	< 1 gram	
Protein	2 grams	
Sodium	45 milligrams	

Shopping List: 8 ounces fat-free strawberry yogurt, 8 ounces strawberry applesauce, honey.

TROPICAL FRUIT SHERBET

EASY - DO AHEAD - FREEZE

ingredients: 20 oz. frozen Tropical Fruit Medley
8 oz. fat-free vanilla yogurt
1 cup lemon powdered sugar
1 tbsp. lemon juice
1/4 tsp. almond extract

directions: Place tropical fruit mix in blender and process on high speed until fruit is thinly shaved. Add remaining ingredients and process until mixture is smooth and creamy.

Serves: 6

<u>**Nutrition per Serving**</u>   <u>**Exchanges**</u>
Calories   178   3 fruit
Carbohydrate   43 grams
Cholesterol   1 milligram
Dietary Fiber   1 gram
Fat   < 1 gram
Protein   2 grams
Sodium   29 milligrams

Shopping List: 20 ounces frozen Tropical Fruit Medley, 8 ounces fat-free vanilla yogurt, 1/2 pound lemon powdered sugar, lemon juice, almond extract.

BLENDER CHEESE SANDWICH SPREAD

EASY - DO AHEAD

ingredients:
1 cup fat-free cottage cheese
1 tbsp. skim milk
1/2 cup shredded zucchini
1/2 cup shredded carrots
1/2 cup fat-free shredded Cheddar cheese
1/2 tsp. onion powder
1/4 tsp. garlic powder
1/2 tsp. dill weed
1/8 tsp. pepper
2 fat-free pita pockets

directions:
Combine all ingredients except pita pockets in the blender and process on high speed until creamy and smooth.
Cut pita pockets in half to form 2 pockets. Fill each pocket with cottage cheese mixture.
Wrap in plastic wrap and refrigerate several hours or overnight.

Serves: 4

Nutrition per Serving		Exchanges
Calories	97	1/2 milk
Carbohydrate	14 grams	2 vegetable
Cholesterol	1 milligram	
Dietary Fiber	1 gram	
Fat	< 1 gram	
Protein	8 grams	
Sodium	301 milligrams	

Shopping List: 8 ounces fat-free cottage cheese, skim milk, zucchini, packaged shredded carrots, 2 ounces fat-free shredded Cheddar cheese, onion powder, garlic powder, dill weed, pepper, fat-free pita pockets.

CHEESE SPREAD

EASY - DO AHEAD

ingredients: 1 cup fat-free cream cheese
1 cup fat-free shredded Cheddar cheese
1 tsp. Dijon mustard
1 tsp. Worcestershire sauce
1/2 tsp. onion powder
1/4 tsp. garlic powder

directions: Combine all ingredients in the blender and process on high speed until creamy and smooth.
Pour cheese mixture into bowl and cover with plastic wrap.
Refrigerate several hours before serving.
Great with fat-free crackers, cut-up fresh vegetables, or fat-free tortilla chips.

Serves: 6

Nutrition per Serving		Exchanges
Calories	65	1 1/3 meat
Carbohydrate	4 grams	1 vegetable
Cholesterol	0 milligrams	
Dietary Fiber	0 grams	
Fat	< 1 gram	
Protein	11 grams	
Sodium	483 milligrams	

Shopping List: 8 ounces fat-free cream cheese, 4 ounces fat-free shredded Cheddar cheese, Dijon mustard, Worcestershire sauce, onion powder, garlic powder.

CURRY CHEESE SANDWICH SPREAD

EASY - DO AHEAD

ingredients:
3/4 cup fat-free cottage cheese
2 tbsp. fat-free sour cream
1 tbsp. skim milk
1/4 tsp. curry powder
1/4 tsp. onion powder
1/4 tsp. garlic powder
2 tsp. dried parsley
1/2 cup fat-free shredded Cheddar cheese
8 slices fat-free multi-grain bread

directions:
Combine cottage cheese, sour cream, milk, curry powder, onion powder, garlic powder and parsley in blender and process until cottage cheese is creamy and smooth.
Pour mixture into medium bowl; add Cheddar cheese and mix lightly.
Cover and refrigerate several hours or overnight.
Just before serving, lightly toast bread slices.
Spread 2 tablespoons cheese mixture on bread, top with bread slice and serve.

Serves: 4

Nutrition per Serving		Exchanges
Calories	208	2 starch
Carbohydrate	36 grams	1 meat
Cholesterol	0 milligram	
Dietary Fiber	2 grams	
Fat	< 1 gram	
Protein	12 grams	
Sodium	487 milligrams	

Shopping List: 6 ounces fat-free cottage cheese, 1 ounce fat-free sour cream, skim milk, 2 ounces fat-free shredded Cheddar cheese, fat-free multi-grain bread, curry powder, onion powder, garlic powder, dried parsley.

HUMMUS

EASY - DO AHEAD

ingredients: 8 oz. canned garbanzo beans, drained and rinsed
1/4 cup fat-free sour cream
1/4 cup fat-free yogurt
3 tbsp. lemon juice
1 1/2 tsp. garlic powder
1/8 tsp. cumin powder

directions: Combine all ingredients in the blender and process until mixture is smooth.
Serve with fat-free pita or potato chips.

Serves: 4

Nutrition per Serving   **Exchanges**
Calories   80   1 starch
Carbohydrate   12 grams
Cholesterol   0 milligrams
Dietary Fiber   3 grams
Fat   < 1 gram
Protein   5 grams
Sodium   247 milligrams

Shopping List: 8 ounces canned garbanzo beans, 2 ounces fat-free sour cream, 2 ounces fat-free yogurt, lemon juice, garlic powder, cumin powder.

VEGETABLE CREAM DIP

EASY - DO AHEAD

ingredients:
1 cup fat-free sour cream
1 cup fat-free cottage cheese
1 tsp. dried basil
1/8 tsp. garlic powder
1/2 tsp. onion powder
1/2 cup chopped tomatoes
1/2 cup chopped green bell pepper
1/2 cup chopped scallions

directions: Combine tomato, green pepper and scallions in blender and process on low speed (chop) just until vegetables are chopped into small chunks.
Add sour cream, cottage cheese, basil, garlic powder and onion powder; process on purée or blend until mixture is creamy and blended.

Serves: 6

Nutrition per Serving
Calories	47
Carbohydrate	3 grams
Cholesterol	1 milligram
Dietary Fiber	1 gram
Fat	< 1 gram
Protein	4 grams
Sodium	91 milligrams

Exchanges
1/2 meat
1 vegetable

Shopping List: 8 ounces fat-free sour cream, 8 ounces fat-free cottage cheese, 1 medium tomato, 1 small green bell pepper, 4 green onions, dried basil, garlic powder, onion powder.

BUTTERMILK DRESSING

EASY - DO AHEAD

ingredients:
3/4 cup fat-free buttermilk
1/4 cup fat-free mayonnaise
2 tsp. onion powder
1 tsp. dried parsley
1 tbsp. lemon juice
1 tbsp. horseradish
1/8 tsp. pepper

directions:
Combine all ingredients in the blender and process on high speed until creamy and smooth. Refrigerate several hours before serving. Great as salad dressing or dip with fresh vegetables.

Serves: 6

Nutrition per Serving		Exchanges
Calories	21	Free
Carbohydrate	4	
Cholesterol	1 milligram	
Dietary Fiber	0 grams	
Fat	< 1 gram	
Protein	1 gram	
Sodium	119 milligrams	

Shopping List: 6 ounces fat-free buttermilk, 2 ounces fat-free mayonnaise, onion powder, dried parsley, lemon juice, horseradish, pepper.

HONEY MUSTARD SALAD DRESSING

EASY - DO AHEAD

ingredients: 1 cup apple juice
1/4 cup honey
1 1/2 tbsp. Dijon mustard
1/2 tsp. onion powder
1/4 tsp. garlic powder

directions: Combine all ingredients in the blender and process on high speed until creamy and smooth.
Pour into bowl; cover and refrigerate several hours before serving.
Great over salads or as dip with fat-free chicken tenders.

Serves: 6

Nutrition per Serving		Exchanges
Calories	65	1 fruit
Carbohydrate	16 grams	
Cholesterol	0 milligrams	
Dietary Fiber	0 grams	
Fat	< 1 gram	
Protein	<1 gram	
Sodium	31 milligrams	

Shopping List: 8 ounces apple juice, 2 ounces honey, Dijon mustard, onion powder, garlic powder.

SOUTHWEST-STYLE RANCH DRESSING

EASY - DO AHEAD

ingredients: 1/2 cup fat-free buttermilk or yogurt
1/2 cup fat-free yogurt
2 tbsp. lemon juice
1/2 tsp. cayenne pepper
2 tbsp. fresh cilantro, chopped
2 tsp. honey

directions: Combine all ingredients in the blender and purée until blended creamy and smooth.
Great with green leafy salad with corn kernels and diced tomatoes.

Serves: 6

Nutrition per Serving		Exchanges
Calories	27	1/3 milk
Carbohydrate	4 grams	
Cholesterol	1 milligram	
Dietary Fiber	0 grams	
Fat	< 1 gram	
Protein	2 grams	
Sodium	30 milligrams	

Shopping List: 4 ounces fat-free buttermilk, 4 ounces fat-free yogurt, 1 ounce lemon juice, cayenne pepper, fresh cilantro, honey.

TROPICAL FRUIT SALAD DRESSING

EASY - DO AHEAD

ingredients: 1/2 cup fat-free mayonnaise
1/2 cup fat-free vanilla yogurt
1/2 tsp. cinnamon
1/4 tsp. nutmeg
Mango, pineapple chunks, kiwi, peaches

directions: Combine mayonnaise, yogurt, cinnamon and nutmeg in blender and process on high speed until creamy and smooth.
Pour into bowl and refrigerate 1-2 hours before serving with cut-up fruit.

Serves: 4

Nutrition per Serving

Calories	33
Carbohydrate	6 grams
Cholesterol	0 milligrams
Dietary Fiber	0 grams
Fat	< 1 gram
Protein	1 gram
Sodium	228 milligrams

Exchanges
1/2 fruit

Shopping List: 4 ounces fat-free mayonnaise, 4 ounces fat-free vanilla yogurt, cinnamon, nutmeg.

CREAM OF ASPARAGUS SOUP

AVERAGE - DO AHEAD

ingredients:
1 cup chopped onions
4 cups + 2 tbsp. fat-free chicken broth, divided
4 cups chopped asparagus
3/4 tsp. tarragon
1/8 tsp. nutmeg
1/4 tsp. pepper

directions:
Pour 2 tablespoons chicken broth into nonstick Dutch oven and heat over medium heat.
Add onions and cook 5-6 minutes, until onions are clear and soft.
Stir in asparagus and cook, stirring constantly, 2-3 minutes.
Gradually pour 4 cups chicken broth into pan and bring to a boil over high heat; reduce heat to low, cover, and simmer until vegetables are tender, about 25-30 minutes.
Pour soup into blender; add tarragon, nutmeg and pepper; purée until mixture is smooth.
Return soup to pan and cook 3-5 minutes, until heated through.

Serves: 4

Nutrition per Serving

Calories	65
Carbohydrate	12 grams
Cholesterol	0 milligrams
Dietary Fiber	3 grams
Fat	< 1 gram
Protein	5 grams
Sodium	325 milligrams

Exchanges

2 1/2 vegetable

Shopping List: 1 medium onion, 34 ounces fat-free chicken broth, 1 1/4 pounds asparagus, tarragon, nutmeg, pepper.

CREAM OF BROCCOLI SOUP

AVERAGE - DO AHEAD

ingredients:
3 cups broccoli flowerets
2 1/2 cups red potatoes, peeled and cubed
2 tbsp. onion powder
1 cup chopped celery
2 tsp. minced garlic
4 cups fat-free chicken broth
1/4 tsp. pepper

directions:
Combine all ingredients in a soup pot or Dutch oven and bring to a boil over medium-high heat. Reduce heat to low, cover, and simmer 45-50 minutes until vegetables are tender.
Remove 1 cup broccoli from soup and set aside. Pour remaining mixture into blender and purée until smooth.
Pour mixture back into pot; add reserved broccoli flowerets and heat 3-5 minutes over medium heat.

Serves: 4

Nutrition per Serving

Calories	111
Carbohydrate	25 grams
Cholesterol	0 milligrams
Dietary Fiber	4 grams
Fat	< 1 gram
Protein	4 grams
Sodium	349 milligrams

Exchanges
1 1/2 vegetable
1 starch

Shopping List: 1 1/2 pounds broccoli flowerets, 1 pound red potatoes, onion powder, celery, minced garlic, 32 ounces fat-free chicken broth, pepper.

MINTED MELON SOUP

EASY - DO AHEAD

ingredients: 2 cups cubed cantaloupe
2 cups cubed honeydew melon
1 cup apricot nectar
2 tbsp. lemon juice
6 sprigs fresh mint

directions: Combine cantaloupe, honeydew and nectar in blender and purée until smooth.
Pour mixture into bowl and blend in lemon juice.
Cover and refirgerate 4-6 hours before serving.
Garnish with mint sprigs just before serving.

Serves: 6

Nutrition per Serving		Exchanges
Calories	64	1 fruit
Carbohydrate	16 grams	
Cholesterol	0 milligrams	
Dietary Fiber	1 gram	
Fat	< 1 gram	
Protein	1 gram	
Sodium	12 milligrams	

Shopping List: 1 1/2 pounds cantaloupe, 1 1/2 pounds honeydew melon, 8 ounces apricot nectar, 1 ounce lemon juice, fresh mint sprigs.

VICHYSSOISE (POTATO SOUP)

EASY - DO AHEAD

ingredients: 4 1/2 cups red potatoes, peeled and cubed
2 1/2 cups skim milk
1/4 tsp. pepper
1 tbsp. onion powder
2 cups chopped cucumbers
3/4 cup fat-free sour cream

directions: Combine potatoes, milk, pepper and onion powder in soup pot or Dutch oven and bring to a boil over medium-high heat.

Reduce heat to low and simmer, uncovered, 20-25 minutes.

Pour mixture into blender; gradually add chopped cucumbers and purée until smooth.

Pour mixture into large bowl and stir in sour cream until blended smooth.

Refrigerate several hours, or overnight, until chilled.

Top with 1 tablespoon sour cream before serving, if desired.

Serves: 4

Nutrition per Serving

Calories	188
Carbohydrate	31 grams
Cholesterol	3 milligrams
Dietary Fiber	2 grams
Fat	< 1 gram
Protein	11 grams
Sodium	115 milligrams

Exchanges

1 milk
1 starch
1/2 vegetable

Shopping List: 1 3/4 pound red potatoes, 24 ounces skim milk, 6 ounces fat-free sour cream, 1 large cucumber, pepper, onion powder.

RECIPES FOR
FAT FREE LIVING®
BAR-B-QUE

by Jyl Steinback

- Breads
- Chicken & Turkey
- Seafood
- Meats
- Vegetables
- Desserts

BARBEQUE TIPS

Choosing a Grill:

Hibachi: Portable grill that is good for cooking small amounts of food.

Covered kettle cookers: Available in a variety of sizes with airflow vents on top and bottom to help control heat.

Gas grills: Available as portables or stationary - most have instant starters, heat up quickly and are easy to control the temperature. Preheat gas grills according to manufacturer's directions and regulate the heat by using controls.

Electric grills: Fast cooking, but must be close to electric outlet; follow manufacturer's directions for starting grills.

Grilling Utensils:

- Hinged wire basket is great for grilling delicate or small foods.
- Long-handled utensils: tongs, forks, spatulas, basting brushes.
- Spray bottle with cool water; spray very lightly on fire flare ups.
- Fire-resistant mitts or pot holders.
- Stiff wire brush for easy cleaning.

Seasoning Blend for Poultry: 1 teaspoon dried thyme leaves (crushed), 1 teaspoon dried marjoram leaves (crushed), 1/4 teaspoon salt, 1/4 teaspoon onion powder, 1/4 teaspoon garlic powder.

Schilling Grill Mates are wonderful seasoning blends for grilling meat, poultry or vegetables.

Marinades: Add flavor and tenderize foods; turn meat several times in marinade to allow even absorption - use a large self-closing plastic bag for marinating; combine marinade ingredients, add meat, turn bag until well coated and refrigerate; turn several times.

- **Always** marinate foods in a nonmetal dish and do not marinate longer than 24 hours. The acid in marinades will discolor metal dishes. Foods must be removed from marinades before the acid starts to disintegrate. Fish should marinate 15 to 20 minutes; shellfish, 25 to 30 minutes; poultry without bone, 20 to 40 minutes; vegetables, 1 to 2 hours.

- **Do Not** reuse marinades; set some aside to use for table sauce.

- **Never** marinate foods on the counter; it is safer to marinate foods in the refrigerator.

- Lightly spray meats with nonfat cooking spray (flavored or plain) to hold seasonings better.

Honey-Ginger Marinade (6 chicken breasts, 1 1/2 pounds fish fillets):
- 1 1/2 tsp. ground ginger
- 1 1/2 tsp. garlic powder
- 1/2 cup soy sauce
- 1/2 cup orange juice
- 6 tbsp. honey

Southwestern Marinade:
- 12 oz. beer
- 1/2 cup V8 juice
- 2 tsp. onion powder
- 1 tbsp. Worcestershire sauce
- 1 tsp. dried oregano
- 1 tsp. thyme

Asian Marinade:
- 1/3 cup lime juice
- 3 tbsp. low-sodium soy sauce
- 2 tbsp. hoisin sauce
- 1/4 tsp. cayenne pepper
- 2 tsp. ginger
- 2 tbsp. chopped cilantro

Golden Dipt Marinades:
P.O. Box 2227
Rock Island, IL 61204-2227
(Fat-free Honey Mustard, Honey Soy, White Wine Dijon)

Dry Rubs: A mixture of spices and herbs used for tenderizing, flavoring and preservative. Do not use salt, as it tends to dry the meat out. Dry rubs add more flavor than marinades, but take longer than marinades to tenderize foods.
- **Italian rub:** garlic powder, basil, crushed fennel
- **Mexican rub:** cumin, ground red pepper, oregano
- **Indian rub:** curry powder, garlic powder, black pepper

Successful grilling requires organization: make sure to have tongs, sharp knife, pot holder or towel close by.
- Check food frequently for doneness; an accurate cooking time cannot be given because grill temperatures vary.
- Brush sauces (especially those containing tomato or sugar) on meats during last 15 to 20 minutes of grilling to prevent overbrowning or burning.

- **Cover grill** when cooking to ensure even doneness - this is especially important for poultry to prevent drying.

- Use a hinged grill basket lightly sprayed with nonfat cooking spray for the best cooked fish; this makes turning easier and prevents fish from falling into the grill.

- **Never** place food on a cold grill - always preheat according to directions.

- Cooking with the lid on gives food a smokier flavor; cooking with the lid up allows food to sear.

Foil grill pans: Use instead of heavy-duty foil sheets.

Skewers:

- If using wooden skewers instead of metal ones, soak them in water for 30 minutes before threading meat, or they may burn while grilling.

- Square metal skewers will hold the food better than round skewers; they prevent the food from turning when skewers are turned.

Kabobs are a great do-ahead meal. Thread the kabob early in the day, cover with plastic wrap and refrigerate until ready to grill.

- Leave space between foods; tightly packed foods will not cook evenly.

- Brush cooking surface with nonfat cooking spray before grilling.

- If using sauces with sugar, brush kabobs in last 15 minutes of grilling.

Food Safety:

- If you have marinated meat, fish or poultry, discard the marinade before grilling. If you want to use some of the marinade for basting, reserve some in a separate bowl and refrigerate until ready to use, or boil marinade for 3 to 5 minutes.

- Place cooked food on a **clean** plate; do not use the plate used for raw meat or poultry, in order to reduce the risk of contamination or food poisoning.

- Chicken is done when no longer pink and juices run out when it is pierced; fish is done when it is opaque throughout.

Grilling Safety:

- **Do Not** line the bottom of a gas or charcoal grill with aluminum foil as it will block the airflow and the fire may extinguish faster.

- **Only use lighter fluid to start the fire** - never try to ignite a dying fire with lighter fluid.

- **NEVER use gasoline or kerosene** in place of liquid starter for charcoal grilling.
- **Store gas tanks and liquid starters** away from the house.
- **Always** shut off the gas valve when you turn off a gas grill.
- **Grill only in well-ventilated areas**, never in enclosed places.
- **Do not** leave a fire unattended; watch children and pets carefully around grill.
- **Do not** throw water on flames which can produce steam vapors; remove food from the fire or cover grill until the fire subsides; you can spray very lightly with cool water if fire flares up.
- **Use long-handled barbecue utensils**, not regular kitchen utensils.
- **Place the grill on level ground to keep steady.**

Fish: Grilling baskets are wonderful for cooking fish; watch fish closely because it cooks quickly when grilled. The fish is done when it flakes easily when tested with a fork.

Nonstick Tip: Spray foil, foil pans, grilling baskets or grill with nonfat cooking spray. If using a foil packet, remember to spray the top foil (facing inward) to prevent sticking to the packet. This is especially good when cooking with cheese.

Vegetable/Fruit Grilling Guide:
6 to 10 minutes:
Carrots, small whole, partially cooked
Cherry tomatoes, whole
Mushrooms, whole
Onions, cut in 1/2-inch slices
Apples, cored, cut in half or in thick slices
Potatoes, cut in 1-inch wedges, partially cooked

15 minutes:
Bell peppers, cut in 1-inch strips
Eggplant, cut in 3/4-inch slices
Green beans, whole
Patty pan squash, whole
Zucchini, cut in 3/4-inch pieces

20 minutes:
Asparagus spears, whole
Broccoli spears, cut in half lengthwise
Cauliflowerets, cut in half lengthwise
Corn on the cob, husked and wrapped in foil

GRILLED BRUSCHETTE

EASY - DO AHEAD

---

ingredients:　8 slices fat-free French bread*
2 tsp. garlic purée
2 tsp. dried basil
4 plum tomatoes, halved

directions:　Prepare a medium-hot grill and lightly spray with nonfat cooking spray. Lightly spray cut-side of tomatoes with nonfat cooking spray; place on grill and cook 4-6 minutes, turning 1-2 times, until slightly charred.
Remove from grill and chop tomatoes; keep warm. In a small bowl, combine garlic and basil; mix well. Cut loaf in half horizontally; brush garlic mixture on both cut sides of bread. Grill, turning once, 6-8 minutes until golden brown.
Top bread slices with grilled tomatoes; slice and serve.

Serves: 8

BRAVO BAR-B-QUE

Nutrition per Serving		Exchanges
Calories	93	1 starch
Carbohydrate	19 grams	1/2 vegetable
Cholesterol	0 milligrams	
Dietary Fiber	1 gram	
Fat	< 1 gram	
Protein	3 grams	
Sodium	155 milligrams	

Shopping List: *1 loaf fat-free French, sourdough, or Italian bread, garlic purée, dried basil, 4 plum tomatoes.

PIZZA BREAD

EASY - DO AHEAD

BRAVO
BAR-B-QUE

ingredients: 6 slices fat-free French bread
3/4 cup fat-free pizza sauce
1 1/2 tbsp. onion flakes
1/2 tsp. garlic powder
3/4 cup fat-free Mozzarella cheese,
    finely shredded

directions: Prepare a medium-hot grill. Cut 2 large pieces of heavy-duty foil and lightly spray 1 piece with nonfat cooking spray.
Arrange bread slices in a single layer on 1 piece of foil.
In a small bowl, combine pizza sauce, onion flakes and garlic powder; mix well.
Spread sauce on cut-sides of bread; sprinkle with Mozzarella cheese.
Loosely place remaining foil piece, with sprayed-side down, over top of bread and seal securely on sides.
Place foil packet on grill and cook 8-10 minutes, turning once, until cheese is melted.
Remove top foil and cook 3-5 minutes longer.

Serves: 6

Nutrition per Serving		Exchanges
Calories	123	1 starch
Carbohydrate	20 grams	1 vegetable
Cholesterol	0 milligrams	1/2 meat
Dietary Fiber	1 gram	
Fat	< 1 gram	
Protein	8 grams	
Sodium	341 milligrams	

Shopping List: fat-free French bread loaf, 6 ounces fat-free pizza sauce, onion flakes, garlic powder, 3 ounces fat-free shredded Mozzarella cheese.

BUFFALO TENDERS

EASY - DO AHEAD - FREEZE

ingredients:
2 lb. fat-free chicken tenders
1 cup pineapple juice
2 tbsp. white wine vinegar
2 tbsp. brown sugar
2 tsp. garlic powder
1 tbsp. chopped jalapeño pepper
1/4 tsp. cinnamon
1/8 tsp. cloves
1/4 tsp. pepper
2 tbsp. cold water
3/4 lb. celery hearts, cut in half
1 1/2 cups fat-free blue cheese or ranch salad dressing

directions:
Combine all ingredients except chicken, celery and salad dressing, in a medium saucepan and cook over medium-high heat until mixture comes to boil; cook 2-3 minutes, stirring frequently. Remove from heat and stir in very cold water. Arrange chicken tenders in 9x13-inch baking dish; pour sauce over chicken and coat well.

Cover with plastic wrap and refrigerate 4-6 hours, or overnight. Prepare a medium-hot grill and lightly spray with nonfat cooking spray.

Remove chicken from marinade and cook 10-15 minutes, turning 2-3 minutes until no longer pink and cooked through.

Serve with sliced celery and blue cheese or ranch salad dressing.

Serves: 6

Nutrition per Serving		Exchanges
Calories	253	1 vegetable
Carbohydrate	28 grams	1 2/3 fruit
Cholesterol	95 milligrams	4 meat
Dietary Fiber	2 grams	
Fat	< 1 gram	
Protein	32 grams	
Sodium	970 milligrams	

Shopping List:
2 pounds fat-free chicken tenders, 8 ounces pineapple juice, 3/4 pound celery hearts, 12 ounces fat-free blue cheese or ranch salad dressing, canned jalapeño peppers, white wine vinegar, brown sugar, garlic powder, cinnamon, cloves, pepper.

CAJUN GRILLED CHICKEN

EASY - DO AHEAD

ingredients:
2 1/2 lb. fat-free chicken breasts
1 1/2 cups fat-free chicken broth
2 tbsp. Worcestershire sauce
1 1/2 tsp. cayenne pepper
1 1/2 tsp. pepper
1 1/2 tsp. hot pepper sauce

directions:
Place chicken breasts in a shallow baking dish.
Combine chicken broth, Worcestershire sauce, cayenne pepper, pepper and pepper sauce in a medium bowl; mix well.
Pour sauce over chicken and coat well. Cover and refrigerate 1 hour.
Prepare a medium-hot grill and lightly spray with nonfat cooking spray.
Remove chicken from marinade and cook 12-15 minutes, turning once, until chicken is no longer pink and cooked through.

Serves: 6

Nutrition per Serving		Exchanges
Calories	178	5 1/2 meat
Carbohydrate	2 grams	
Cholesterol	118 milligrams	
Dietary Fiber	< 1 gram	
Fat	< 1 gram	
Protein	39 grams	
Sodium	585 milligrams	

Shopping List: 2 1/2 pounds fat-free chicken breasts, 12 ounces fat-free chicken broth, Worcestershire sauce, cayenne pepper, pepper, hot pepper sauce.

GRILLED CHICKEN AND CHEESE MELTS

AVERAGE

ingredients:
1 1/2 lb. fat-free chicken breasts
1 tbsp. onion powder
1 tbsp. garlic powder
1 medium onion, sliced 1/2-inch thick
1 medium red bell pepper, cut into rings
1 1/2 cups fat-free shredded Mexican cheese
1/2 cup spicy brown mustard
1/2 cup fat-free mayonnaise
12 slices fat-free multi-grain bread*

directions:
Combine brown mustard and mayonnaise in small bowl; mix until blended smooth. Prepare medium-hot grill; lightly spray with nonfat cooking spray. Sprinkle chicken breasts with onion and garlic powder. Brush mustard sauce over chicken, onion and pepper slices. Place chicken on grill; cook 10-15 minutes, until no longer pink and cooked through; top each chicken breast with cheese; cook until cheese is melted. Arrange onions and peppers on grill; cook 3-5 minutes, turning often until lightly browned and tender. Place bread or rolls on grill and cook 1-2 minutes, just until lightly browned.
To prepare sandwiches: Spread remaining mustard sauce on bread slices; stack chicken breast, sliced onion, sliced pepper and bread slice.

Serves: 6

Nutrition per Serving		Exchanges
Calories	371	2 starch
Carbohydrate	44 grams	3 vegetable
Cholesterol	72 milligrams	4 meat
Dietary Fiber	5 grams	
Protein	39 grams	
Sodium	1179 milligrams	

Shopping List: 1 1/2 pounds fat-free chicken breasts, 1 onion, 1 red bell pepper, 6 ounces fat-free shredded Mexican cheese, 4 ounces spicy brown mustard, 4 ounces fat-free mayonnaise, 1 loaf fat-free multi-grain bread (*or other fat-free bread or rolls of choice), onion powder, garlic powder.

GRILLED CHICKEN NUGGETS

EASY - DO AHEAD

ingredients: 1 1/2 cups fat-free bread crumbs
1 tsp. garlic powder
1 tsp. onion powder
1/3 cup fat-free Parmesan cheese
1 tsp. dried parsley
1/4 tsp. pepper
1/2 cup egg substitute
2 lb. fat-free chicken tenders, cut in 1 1/2-inch cubes

directions: Combine bread crumbs, garlic powder, onion powder, Parmesan cheese, parsley and pepper in a shallow baking dish and mix until ingredients are blended. Pour egg substitute into shallow dish.
Dip chicken pieces into egg substitute and roll in crumb mixture until thoroughly coated; place nuggets on large platter, cover, and refrigerate 1-2 hours. Prepare a medium-hot grill and lightly spray with nonfat cooking spray. Grill chicken nuggets 10-15 minutes, turning 2-3 times, until no longer pink and lightly browned.
Serve nuggets with honey-mustard sauce, barbecue sauce, or fat-free ranch dressing.

Serves: 6

Nutrition per Serving		**Exchanges**
Calories	190	1/2 starch
Carbohydrate	8 grams	4 1/2 meat
Cholesterol	95 milligrams	
Dietary Fiber	< 1 gram	
Fat	< 1 gram	
Protein	35 grams	
Sodium	489 milligrams	

Shopping List: fat-free bread crumbs, fat-free Parmesan cheese, 4 ounces egg substitute, 2 pounds fat-free chicken tenders, garlic powder, onion powder, dried parsley, pepper.

BRAVO
BAR-B-QUE

GRILLED CHICKEN WITH FRUIT SALSA

EASY - DO AHEAD

ingredients: 2 1/2 lb. fat-free chicken breasts
1 cup pineapple tidbits in juice
1 tsp. onion powder
1/3 cup low-sodium teriyaki sauce
1 tsp. garlic powder
1 tsp. minced garlic
6 large strawberries, chopped
1 peach, peeled and chopped
2 tbsp. sliced green onions
2 tbsp. chopped cilantro
1 tbsp. sugar
1 tbsp. red wine vinegar
1 tbsp. low-sodium soy sauce

directions: Drain pineapple, reserving liquid; place pineapple in medium bowl. Place chicken in 9x13-inch baking dish; sprinkle chicken with onion and garlic powder.
In a small bowl, combine pineapple liquid, teriyaki sauce and minced garlic; mix well. Pour over chicken and turn to coat well. Cover with plastic wrap and refrigerate several hours. Add strawberries, peaches, green onions, cilantro, sugar, vinegar and soy sauce to pineapple tidbits; mix well. Cover and refrigerate several hours. Prepare medium-hot grill and lightly spray with nonfat cooking spray. Remove chicken from marinade and grill 10-15 minutes, until no longer pink and cooked through; turn once while grilling. Serve chicken with fruit salsa.

Serves: 6

Nutrition per Serving		Exchanges
Calories	230	1 fruit
Carbohydrate	15 grams	5 1/4 meat
Cholesterol	118 milligrams	
Dietary Fiber	1 gram	
Fat	< 1 gram	
Protein	40 grams	
Sodium	1023 milligrams	

Shopping List: 2 1/2 pounds fat-free chicken breasts, 8 ounces pineapple tidbits in juice, low-sodium teriyaki sauce, strawberries, 1 peach, green onions, sugar, red wine vinegar, low-sodium soy sauce, onion powder, garlic powder, minced garlic, cilantro.

ORANGE GRILLED CHICKEN
EASY - DO AHEAD

ingredients: 3/4 cup barbecue sauce
3/4 cup orange marmalade
3 tsp. onion powder, divided
1 tsp. garlic powder
1/4 tsp. pepper
1 1/2 lb. fat-free chicken breasts

directions: Prepare a medium-hot grill and lightly spray with nonfat cooking spray.
In a medium saucepan, combine barbecue sauce, orange marmalade and 2 teaspoons onion powder; mix until blended.
Sprinkle chicken with remaining onion powder, garlic powder and pepper; place on grill and cook 5-8 minutes, turning once.
Generously brush chicken with sauce and cook an additional 5-8 minutes, brushing frequently, until chicken is no longer pink and cooked through.
While chicken is cooking, place saucepan on grill and heat remaining sauce (or heat in microwave); serve chicken with grilled vegetables and rice.

Serves: 6

Nutrition per Serving
Calories	256
Carbohydrate	39 grams
Cholesterol	71 milligrams
Dietary Fiber	< 1 gram
Fat	< 1 gram
Protein	23 grams
Sodium	538 milligrams

Exchanges
2 2/3 fruit
3 meat

Shopping List: 6 ounces barbecue sauce, 6 ounces orange marmalade, 1 1/2 pounds fat-free chicken breasts, onion powder, garlic powder, pepper.

SPINACH-STUFFED CHICKEN ROLLS

AVERAGE - DO AHEAD - FREEZE

ingredients:
1 cup frozen, chopped spinach, thawed and drained
2 tsp. onion powder
1/3 cup fat-free Parmesan cheese
1 1/2 tbsp. + 1 tsp. garlic powder
2 tsp. dried basil
1 1/2 cups fat-free seasoned croutons, crushed
1/3 cup fat-free mayonnaise
3/4 tsp. Tabasco sauce
2 lb. fat-free chicken breasts
2 tbsp. reconstituted Butter Buds

directions:
Prepare a medium-hot grill and lightly spray with nonfat cooking spray. Combine spinach, onion powder, Parmesan cheese, 1 1/2 tablespoons garlic powder, basil, croutons, mayonnaise and Tabasco sauce in a medium bowl and mix until blended. In a small bowl, combine Butter Buds and 1 teaspoon garlic powder and mix until blended.

Lay chicken breasts flat on work surface; divide spinach mixture evenly and spoon down the center of each chicken breast. Fold chicken breast and roll around filling and secure with toothpick.

Brush chicken breasts with garlic-butter mixture and place on grill. Grill chicken 10-15 minutes, turning 1-2 times, until no longer pink and cooked through.

Serves: 6

Nutrition per Serving		Exchanges
Calories	196	2 vegetable
Carbohydrate	12 grams	4 meat
Cholesterol	95 milligrams	
Dietary Fiber	< 1 gram	
Fat	< 1 gram	
Protein	35 grams	
Sodium	542 milligrams	

Shopping List: 10 ounces frozen chopped spinach, fat-free Parmesan cheese, fat-free seasoned croutons, fat-free mayonnaise, Tabasco sauce, 2 pounds fat-free chicken breasts, Butter Buds, onion powder, garlic powder, dried basil.

SWEET 'N SPICY CHICKEN
EASY

ingredients:
1 1/2 lb. fat-free chicken breasts
1 1/2 tsp. onion powder
1 1/2 tsp. garlic powder
1/2 cup mustard
1/2 cup pineapple juice
1/4 cup brown sugar
1 tsp. horseradish

directions: Prepare a medium-hot grill and lightly spray with nonfat cooking spray.
Combine pineapple juice, brown sugar, mustard and horseradish in a small saucepan; place directly on grill and cook 5-10 minutes.
Sprinkle chicken breasts with onion and garlic powder.
Cook chicken breasts 10-15 minutes, brushing frequently with sauce, until no longer pink and cooked through.
Turn chicken once while grilling.
Serve remaining sauce with chicken.

Serves: 6

Nutrition per Serving		Exchanges
Calories	171	1 fruit
Carbohydrate	13 grams	3 meat
Cholesterol	71 milligrams	
Dietary Fiber	< 1 gram	
Fat	< 1 gram	
Protein	29 grams	
Sodium	546 milligrams	

Shopping List: 1 1/2 pounds fat-free chicken breasts, 4 ounces mustard, 4 ounces pineapple juice, onion powder, brown sugar, horseradish, garlic powder.

BRAVO BAR-B-QUE

BREADED ITALIAN SOLE

EASY - DO AHEAD

ingredients: 1 1/2 lb. cod fillets
2 cups fat-free croutons, crushed
1 tsp. garlic powder
1 tbsp. onion powder
1 1/2 tsp. dry mustard
1/2 tsp. cayenne pepper
1/4 cup egg substitute
1 1/2 tbsp. skim milk
1/4 cup reconstituted Butter Buds

directions: Cut fillets into 6 equal pieces.
Combine croutons, garlic powder, onion powder, mustard and cayenne pepper in a shallow baking dish and mix well.
Combine egg substitute and milk in a shallow baking dish and mix until blended.
Prepare a medium-hot grill and lightly spray grill basket with nonfat cooking spray (or spray grill directly).
Dip fish fillets in egg mixture; roll in crumb mixture until well coated.
Place fish in grill basket and cook 10-15 minutes, turning once, until fish flakes easily.
Brush or sprinkle fish with Butter Buds several times while cooking, if desired.

Serves: 6

Nutrition per Serving		**Exchanges**
Calories	129	1/3 starch
Carbohydrate	7 grams	3 meat
Cholesterol	41 milligrams	
Dietary Fiber	0 grams	
Fat	< 1 gram	
Protein	22 grams	
Sodium	207 milligrams	

Shopping List: 1 1/2 pounds cod fillets, fat-free croutons, garlic powder, onion powder, dry mustard, cayenne pepper, 2 ounces egg substitute, skim milk, Butter Buds.

BRAVO BAR-B-QUE

GRILLED SHRIMP CAESAR SALAD

EASY - DO AHEAD

ingredients:
1 1/2 lb. fat-free frozen shrimp, thawed
1 small red onion, sliced
3/4 cup + 2 tbsp. fat-free Caesar salad
    dressing, divided
10-12 cups romaine lettuce, cut in bite-size pieces
1 cup cherry tomatoes, cut in half
1 cup artichoke hearts, chopped
1 1/2 cups fat-free seasoned croutons (2 oz.)
3/4 cup fat-free Parmesan cheese (3 oz.)

directions:
Prepare a medium-hot grill.
Lightly spray wire hinged grill basket with nonfat cooking spray or directly spray grill.
Brush shrimp and onion slices lightly with Caesar dressing. Place shrimp and onions in grill basket. Cook 8-10 minutes, turning once, and brushing with additional dressing until shrimp are pink and firm.
Combine lettuce, tomatoes, artichoke hearts, croutons, shrimp and onions in a large mixing bowl; sprinkle with Parmesan cheese and toss lightly.
Gradually pour Caesar dressing over salad and toss until well mixed.

Serves: 6

Nutrition per Serving		Exchanges
Calories	292	1 starch
Carbohydrate	51 grams	7 vegetable
Cholesterol	13 milligrams	1 meat
Dietary Fiber	3 grams	
Fat	< 1 gram	
Protein	22 grams	
Sodium	1649 milligrams	

Shopping List: 1 1/2 pounds fat-free shrimp (medium), 7 ounces fat-free Caesar salad dressing, 2 bunches romaine or prepackaged romaine salad mix, 1/2 pint cherry tomatoes, canned artichoke hearts (packed in water), fat-free seasoned croutons, 3 ounces fat-free Parmesan cheese, 1 red onion.

JAMAICAN COD
EASY - DO AHEAD

ingredients:
1 1/2 lb. cod fillets
2 tbsp. chopped green onions
1 tbsp. chopped jalapeño pepper
2 tbsp. white wine vinegar
2 tbsp. Worcestershire sauce
1 tsp. ginger
1 tsp. thyme
1/2 tsp. cinnamon
1/8 tsp. cloves

directions:
Combine all ingredients, except fish, in a shallow baking dish and mix well; add fish and turn to coat.
Let stand at room temperature 5-10 minutes.
Prepare a medium-hot grill and lightly spray with nonfat cooking spray.
Place fish on grill and top with half the seasoning sauce; grill 5 minutes. Turn fish over, top with remaining sauce and grill 5 6 minutes, until fish flakes easily when tested with a fork.

Serves: 6

Nutrition per Serving		Exchanges
Calories	93	3 meat
Carbohydrate	2 grams	
Cholesterol	45 milligrams	
Dietary Fiber	< 1 gram	
Fat	< 1 gram	
Protein	19 grams	
Sodium	13 milligrams	

Shopping List: 1 1/2 pounds cod fillets, green onions, canned chopped jalapeño peppers, white wine vinegar, Worcestershire sauce, ginger, thyme, cinnamon, cloves.

BRAVO BAR-B-QUE

SEAFOOD-MELON KABOBS
EASY - DO AHEAD

ingredients: 3/4 lb. fat-free shrimp
3/4 lb. fat-free scallops
1 1/2 cups cantaloupe balls
1 1/2 cups honeydew melon balls
1 cup pineapple chunks in juice
1 large green bell pepper, cut in 1-inch pieces
1/4 cup honey
2 tbsp. low-sodium teriyaki sauce

directions: Prepare a medium-hot grill and lightly spray with nonfat cooking spray.
Drain pineapple and reserve 2 teaspoons juice.
In a small bowl, combine reserved pineapple juice, honey and teriyaki sauce.
Thread shrimp, scallops, cantaloupe, honeydew, pineapple and green pepper onto large metal skewers and place on grill.
Brush kabobs generously with sauce mixture and cook 8-10 minutes, turning 2-3 times, until shrimp and scallops are cooked through.
Brush kabobs frequently with sauce while grilling. Serve with fat-free rice.

Serves: 6

Nutrition per Serving		Exchanges
Calories	202	2 meat
Carbohydrate	39 grams	2 1/3 fruit
Cholesterol	3 milligrams	
Dietary Fiber	1 gram	
Fat	< 1 gram	
Protein	13 grams	
Sodium	986 milligrams	

Shopping List: 3/4 pounds fat-free shrimp (medium-large), 3/4 pounds fat-free scallops (medium-large), cantaloupe*, honeydew*, 8 ounces pineapple chunks in juice, 1 green bell pepper, 2 ounces honey, low-sodium teriyaki sauce
*look for prepackaged melon balls in fruit section of your grocery store.

TROPICAL GRILLED COD

EASY - DO AHEAD

---

ingredients: 3 tbsp. frozen pine-orange banana concentrate, thawed
1 1/2 tbsp. low-sodium soy sauce
1 1/2 tbsp. honey
3/4 tsp. onion powder
1 1/2 lb. cod fillet, 1/2- to 3/4-inch thick

directions: Combine juice concentrate, soy sauce, honey and onion powder in a shallow baking dish and mix until blended.
Place cod fillets in sauce and turn to coat well. Cover and refrigerate 1 hour.
Prepare a medium-hot grill and lightly spray with nonfat cooking spray (or spray hinged grill basket).
Remove fish from marinade and cook 15-20 minutes, turning once, until fish flakes easily.
Brush fish several times while cooking with reserved marinade.

Serves: 6

Nutrition per Serving
Calories	129
Carbohydrate	9 grams
Cholesterol	49 milligrams
Dietary Fiber	< 1 gram
Fat	< 1 gram
Protein	21 grams
Sodium	212 milligrams

Exchanges
3 meat
1/2 fruit

Shopping List: 1 1/2 pounds cod fillets, frozen pine-orange banana concentrate, low-sodium soy sauce, honey, onion powder.

CHILI-CHEESE BURRITOS

EASY

ingredients:
2 cups fat-free chili
3/4 cup garden-style salsa
1 1/2 cups fat-free shredded Cheddar cheese
6 (10-inch) fat-free flour tortillas
6 tbsp. fat-free sour cream (optional)

directions:
Prepare a medium-hot grill and lightly spray with nonfat cooking spray.

Lightly spray a small saucepan with nonfat cooking spray; add chili and salsa to pan and place on grill.

Cook chili, stirring constantly, 5-10 minutes until thoroughly heated; remove from heat and keep warm.

Place tortillas on grill and cook 1-3 minutes, turning 2-3 times, just until soft and warm.

Remove tortillas from grill; top each tortilla with chili, 1/4 cup cheese and 1 tablespoon sour cream, if desired.

Roll tortilla up and serve with additional salsa, or wrap in foil and grill 1-2 minutes, until cheese is melted.

Serves: 6

Nutrition per Serving		Exchanges
Calories	270	2 starch
Carbohydrate	45 grams	3 vegetable
Cholesterol	0 milligrams	1 meat
Dietary Fiber	5 grams	
Fat	< 1 gram	
Protein	19 grams	
Sodium	1024 milligrams	

Shopping List: 16 ounces fat-free chili, 6 ounces garden-style salsa, 6 ounces fat-free shredded Cheddar cheese, fat-free 10-inch flour tortillas, 3 ounces fat-free sour cream (optional).

HOT AND SPICY
HOT DOG BITES

EASY - DO AHEAD

ingredients: 6 fat-free hot dogs
1/2 cup brown sugar
1/4 cup white horseradish

directions: **Combine horseradish** and brown sugar in a small bowl and mix until blended smooth; set aside.
Prepare a medium-hot grill and lightly spray with nonfat cooking spray. Cook hot dogs 10-15 minutes, turning several times, until browned and cooked through.
Cut each hot dog into 4 equal pieces.
Place toothpick in center of each hot dog piece and serve with horseradish sauce.

Serves: 6

Nutrition per Serving		Exchanges
Calories	117	1 meat
Carbohydrate	23 grams	1 1/3 fruit
Cholesterol	15 milligrams	
Dietary Fiber	0 grams	
Fat	< 1 gram	
Protein	6 grams	
Sodium	596 milligrams	

Shopping List: fat-free hot dogs, brown sugar, 2 ounces horseradish.

HOT DOG KABOBS

EASY - DO AHEAD

ingredients:
1/2 cup fat-free pasta sauce
1 tsp. basil
1 tsp. garlic powder
6 fat-free hot dogs, cut in 4 pieces
1 large onion, cut in 1-inch pieces
1 large zucchini, cut in 1-inch pieces
1 large red bell pepper, cut in 1-inch pieces
6 cherry tomatoes

directions:
In a small bowl, combine pasta sauce, basil and garlic powder; mix until blended.

Prepare a medium-hot grill and lightly spray with nonfat cooking spray.

To prepare kabobs: Alternate hot dog pieces, onion, zucchini and bell pepper on 6 metal skewers and top with cherry tomato.

Cook kabobs over medium-high heat, brushing frequently with pasta sauce, until hot dogs are browned and vegetables are tender, about 15-20 minutes.

Serves: 6

Nutrition per Serving

		Exchanges
Calories	74	2 vegetable
Carbohydrate	10 grams	1/2 meat
Cholesterol	15 milligrams	
Dietary Fiber	1 gram	
Fat	< 1 gram	
Protein	7 grams	
Sodium	572 milligrams	

Shopping List: 4 ounces fat-free pasta sauce, fat-free hot dogs, 1 large onion, 1 large zucchini, 1 large red bell pepper, cherry tomatoes, basil, garlic powder.

ORIENTAL HOT DOG BITES

EASY

ingredients: 6 fat-free hot dogs
1 1/2 cups mandarin oranges in juice, drained
6 slices fat-free turkey bacon
1 cup sweet and sour sauce

directions: Prepare a medium-hot grill and lightly spray with nonfat cooking spray.
Cook hot dogs 10-15 minutes, turning several times, until browned and cooked through.
Cut hot dogs into 4 equal pieces.
Lightly spray large nonstick skillet with nonfat cooking spray and heat over medium-high heat. Add turkey bacon to skillet; cook 4-5 minutes, turning once. Cut each piece into 4 equal pieces. Arrange hot dog bites on platter by stacking hot dog, bacon and mandarin orange; secure with toothpick and serve with sweet and sour sauce.

Serves: 6

BRAVO BAR-B-QUE

Nutrition per Serving		Exchanges	
Calories	135	1 1/3 fruit	
Carbohydrate	21 grams	1 1/3 meat	
Cholesterol	30 milligrams		
Dietary Fiber	< 1 gram		
Fat	< 1 gram		
Protein	9 grams		
Sodium	740 milligrams		

Shopping List: fat-free hot dogs, 15 ounces mandarin oranges, fat-free turkey bacon, 8 ounces sweet and sour sauce.

SPICY PIZZA DOGS
EASY - DO AHEAD

ingredients: 12 slices Italian bread
3 fat-free smoked sausages
6 tbsp. fat-free pizza sauce
6 tbsp. fat-free Mozzarella cheese,
    finely shredded

directions: Cut sausage in half; slice each half vertically to open, but do not cut all the way through.
Prepare a medium-hot grill and lightly spray with nonfat cooking spray.
Place sausage, cut-side down, on grill and cook 10-15 minutes, turning frequently.
Heat pizza sauce in microwave, or in small saucepan on grill and keep warm.
Lightly spray bread slices with nonfat cooking spray and grill 1-2 minutes, turning once.
Arrange sausage on bread; top with pizza sauce, cheese and remaining bread.

Serves: 6

Nutrition per Serving		Exchanges
Calories	344	3 1/2 starch
Carbohydrate	55 grams	2 meat
Cholesterol	44 milligrams	
Dietary Fiber	2 grams	
Fat	< 1 gram	
Protein	27 grams	
Sodium	1742 milligrams	

Shopping List: 1 loaf Italian bread, 21 ounces fat-free smoked sausage, fat-free pizza sauce, fat-free shredded Mozzarella cheese.

CAJUN SPICE
CORN ON THE COB

EASY - DO AHEAD

ingredients: 6 ears of corn, husked
1/4 cup reconstituted Butter Buds
1 1/2 tbsp. Cajun seasoning
3 tbsp. water

BRAVO
BAR-B-QUE

directions: Prepare a medium-hot grill.
Cut heavy-duty foil sheet for each ear of corn and
lightly spray with nonfat cooking spray.
In a small bowl, combine Butter Buds and Cajun
seasoning; stir to mix until blended.
Place corn on foil; brush thoroughly with butter
mixture and sprinkle with water.
Seal foil packets and grill 15-25 minutes, turning
once, until tender.

Serves: 6

Nutrition per Serving

Calories	95
Carbohydrate	21 grams
Cholesterol	0 milligrams
Dietary Fiber	3 grams
Fat	< 1 gram
Protein	3 grams
Sodium	245 milligrams

Exchanges
1 1/3 starch

Shopping List: 6 ears of corn, Butter Buds, Cajun seasoning blend.

CHEESY POTATO PACKETS
EASY - DO AHEAD

ingredients: 6 medium baking potatoes, sliced 1/2-inch thick
6 tbsp. fat-free Italian salad dressing
3/4 cup fat-free Mozzarella cheese, finely shredded
3/4 cup fat-free Cheddar cheese, finely shredded
6 tbsp. fat-free Parmesan cheese

directions: Cut potatoes in half and slice vertically 1/2-inch thick. Cut 6 pieces of heavy-duty foil and lightly spray with nonfat cooking spray.
Arrange potatoes on foil sheets; drizzle each potato with 1 tablespoon salad dressing and sprinkle with Mozzarella and Cheddar cheese.
Sprinkle Parmesan cheese over potatoes.
Wrap foil securely around potatoes and pierce top with fork in several places.
Place foil packets on grill seam-side up, cover grill and cook 45-60 minutes, until potatoes are tender and cooked through.

Serves: 6

Nutrition per Serving		**Exchanges**
Calories	214	2 1/2 starch
Carbohydrate	39 grams	1/2 meat
Cholesterol	0 milligrams	
Dietary Fiber	4 grams	
Fat	< 1 gram	
Protein	13 grams	
Sodium	346 milligrams	

Shopping List: 6 baking potatoes, 3 ounces fat-free Italian salad dressing, 3 ounces fat-free shredded Mozzarella cheese, 3 ounces fat-free shredded Cheddar cheese, fat-free Parmesan cheese.

GRILLED EGGPLANT PARMESAN

EASY - DO AHEAD

ingredients: 2 lb. eggplant, cut in 1 1/2-inch slices
1/2 cup fat-free Italian salad dressing
1 tsp. garlic powder
4 oz. fat-free Mozzarella cheese, sliced

directions: Combine Italian salad dressing and garlic powder in a small bowl and mix well.
Prepare a medium-hot grill and lightly spray with nonfat cooking spray.
Dip eggplant slices into salad dressing and coat well on all sides.
Arrange eggplant on grill, cover and cook 8-10 minutes; turn eggplant several times while grilling and brush with salad dressing.
Top eggplant with cheese and cook 2-4 minutes until cheese is melted.
Serve with fat-free pasta sauce, if desired.

Serves: 6

Nutrition per Serving		Exchanges
Calories	80	2 vegetables
Carbohydrate	11 grams	1/2 meat
Cholesterol	0 milligrams	
Dietary Fiber	4 grams	
Fat	< 1 gram	
Protein	7 grams	
Sodium	219 milligrams	

Shopping List: 2 pounds eggplant, 4 ounces fat-free Italian salad dressing, 4 ounces fat-free Mozzarella cheese (whole or sliced), garlic powder.

BRAVO BAR-B-QUE

GRILLED PORTABELLO MUSHROOM SANDWICH

EASY - DO AHEAD

ingredients:
4 large portabello mushrooms, stemmed
1/4 cup low-sodium teriyaki sauce
4 slices tomato
4 lettuce leaves
2 1/2 tbsp. fat-free honey mustard sauce
8 slices fat-free sourdough bread

directions:
Place mushrooms in a shallow baking dish; pour teriyaki sauce on top and turn mushrooms until thoroughly coated. Cover and refrigerate at least 1 hour.

Prepare a medium-hot grill and lightly spray with nonfat cooking spray.

Grill mushrooms 6-8 minutes, turning once, brushing several times with teriyaki sauce.

Place bread slices on grill during last 1-2 minutes and cook just until lightly browned.

Spread each bread slice with 1 teaspoon honey-mustard sauce; top with lettuce leaf, tomato, portabello mushroom and remaining bread.

Serves: 4

Nutrition per Serving		Exchanges
Calories	200	2 starch
Carbohydrate	40 grams	2 vegetables
Cholesterol	0 milligrams	
Dietary Fiber	3 grams	
Fat	< 1 gram	
Protein	8 grams	
Sodium	740 milligrams	

Shopping List: 4 large portabello mushrooms, 2 ounces low-sodium teriyaki sauce, 1 medium tomato, lettuce, fat-free honey-mustard sauce, fat-free sourdough bread.

GRILLED TOMATOES

EASY

---

ingredients: 6 whole tomatoes
2 tbsp. fat-free Parmesan cheese

directions: Prepare a medium-hot grill and lightly spray with nonfat cooking spray.
Remove stem from tomato and cut a thin slice off the top.
Sprinkle tomato with Parmesan cheese.
Place tomatoes on grill; cover, and cook 10-15 minutes, until cheese is browned and tomato is cooked through.

Serves: 6

BRAVO
BAR-B-QUE

Nutrition per Serving

Calories	31
Carbohydrate	6 grams
Cholesterol	0 milligrams
Dietary Fiber	2 grams
Fat	< 1 gram
Protein	2 grams
Sodium	26 milligrams

Exchanges
1 vegetable

Shopping List: 6 tomatoes, fat-free Parmesan cheese.

HONEY-DIJON
VEGETABLE KABOBS

EASY - DO AHEAD

BRAVO
BAR-B-QUE

ingredients: 3 medium zucchini, cut in 3/4-inch slices
1 large green bell pepper, cut in 1 1/2-inch
   pieces
1 large red bell pepper, cut in 1 1/2-inch pieces
1 pint cherry tomatoes, stemmed
1 medium onion, cut in 1 1/2-inch pieces
3/4 cup fat-free honey-mustard salad dressing
1 tsp. garlic powder

directions: Prepare a medium-hot grill and lightly spray with
nonfat cooking spray.
Arrange vegetables on 6 metal skewers, alternat-
ing zucchini, peppers, tomatoes and onions;
sprinkle kabobs with garlic powder and brush
with dressing.
Place kabobs on grill, cover and cook 10-15 minutes.
Turn and baste kabobs 2-3 times while grilling.
Serve over cooked rice or pasta.

Serves: 6

Nutrition per Serving

Calories	73
Carbohydrate	16 grams
Cholesterol	0 milligrams
Dietary Fiber	2 grams
Fat	< 1 gram
Protein	2 grams
Sodium	339 milligrams

Exchanges
3 vegetable

Shopping List: 3 zucchini, 1 green bell pepper, 1 red bell pepper,
1 pint cherry tomatoes, 1 onion, 6 ounces fat-free
honey mustard salad dressing, garlic powder.

ZUCCHINI-TOMATO SALAD

AVERAGE - DO AHEAD

ingredients: 6 large roma tomatoes, cut in half lengthwise
3 large zucchini, cut in 1/2-inch slices
2 small red onions, cut in 1/2-inch slices
1 small green bell pepper, cut in 1-inch strips
1 small red bell pepper, cut in 1-inch strips
2 tsp. Italian seasoning
1 cup fat-free Italian salad dressing, divided

directions: Prepare a medium-hot grill and lightly spray with nonfat cooking spray.
Place peppers and onions on grill; brush with salad dressing and sprinkle lightly with Italian seasoning.
Grill peppers and onion 8-10 minutes, turning once, until tender. When peppers and onions are turned, add tomatoes and zucchini to grill; brush with salad dressing and sprinkle lightly with Italian seasoning.
Grill tomatoes and zucchini 5-6 minutes, turning once, until tender.
Remove vegetables from grill and cool slightly.
Chop vegetables into bite-size chunks and toss with remaining Italian salad dressing in a large mixing bowl.
Serve warm or refrigerate 1-2 hours.

Serves: 6

Nutrition per Serving		Exchanges
Calories	56	3 vegetable
Carbohydrate	19 grams	
Cholesterol	0 milligrams	
Dietary Fiber	4 grams	
Fat	< 1 gram	
Protein	3 grams	
Sodium	175 milligrams	

Shopping List: 6 roma tomatoes, 3 zucchini, 2 red onions, 1 green bell pepper, 1 red bell pepper, Italian seasoning, 8 ounces fat-free Italian salad dressing.

BRAVO BAR-B-QUE

101

APPLE-BERRY BROWN BETTY

AVERAGE - DO AHEAD

ingredients:
3 cups fat-free bread crumbs
1 tbsp. sugar
6 tbsp. reconstituted Butter Buds
2 cups apples, peeled and sliced 1/2-inch thick
2 cups blueberries, rinsed and drained
1/3 cup brown sugar
1 tbsp. lemon juice
3/4 tsp. cinnamon, divided
1/4 tsp. nutmeg
1/4 cup hot apple juice
1/4 cup water

directions:
Prepare a medium-hot grill. Brush apple slices with Butter Buds; grill 8-10 minutes, turning several times until tender; remove from grill. Lightly spray 9-inch baking dish with nonfat cooking spray. In a medium bowl, combine bread crumbs, sugar and 1/4 teaspoon cinnamon; mix well. Sprinkle Butter Buds over crumb mixture and mix with hands until crumbs form. Spread half crumb mixture in bottom of baking dish. In medium bowl, combine grilled apples, blueberries, brown sugar, lemon juice, cinnamon and nutmeg; mix well. Spoon half the apple-berry mixture over crumb crust; sprinkle with 1/2 the remaining crumb mixture. Repeat layers and top with crumbs. Heat apple juice and water in microwave or saucepan until heated through; do not boil. Pour hot liquid over apple-berry pie, cover tightly with foil and bake on covered grill 15 minutes. Remove foil; cook an addition 10-15 minutes, until lightly browned.

Serves: 6

Nutrition per Serving

Calories	183	
Carbohydrate	42 grams	
Cholesterol	0 milligrams	
Dietary Fiber	3 grams	
Fat	< 1 gram	
Protein	2 grams	
Sodium	208 milligrams	

Exchanges
3 fruit

Shopping List:
fat-free bread crumbs, sugar, Butter Buds, 2 medium-large apples, 1 pint blueberries, brown sugar, lemon juice, cinnamon, nutmeg, 2 ounces apple juice.

APPLE SPICE BURRITOS

AVERAGE - DO AHEAD

ingredients:
2 cups cinnamon 'n spice apples, chopped
3 tbsp. reconstituted Butter Buds, divided
3/4 cup sugar, divided
1/4 cup brown sugar
3 tsp. cinnamon, divided
1 1/2 T. lemon juice
6 fat-free 10-inch flour tortillas

directions:
Prepare a medium-hot grill.
Pour 1 tablespoon Butter Buds into medium sauce-pan; add chopped apples, 1/2 cup sugar, brown sugar and 2 teaspoons cinnamon.
Place saucepan on grill and cook 5-8 minutes, stirring frequently, until mixture thickens. Stir in lemon juice and mix well. Remove saucepan from grill and cool slightly.
Lightly spray grill with nonfat cooking spray.
Spoon apple mixture into center of tortilla; fold up bottom and sides; roll from the bottom so the tortilla is tightly sealed.
Brush rolled tortillas with remaining Butter Buds and grill 5-7 minutes, until tortillas are lightly browned and filling is hot.
In a small bowl, combine remaining cinnamon and sugar; mix well.
Sprinkle cinnamon-sugar mixture over cooked burritos.

Serves: 6

Nutrition per Serving		Exchanges
Calories	401	2 starch
Carbohydrate	94 grams	4 1/4 fruit
Cholesterol	0 milligrams	
Dietary Fiber	4 grams	
Fat	< 1 gram	
Protein	6 grams	
Sodium	566 milligrams	

Shopping List: 20 ounce can cinnamon 'n spice apples, Butter Buds, sugar, brown sugar, cinnamon, lemon juice, 10-inch fat-free flour tortillas.

CARROT CAKE

AVERAGE - DO AHEAD - FREEZE

ingredients:
1 cup Pioneer baking mix
2 tbsp. brown sugar
1/4 cup sugar
3/4 tsp. cinnamon
1/2 cup shredded carrots
2 tbsp. skim milk
1/4 cup egg substitute
3/4 tsp. vanilla, divided
1/4 cup raisins
Powdered sugar

directions:
Prepare a medium-hot grill.
Lightly spray tinfoil pie pan with nonfat cooking spray; cut a foil sheet to cover pan and lightly spray with nonfat cooking spray.
In a large bowl, combine baking mix, brown sugar, sugar, cinnamon, carrots, milk, egg substitute, vanilla and raisins; mix until blended. Pour batter into prepared pan; cover with foil sheet (sprayed-side down) and secure tightly.
Cook over hot grill 10-12 minutes; turn pan over and cook an additional 5-10 minutes, until cake springs back when touched in the center. Remove from grill; let cool 5-10 minutes. Invert onto serving platter. Sprinkle with powdered sugar; cut and serve.

Serves: 6

Nutrition per Serving		Exchanges
Calories	179	1/2 starch
Carbohydrate	46 grams	2 1/2 fruit
Cholesterol	<1 milligram	
Dietary Fiber	1 gram	
Fat	< 1 gram	
Protein	3 grams	
Sodium	363 milligrams	

Shopping List: Pioneer baking mix, brown sugar, sugar, cinnamon, packaged shredded carrots, skim milk, egg substitute, vanilla, powdered sugar, raisins.

CHERRY-PINEAPPLE CAKE KABOBS

EASY - DO AHEAD

ingredients:
1 angel food cake, cut in 1-inch pieces
1 cup pineapple chunks in juice, drained
1 cup maraschino cherries
3/4 cup fat-free cherry-vanilla yogurt

directions:
Prepare a medium-hot grill and lightly spray with nonfat cooking spray.
Drain cherries, reserving 1 teaspoon juice.
In a small bowl, combine yogurt and cherry juice, stir until blended.
Alternate cake, pineapple and cherries on metal skewers and brush with yogurt-blend.
Place on grill, cover and cook 5-7 minutes, turning once, until cake and pineapple are lightly browned.
Serve with additional cherry yogurt for dipping, if desired.

Serves: 6

BRAVO BAR-B-QUE

Nutrition per Serving
Calories	245
Carbohydrate	56 grams
Cholesterol	1 milligram
Dietary Fiber	< 1 gram
Fat	< 1 gram
Protein	5 grams
Sodium	439 milligrams

Exchanges
1 2/3 starch
2 fruit

Shopping List: angel food cake, 8 ounces pineapple chunks in juice, maraschino cherries, 6 ounces fat-free cherry-vanilla yogurt.

CHOCOLATE-ALMOND PUDDING SUNDAES

AVERAGE - DO AHEAD

BRAVO BAR-B-QUE

ingredients:

2 tbsp. cornstarch
3/4 cup sugar
3/4 cup egg substitute
1 tsp. almond extract
1 3/4 cups skim milk
1 3/4 tbsp. reduced-fat chocolate chips
2 tsp. reconstituted Butter Buds
1 cup fat-free Cool Whip, thawed
8 maraschino cherries
2 1/2 tbsp. lite chocolate syrup

directions:

Prepare a medium-hot grill.
In a medium bowl, combine cornstarch and sugar; mix well. Add egg substitute and almond extract and mix until blended. Lightly spray medium saucepan with nonfat cooking spray and place on grill; combine milk, chocolate chips and butter in saucepan and cook, stirring constantly, until mixture comes to a boil. Pour chocolate mixture into cornstarch mixture and mix well. Return mixture to saucepan and bring to a boil, stirring frequently. Remove saucepan from grill. Divide chocolate pudding among 8 dessert cups or dishes and refrigerate 4-6 hours, until set. Just before serving, top each pudding dish with 1 tablespoon Cool Whip and 1 cherry; drizzle with 1 teaspoon lite chocolate syrup.

Serves: 8

Nutrition per Serving		Exchanges
Calories	152	1 1/3 starch
Carbohydrate	33 grams	2/3 fruit
Cholesterol	1 milligram	
Dietary Fiber	< 1 gram	
Fat	< 1 gram	
Protein	4 grams	
Sodium	70 milligrams	

Shopping List: cornstarch, sugar, 6 ounces egg substitute, almond extract, 14 ounces skim milk, reduced-fat chocolate chips, Butter Buds, 8 ounces fat-free Cool Whip, maraschino cherries, lite chocolate syrup.

GRILLED S'MORES

EASY

ingredients: 12 slices angel food cake
3/4 cup marshmallow creme
3/4 cup lite chocolate syrup

directions: Prepare a medium-hot grill and lightly spray with nonfat cooking spray.
Cut angel food cake into 12 equal square slices and place on grill; cook 3-4 minutes, turning once, until golden brown.
Remove cake slices from grill; spoon 2 tablespoons marshmallow creme on 6 cake slices and drizzle with 2 tablespoons chocolate syrup.
Top with remaining cake slices and serve.

Serves: 6

Nutrition per Serving

		Exchanges
Calories	413	3 starch
Carbohydrate	97 grams	3 fruit
Cholesterol	0 milligrams	
Dietary Fiber	< 1 gram	
Fat	< 1 gram	
Protein	9 grams	
Sodium	307 milligrams	

Shopping List: angel food cake, 6 ounces marshmallow creme, 6 ounces lite chocolate syrup.

107

RASPBERRY-PEACHES

EASY - DO AHEAD

ingredients:
6 peaches, cut in half
3/4 cup raspberries
1/4 cup brown sugar
1 1/2 tbsp. peach nectar
1 1/2 cups fat-free Cool Whip

directions:
Prepare a medium-hot grill.
Remove pits from peach halves.
Place each peach half on heavy-duty foil square.
Spoon 2 teaspoons raspberries into the center of each peach half; sprinkle with 1 teaspoon brown sugar and drizzle with peach nectar.
Wrap peach securely in foil and grill 10-15 minutes, turning once.
Top each peach half with 1 tablespoon Cool Whip just before serving.

Serves: 6

Nutrition per Serving

Calories	111
Carbohydrate	27 grams
Cholesterol	0 milligrams
Dietary Fiber	2 grams
Fat	< 1 gram
Protein	1 gram
Sodium	7 milligrams

Exchanges
2 fruit

Shopping List: 6 peaches, 1/2 pint raspberries, brown sugar, peach nectar, fat-free Cool Whip.

RECIPES FOR

FAT FREE LIVING®

FOOD PROCESSORS

by Jyl Steinback

FOOD PROCESSOR TIPS

Food processors provide you with efficiency, speed, and the ability to create a variety of recipes from appetizers to desserts. The best method for perfecting your use of the food processor is to practice slicing, shredding, or chopping a variety of fruits, vegetables, and other foods. You need to establish the most efficient sequence for processing the foods you need for your recipe. Start with the dry ingredients and finish with any liquid ingredients; this way you can usually avoid washing the bowl or attachments until you are finished. The following are some basic tips for efficient use of your food processor:

- Determine the amount of pressure needed for the particular food by guiding the food through the feed tube - never force the food through! Carrots, potatoes, or apples will require more pressure than mushrooms or tomatoes. This applies to foods that are sliced or shredded.

- Fit foods firmly and tightly packed in the feed tube to create even slices. Foods that are processed at an angle will be uneven.

- The pulse control button on the food processor allows you to determine how finely chopped the foods will be processed. Several quick pulses will perfectly chop onions, celery, parsley, etc. without crushing them. Brush the foods down if necessary in between pulses. If you need foods minced or very finely chopped, pulse 1 or 2 additional times.

The food processor is especially efficient for creating fat-free foods because you can use fresh fruits and vegetables and slice, dice, shred or chop as needed. It is wonderful for blending batters for quick breads, muffins and cakes, as well as puréeing a variety of fat-free hot and cold soups.

APPLE BUTTER

EASY - DO AHEAD

ingredients: 6 cups canned Cinnamon 'n Spice apples, drained
1/3 cup frozen apple juice concentrate
2/3 cup water
1 tsp. cinnamon
1/4 tsp. nutmeg
1/4 tsp. ginger

directions: Insert metal blade into food processor bowl. Combine all ingredients in bowl of food processor and process until smooth and creamy. Refrigerate several hours before using. Apple butter is a great substitute for "fat" in most baked goods or as a spread on bagels or toast.

Serves: 24

FABULOUS FOODPROCESSOR

Nutrition per Serving

Calories	89
Carbohydrate	22
Cholesterol	0 milligrams
Dietary Fiber	1 gram
Fat	< 1 gram
Protein	0 grams
Sodium	46 grams

Exchanges
1 1/2 fruit

Shopping List: 3 - 21 oz. cans Cinnamon 'n Spice apples, frozen apple juice concentrate, cinnamon, nutmeg, ginger.

BAGEL CRISPS WITH FRUITY CREAM CHEESE SPREAD

EASY - DO AHEAD

---

ingredients: 6 fat-free bagels
1 cup fat-free cream cheese, softened
1/4 cup apricot preserves

directions: Preheat oven to 400 degrees.
Slice each bagel into three or four thin slices. Arrange slices on baking sheet and bake 8 minutes; turn slices over and bake 5-8 minutes until crisp.
Insert metal blade into food processor bowl.
Combine cream cheese and preserves in bowl of food processor; process until blended, creamy and smooth.
Dip bagel chips into cheese mixture or spread with knife.

Serves: 6

Nutrition per Serving:

		Exchanges:
Calories	249	2 starch
Carbohydrate	52 grams	1 1/3 fruit
Cholesterol	0 milligrams	1/2 meat
Dietary Fiber	2 grams	
Fat	< 1 gram	
Protein	11 grams	
Sodium	536 milligrams	

Shopping List: 1/2 dozen fat-free bagels, 8 oz. fat-free cream cheese, 2 oz. apricot preserves.

TUNA APPETIZER SPREAD

EASY - DO AHEAD

ingredients: 1 cup fat-free cream cheese, softened
2 tbsp. fat-free chili sauce
2 tsp. dried parsley
1 tsp. onion powder
1/4 tsp. cayenne pepper
2 (6 1/2 oz.) cans fat-free tuna
fat-free crackers

directions: Insert metal blade into bowl of food processor.
Combine all ingredients in bowl and pulse several times until ingredients are blended.
Scrape bowl to blend ingredients and pulse several more times.
Spoon mixture into medium bowl, cover with plastic wrap, and refrigerate several hours before serving.
Serve with fat-free crackers.

Serves: 8

__Nutrition per Serving (no crackers)__		__Exchanges__
Calories	89	2 meat
Carbohydrate	3 grams	1/3 starch
Cholesterol	8 milligrams	
Dietary Fiber	< 1 gram	
Fat	< 1 gram	
Protein	18 grams	
Sodium	415 milligrams	

Shopping List: 8 oz. fat-free cream cheese, fat-free chili sauce, dried parsley, onion powder, cayenne pepper, 2 - 6 1/2 oz. cans fat-free tuna, fat-free crackers.

VEGETABLE-CHIVE DIP

EASY - DO AHEAD

ingredients: 1 cup fat-free cottage cheese
1 tbsp. lemon juice
1 tbsp. skim milk
1/2 tsp. garlic powder
1/4 tsp. onion powder
1 large carrot, peeled and trimmed
2 whole green onions, trimmed
1/2 small cucumber, peeled and halved

directions: Insert shredding disc into food processor.
Place carrot in feed tube and process until finely
shredded; remove from bowl and set aside. Insert
metal blade into food processor. Place green onions and cucumbers in bowl and pulse several
times until onions and cucumber are chopped;
remove from bowl and set aside.
Combine cottage cheese, lemon juice, milk, garlic
powder and onion powder in bowl of food processor and process until creamy and smooth. Spoon
mixture into medium bowl.
Add carrots and green onions and mix until
blended.
Cover and refrigerate several hours before serving.

Serves: 6

Nutrition per Serving

Calories	19	
Carbohydrate	3 grams	
Cholesterol	1 milligram	
Dietary Fiber	1 gram	
Fat	< 1 gram	
Protein	2 grams	
Sodium	38 milligrams	

Exchanges
Free

Shopping List: 8 oz. fat-free cottage cheese, lemon juice, skim
milk, garlic powder, onion powder, 1 carrot, 2
green onions, 1 small cucumber.

CINNAMON-SPICE
BANANA BREAD
EASY - DO AHEAD - FREEZE

ingredients:
2 large bananas, cut in half
1/3 cup fat-free banana yogurt
3/4 tsp. vanilla
1/4 cup egg substitute
2 tbsp. corn syrup
1/3 cup sugar
1/3 cup brown sugar
1 tsp. cinnamon
1/4 tsp. nutmeg
1/8 tsp. allspice
1 1/2 cups flour
1 tsp. baking powder
1 tsp. baking soda

directions:
Preheat oven to 375 degrees. Lightly spray 4x8-inch loaf pan with nonfat cooking spray.
Place metal blade in bowl of food processor.
Add bananas, yogurt, vanilla, egg substitute, corn syrup, sugar, brown sugar, cinnamon, nutmeg and allspice; process 30 seconds until mixture is creamy and smooth.
Remove top of food processor; add flour, baking powder and baking soda; replace top and process 30-45 seconds, until mixture is blended smooth. Scrape batter into loaf pan and bake in preheated oven 45-50 minutes, until knife inserted in center comes out clean.

Serves: 8

Nutrition per Serving		Exchanges
Calories	201	1 1/3 starch
Carbohydrate	46 grams	1 2/3 fruit
Cholesterol	< 1 milligram	
Dietary Fiber	1 gram	
Fat	< 1 gram	
Protein	4 grams	
Sodium	90 milligrams	

Shopping List: 2 bananas, fat-free banana yogurt, 2 oz. egg substitute, 1 oz. corn syrup, sugar, brown sugar, vanilla, cinnamon, nutmeg, allspice, flour, baking powder, baking soda.

DOUBLE CORNBREAD

EASY - DO AHEAD

ingredients: 1 cup flour
1 cup cornmeal
1/3 cup sugar
1 tbsp. baking powder
1/4 cup egg substitute
1 cup fat-free sour cream
1/3 cup unsweetened applesauce
1/2 cup corn kernels, drained

directions: Preheat oven to 375 degrees.
Lightly spray 8-inch square baking dish with non-fat cooking spray.
Place metal blade in bowl of food processor.
Combine all ingredients except corn kernels in bowl; replace top and process 30-45 seconds until blended creamy and smooth.
Remove top and fold in corn kernels. Spoon batter into prepared pan and bake in preheated oven 20-25 minutes, until knife inserted in center comes out clean.

Serves: 8

Nutrition per Serving		Exchanges
Calories	189	2 starch
Carbohydrate	39 grams	2/3 fruit
Cholesterol	0 milligrams	
Dietary Fiber	2 grams	
Fat	< 1 gram	
Protein	6 grams	
Sodium	190 milligrams	

Shopping List: flour, cornmeal, sugar, baking powder, 2 oz. egg substitute, 8 oz. fat-free sour cream, unsweetened applesauce, 6 oz. corn kernels.

FABULOUS FOOD PROCESSOR

FRENCH BREAD

DIFFICULT - DO AHEAD - FREEZE

ingredients:
1 tbsp. active dry yeast
1/2 tsp. sugar
1/4 cup warm water
1 1/4 cups cold water
1 1/2 cups flour
1 3/4 cups bread flour
1 1/2 tsp. salt
1 tsp. garlic powder (optional)

directions: Pour water in small bowl, sprinkle yeast and sugar over warm water and mix until dissolved. Set mixture aside until it becomes bubbly, then stir in cold water. Insert dough blade into food processor. Combine flour, bread flour and salt in food processor bowl and pulse several times until mixed.
Gradually pour yeast mixture through feed tube as machine is running, and process until liquid is absorbed and dough forms into a ball. If dough is too sticky, add a little more flour; if dough is too dry, gradually add water until dough is smooth.
Lightly spray large glass bowl with nonfat cooking spray. Transfer dough to bowl and turn to coat. Cover bowl with plastic wrap and place in warm spot until dough has tripled in size (2 1/2-3 hours). Turn dough on lightly-floured work surface and knead lightly. Reshape dough back into ball. Place in bowl; cover with plastic wrap. Let dough rise at room temperature another 2 hours, until doubled in size. Turn dough on lightly-floured surface; knead lightly. Divide dough in half and shape into logs; using serrated knife, cut diagonal slashes in top of bread loaf.
Lightly spray plastic wrap with nonfat cooking spray and cover bread loaves. Let loaves rise 45-55 minutes, until doubled in size. Preheat oven to 450 degrees. Lightly spray cookie sheet with nonfat cooking spray. Arrange loaves on cookie sheet; lightly spray with nonfat cooking spray and immediately sprinkle with garlic powder, if desired. Bake in preheated oven 20-22 minutes until loaves are lightly browned and sound hollow when tapped.

Serves: 12

Nutrition per Serving		Exchanges
Calories	118	1 1/2 starch
Carbohydrate	24 grams	
Cholesterol	0 milligrams	
Dietary Fiber	1 gram	
Fat	< 1 gram	
Protein	4 grams	
Sodium	268 milligrams	

Shopping List: 1/4 oz. active dry yeast, sugar, flour, bread flour, salt, garlic powder (optional).

PEACHY BRAN MUFFINS
AVERAGE - DO AHEAD - FREEZE

ingredients: 6 dried peaches
3/4 cup skim milk
1/4 cup fat-free peach-flavored yogurt
2 tbsp. egg substitute
2 tbsp. applesauce
1/4 cup sugar
1/2 cup brown sugar
2 cups flour
1/2 cup Bran Buds
2 tsp. baking powder

directions: Preheat oven to 350 degrees.
Lightly spray muffin pan with nonfat cooking spray.
Insert metal blade into food processor bowl. Place
peaches in bowl and pulse several times, just until
peaches are chopped.
Combine milk and yogurt in large mixing bowl;
add peaches and toss lightly.
Combine flour, Bran Buds, baking powder, egg
substitute, applesauce, sugar and brown sugar in
food processor bowl; process until blended (batter
will be thick). Gradually pour in milk and peaches
and pulse several times, just until batter is blended.
Fill muffin cups and bake in preheated oven 20-25
minutes, until knife inserted in center comes out clean.

Serves: 12

Nutrition per Serving		Exchanges
Calories	178	1/2 milk
Carbohydrate	42 grams	2 1/3 fruit
Cholesterol	< 1 milligram	
Dietary Fiber	3 grams	
Fat	< 1 gram	
Protein	4 grams	
Sodium	92 milligrams	

Shopping List: dried peaches, 6 oz. skim milk, 2 oz. fat-free peach
yogurt, 1 oz. egg substitute, 1 oz. applesauce, sugar,
brown sugar, flour, Bran Buds, baking powder.

ZUCCHINI-APPLE BREAD

EASY - DO AHEAD - FREEZE

ingredients:
2 small apples, peeled and cored
2 small zucchini, trimmed
1 1/2 cups sugar
1 cup brown sugar
1/4 cup corn syrup
1/2 cup fat-free vanilla yogurt
1 1/2 tbsp. vanilla
1/2 cup cinnamon-flavored applesauce
2 1/2 tsp. cinnamon
1 cup egg substitute
3 cups flour
1 tsp. baking soda
1 tsp. baking powder
1/4 tsp. nutmeg
1/2 cup raisins

directions:
Preheat oven to 350 degrees. Lightly spray two 5x9-inch loaf pans with nonfat cooking spray. Insert shredding disc into food processor.
Cut apples and zucchini into vertical slices to fit feed tube. Place apples in feed tube and process until shredded; repeat process with zucchini.
Remove apples and zucchini and set aside. Insert metal blade into food processor bowl. Combine sugar, brown sugar, corn syrup, yogurt, applesauce, egg substitute, vanilla, flour, cinnamon, baking soda, baking powder and nutmeg in bowl of food processor; process until blended smooth; scrape bowl down several times to blend all ingredients. Spoon batter in large mixing bowl; fold in apples, zucchini and raisins; mix well. Divide batter between loaf pans; bake in preheated oven 1 hour, until knife inserted in center comes out clean.

Serves: 16

Nutrition per Serving		Exchanges
Calories	265	1 starch
Carbohydrate	63 grams	3 fruit
Cholesterol	< 1 milligram	
Dietary Fiber	2 grams	
Fat	< 1 gram	
Protein	4 grams	
Sodium	106 milligrams	

Shopping List: 2 apples, 2 zucchini, sugar, brown sugar, 2 oz. corn syrup, 4 oz. fat-free vanilla yogurt, 4 oz. cinnamon-flavored applesauce, 8 oz. egg substitute, vanilla, cinnamon, flour, baking powder, baking soda, nutmeg, raisins.

COLD BLUEBERRY SOUP

EASY - DO AHEAD

ingredients: 1 cup fat-free sour cream
30 oz. frozen blueberries
1/3 cup sugar

directions: Insert metal blade into food processor bowl.
Combine all ingredients in bowl and process until
blended creamy and smooth.
Refrigerate several hours before serving.

Serves: 6

Nutrition per Serving		Exchanges
Calories	139	1/3 milk
Carbohydrate	31 grams	1 2/3 fruit
Cholesterol	0 milligrams	
Dietary Fiber	5 grams	
Fat	< 1 gram	
Protein	3 grams	
Sodium	28 milligrams	

Shopping List: 8 oz. fat-free sour cream, 3 - 10 oz. pkg. frozen
blueberries, sugar.

CREAM OF CORN SOUP

AVERAGE - DO AHEAD - FREEZE

ingredients: 2 medium potatoes, peeled and cubed
1 1/2 cups evaporated skim milk
32 oz. frozen corn kernels, thawed and drained
1 tbsp. onion powder
1 tsp. garlic powder
2 tsp. sugar
2 tbsp. Dijon mustard
1/4 tsp. pepper
1 cup skim milk

directions: Place potatoes in a large soup pot and cover with water; bring to boil over high heat. Cook until tender. Remove saucepan from heat, drain potatoes and set aside.

Lightly spray soup pot with nonfat cooking spray. Combine evaporated skim milk, corn, onion powder, garlic powder, sugar, mustard and pepper in soup pot and cook over medium heat, stirring frequently, until ingredients are blended and thickened.

Insert metal blade into bowl of food processor. Place 1/2 potatoes and 1/2 soup mixture into food processor; process until smooth. Spoon mixture back into soup pot and add remaining potatoes. Gradually add skim milk and cook over medium heat until thickened and heated through.

Serves: 6

Nutrition per Serving		**Exchanges**
Calories	252	1/3 milk
Carbohydrate	54 grams	3 starch
Cholesterol	3 milligrams	
Dietary Fiber	4 grams	
Fat	< 1 gram	
Protein	12 grams	
Sodium	231 milligrams	

Shopping List: 2 potatoes, 12 oz. evaporated skim milk, 32 oz. frozen corn kernels, onion powder, garlic powder, sugar, Dijon mustard, pepper, 8 oz. skim milk.

CREAM OF MUSHROOM SOUP

AVERAGE - DO AHEAD - FREEZE

ingredients:
10 cups sliced mushrooms
3/4 cup chopped onions
1 3/4 cups fat-free chicken broth, divided
1 1/2 cups evaporated skim milk
3 tbsp. cornstarch
1/8 tsp. pepper

directions:
Lightly spray large saucepan with nonfat cooking spray. Add 1/4 cup chicken broth to saucepan and heat over medium-high heat.
Add mushrooms and onions; cook until tender and soft. Gradually pour remaining chicken broth into saucepan and mix well.
Insert metal blade into bowl of food processor; remove 1 cup mushrooms from saucepan and set aside.
Pour soup mixture into food processor bowl and process 25-30 seconds until mixture is smooth. Pour soup back into saucepan.
In small cup, combine 1/2 cup milk and cornstarch; mix until blended smooth. Stir into soup mixture; add remaining milk. Cook over medium heat, stirring frequently, until soup is thick and bubbly.
Add reserved mushrooms and cook 2-3 minutes until heated through.

Serves: 6

Nutrition per Serving		Exchanges
Calories	103	1/2 milk
Carbohydrate	18 grams	2 vegetable
Cholesterol	3 milligrams	
Dietary Fiber	2 grams	
Fat	< 1 gram	
Protein	8 grams	
Sodium	229 milligrams	

Shopping List: 2 lb. sliced mushrooms, 1 medium onion, 16 oz. fat-free chicken broth, 12 oz. evaporated skim milk, cornstarch, pepper.

FABULOUS FOOD PROCESSOR

GAZPACHO SOUP
AVERAGE -D O AHEAD

ingredients:
1 medium onion
1 green bell pepper
1 red bell pepper
2 large cucumbers
10 cups Mexican stewed tomatoes
fat-free croutons (optional)
1 tsp. garlic powder
1 (4 oz.) can chopped green chilies
1 1/2 tsp. Worcestershire sauce
1 tbsp. red wine vinegar
1/4 tsp. pepper

directions:
Insert metal blade into food processor bowl. Add onion and pulse several times until onion is chopped. Remove onion and place in large mixing bowl.
Add peppers to food processor bowl and pulse several times until chopped into medium-sized pieces. Remove and add to mixing bowl.
Insert slicing disc into food processor bowl. Cut cucumbers in half lengthwise; stand cucumbers in feeding tube and process into medium slices. Remove cucumbers and add to mixing bowl.
Replace metal blade into food processor bowl. Pour 4 cups stewed tomatoes into bowl; add garlic powder, Tabasco sauce, vinegar and pepper; pulse several times until tomatoes are diced. Pour mixture into mixing bowl. Add remaining stewed tomatoes and green chilies to mixing bowl and stir until ingredients are blended.
Cover; refrigerate several hours before serving. Top with fat-free croutons, just before serving, if desired.

Serves: 8

Nutrition per Serving

Calories	75
Carbohydrate	18 grams
Cholesterol	0 milligrams
Dietary Fiber	3 grams
Fat	< 1 gram
Protein	3 grams
Sodium	1386 milligrams

Exchanges
3 vegetable

Shopping List: 6 - 14 1/2 oz. cans Mexican stewed tomatoes, 1 onion, 1 green bell pepper, 1 red bell pepper, 2 large cucumbers, green chilies, garlic powder, Worcestershire sauce, red wine vinegar, pepper, fat-free croutons.

SEAFOOD GUMBO

AVERAGE - DO AHEAD - FREEZE

ingredients:
3 green onions, trimmed
1 medium onion, peeled and quartered
2 stalks celery, trimmed
1 red bell pepper, cored, seeded, cut in half
2 carrots, peeled and trimmed
1 cup canned corn kernels, drained
1 1/2 cups canned red kidney beans, drained
1 tsp. garlic powder
1/4 tsp. cayenne pepper
15 oz. fat-free chicken broth
3/4 lb. fat-free scallops
1/2 lb. crabmeat

directions:
Insert metal blade into food processor bowl.
Cut green onions, onion, celery and red bell pepper into large pieces. Place vegetables in food processor bowl; pulse several times until all vegetables are chopped fine.
Lightly spray large nonstick saucepan with nonfat cooking spray and heat over medium-high heat. Add chopped vegetables to pan; cook over medium heat until vegetables are tender, about 3-5 minutes.
Sprinkle vegetables with garlic powder and cayenne pepper. Insert shredding disc into food processor. Place carrots in feed tube; process until finely shredded. Add carrots to saucepan and cook until softened, about 3-5 minutes.
Add chicken broth to saucepan and bring to a boil over high heat; add beans and corn. Cover pan and simmer over low heat 40-45 minutes.
Stir in scallops and crabmeat and cook over medium heat until scallops are cooked through and tender.

Serves: 6

Nutrition per Serving		Exchanges
Calories	196	1 starch
Carbohydrate	29 grams	3 vegetable
Cholesterol	27 grams	1 meat
Dietary Fiber	2 grams	
Fat	< 1 gram	
Protein	19 grams	
Sodium	879 milligrams	

Shopping List: green onions, 1 onion, celery, red bell pepper, 2 carrots, 8 oz. canned corn kernels, 15 oz. can red kidney beans, 15 oz. fat-free chicken broth, 3/4 lb. fat-free scallops, 1/2 lb. crabmeat, garlic powder, cayenne pepper.

FABULOUS
FOOD PROCESSOR

CREAMY DILL SALAD DRESSING

EASY - DO AHEAD

ingredients:
- 1/2 cup fat-free yogurt
- 1/4 cup fat-free sour cream
- 1 tsp. dill weed
- 1 1/2 tbsp. lemon juice
- 1/4 tsp. onion powder
- 1/4 tsp. pepper

directions:
Insert metal blade in food processor bowl.
Combine all ingredients and process until creamy and smooth.
Spoon into bowl, cover and refrigerate several hours before serving.

Serves: 6

Nutrition per Serving		Exchanges
Calories	19	Free
Carbohydrate	3 grams	
Cholesterol	<1 milligram	
Dietary Fiber	0 grams	
Fat	< 1 gram	
Protein	2 grams	
Sodium	22 milligrams	

Shopping List: 4 oz. fat-free yogurt, 2 oz. fat-free sour cream, dill weed, onion powder, pepper, lemon juice.

CREAMY ITALIAN DRESSING

EASY - DO AHEAD

ingredients:
1/4 cup fat-free yogurt
1/4 cup fat-free sour cream
1/2 cup skim milk
1/2 tsp. garlic powder
1/8 tsp. onion powder
1 tsp. Italian seasoning

directions:
Insert metal blade into food processor bowl.
Combine all ingredients and purée until creamy and smooth.
Cover and refrigerate several hours before serving.

Serves: 6

FABULOUS FOOD PROCESSOR

Nutrition per Serving		Exchanges
Calories	21	Free
Carbohydrate	3 grams	
Cholesterol	1 milligram	
Dietary Fiber	0 grams	
Fat	< 1 gram	
Protein	2 grams	
Sodium	24 milligrams	

Shopping List: 2 oz. fat-free yogurt, 2 oz. fat-free sour cream, 4 oz. skim milk, garlic powder, onion powder, Italian seasoning.

GREEN GODDESS SALAD DRESSING

EASY - DO AHEAD

ingredients:
1 cup fat-free mayonnaise
1 cup fat-free sour cream
1/2 cup parsley
1 tbsp. anchovy paste
3 tbsp. white wine vinegar
2 tbsp. lemon juice
1 tbsp. Worcestershire sauce
1 1/2 tsp. minced garlic
1/2 tsp. dry mustard
1/4 tsp. pepper
1/4 tsp. tarragon

directions:
Insert metal blade into food processor bowl.
Add fresh parsley to bowl and pulse 2-3 times until finely chopped.
Combine remaining ingredients and process until blended creamy and smooth.
Refrigerate several hours, or overnight, before serving.

Serves: 8

Nutrition per Serving		Exchanges
Calories	52	2/3 starch
Carbohydrate	8 grams	
Cholesterol	< 1 milligram	
Dietary Fiber	< 1 gram	
Fat	< 1 gram	
Protein	2 grams	
Sodium	278 milligrams	

Shopping List: 8 oz. fat-free mayonnaise, 8 oz. fat-free sour cream, fresh parsley, anchovy paste, white wine vinegar, lemon juice, Worcestershire sauce, minced garlic, dry mustard, pepper, tarragon.

TOMATO RED WINE VINAIGRETTE

EASY - DO AHEAD

ingredients: 2 medium tomatoes, quartered
1/4 cup red wine vinegar
1 tsp. dried basil
1 tsp. dried thyme
1/8 tsp. garlic powder
1 tsp. Dijon mustard

directions: Insert metal blade into food processor bowl.
Place tomatoes in bowl and pulse several times until tomatoes are chopped into chunks.
Add remaining ingredients and pulse until ingredients are blended.
Cover and refrigerate several hours before serving.

Serves: 6

FABULOUS FOOD PROCESSOR

Nutrition per Serving		Exchanges
Calories	21	Free
Carbohydrate	5 grams	
Cholesterol	0 milligrams	
Dietary Fiber	< 1 gram	
Fat	< 1 gram	
Protein	< 1 gram	
Sodium	27 milligrams	

Shopping List: 2 tomatoes, 2 oz. red wine vinegar, dried basil, thyme, garlic powder, Dijon mustard.

CHEESY POTATO CASSEROLE

EASY - DO AHEAD

ingredients: 6 medium potatoes, peeled
1 1/2 cups low-fat cream of celery soup
1 cup fat-free sour cream
3/4 cup evaporated skim milk
1 1/2 tsp. onion powder
1 1/2 cups Cornflake crumbs

directions: Preheat oven to 350 degrees. Lightly spray 7x11-inch baking dish with nonfat cooking spray.
Insert shredding disc into food processor.
Replace top of food processor. Cut potatoes into thirds (lengthwise) to fit through feeder.
Place potatoes in feed tube and process until all potatoes are shredded.
Remove potatoes from bowl and set aside. Insert metal blade into bowl of food processor; add soup, sour cream, milk and onion powder to bowl and process 15-20 seconds until blended.
Pour soup mixture over shredded potatoes and toss until mixed.
Spread potato mixture into prepared pan and sprinkle with Cornflake crumbs.
Bake in preheated oven 45-55 minutes, until potatoes are tender and top is lightly browned.

Serves: 8

Nutrition per Serving

Calories	235
Carbohydrate	46 grams
Cholesterol	2 milligrams
Dietary Fiber	3 grams
Fat	< 1 gram
Protein	8 grams
Sodium	414 milligrams

Exchanges
3 starch

Shopping List: 2 lb. potatoes, 15 oz. low-fat cream of celery soup, 8 oz. fat-free sour cream, 6 oz. evaporated skim milk, onion powder, Cornflake crumbs.

FABULOUS FOODPROCESSOR

CREAMY TWICE-BAKED POTATOES

EASY - DO AHEAD

---

ingredients:
3 large baking potatoes
1/2 cup fat-free ricotta cheese
1/2 cup fat-free cottage cheese
1/4 cup fat-free sour cream
2 tsp. dried parsley
3/4 cup fat-free shredded Cheddar cheese, divided

directions:
Preheat oven to 400 degrees.
Prick potatoes with fork in several places and bake in oven 55-60 minutes, until tender. Remove from oven and cool 5-10 minutes.
Insert metal blade into food processor bowl; add ricotta cheese, cottage cheese, sour cream, 1/4 cup Cheddar cheese and parsley to bowl and process 15-20 seconds until smooth and creamy.
Add potato pulp and pulse 10-15 seconds until mixture is blended and smooth.
Arrange potato skins on baking sheet; divide potato mixture among shells and sprinkle with remaining Cheddar cheese.
Bake in 400 degree oven 10-15 minutes, until cheese is melted and lightly browned.

Serves: 6

FABULOUS
FOOD PROCESSOR

Nutrition per Serving
Calories	126
Carbohydrate	21 grams
Cholesterol	4 milligrams
Dietary Fiber	2 grams
Fat	< 1 gram
Protein	10 grams
Sodium	207 milligrams

Exchanges
1 meat
1 1/3 starch

Shopping List: 3 baking potatoes, 4 oz. fat-free ricotta cheese, 4 oz. fat-free cottage cheese, 2 oz. fat-free sour cream, dried parsley, 3 oz. fat-free shredded Cheddar cheese.

NOODLE PUDDING

EASY - DO AHEAD - FREEZE

ingredients: 12 oz. yolk-free noodles, cooked and drained
2 cups skim milk
1 cup fat-free cottage cheese
1 cup fat-free sour cream
3/4 cup egg substitute
1/2 cup sugar
1/4 cup reconstituted Butter Buds

directions: Cook noodles according to package directions and drain well; set aside.
Preheat oven to 350 degrees.
Lightly spray 9x13-inch baking dish with nonfat cooking spray.
Insert metal blade into food processor bowl.
Combine all ingredients except noodles in bowl, and process until blended smooth.
Combine noodles and sauce in baking dish and toss until noodles are well coated.
Bake in preheated oven 45-55 minutes, until lightly browned and cooked through.

Serves: 8

Nutrition per Serving		Exchanges
Calories	263	1 meat
Carbohydrate	49 grams	3 starch
Cholesterol	2 milligrams	
Dietary Fiber	2 grams	
Fat	< 1 gram	
Protein	14 grams	
Sodium	170 milligrams	

Shopping List: 12 oz. yolk-free noodles, 1 pint skim milk, 8 oz. fat-free cottage cheese, 8 oz. fat-free sour cream, 6 oz. egg substitute, sugar, Butter Buds.

SCALLOPED POTATOES

EASY - DO AHEAD

ingredients:

3 medium potatoes, scrubbed
1 medium onion, peeled and quartered
1 cup skim milk
1 tbsp. flour
1/4 tsp. pepper
1 1/2 tsp. Butter Buds, reconstituted

directions:

Insert medium slicer into food processor.
Cut potatoes to fit feeder and process until all potatoes are sliced; remove from bowl and set aside.
Replace slicer and repeat process with onion; remove onion and set aside.
Insert metal blade into bowl of food processor.
Add milk, flour, pepper and Butter Buds to bowl and process until blended smooth.
Preheat oven to 425 degrees. Lightly spray an 8- or 9-inch square baking dish with nonfat cooking spray.
Layer half the potatoes in dish and top with onions; top with remaining potatoes.
Pour milk mixture over casserole and mix lightly.
Cover dish with foil and bake in preheated oven 45 minutes. Remove cover and bake an additional 10 to 15 minutes, until top is lightly browned.

Serves: 6

Nutrition per Serving

Calories	102
Carbohydrate	22 grams
Cholesterol	1 milligram
Dietary Fiber	2 grams
Fat	< 1 gram
Protein	3 grams
Sodium	33 milligrams

Exchanges

1 1/2 starch

Shopping List: 3 potatoes, 1 onion, 8 oz. skim milk, flour, pepper, Butter Buds.

SIMPLE STUFFING

EASY - DO AHEAD

ingredients:
1/2 medium onion, peeled
1/4 cup reconstituted Butter Buds
3/4 cup egg substitute
1 1/4 cups fat-free chicken broth
1/2 tsp. poultry seasoning
1/2 tsp. garlic powder
2 cups fat-free seasoned croutons
1/2 lb. mushrooms, rinsed and dried

directions:
Preheat oven to 350 degrees. Lightly spray 9x13-inch baking dish with nonfat cooking spray. Insert medium slicing disc into food processor.
Cut mushrooms in half and place in feed tube; process until mushrooms are sliced.
Remove mushrooms and set aside.
Insert metal blade into food processor bowl.
Add onion and pulse several times until onions are chopped.
Add Butter Buds, egg substitute, chicken broth, poultry seasoning and garlic powder; process until all ingredients are blended.
Pour mixture into prepared dish; add croutons and mushrooms; mix well. Bake in preheated oven 45 minutes, until lightly browned and cooked through.

Serves: 6

Nutrition per Serving

Calories	54
Carbohydrate	9 grams
Cholesterol	0 milligrams
Dietary Fiber	< 1 gram
Fat	< 1 gram
Protein	4 grams
Sodium	216 milligrams

Exchanges
2/3 starch

Shopping List: onion, Butter Buds, 6 oz. egg substitute, 10 oz. fat-free chicken broth, poultry seasoning, garlic powder, fat-free croutons, mushrooms.

SWEET POTATO SOUFFLÉ

EASY - DO AHEAD

ingredients:
3 cups orange-pineapple yams
1/2 cup egg substitute
1/4 cup sugar
1 tsp. vanilla
5 tbsp. flour, divided
1/2 cup brown sugar
1/2 cup fat-free granola
1 tbsp. fat-free vanilla yogurt

directions:
Preheat oven to 350 degrees. Lightly spray a 6x10-inch baking dish with nonfat cooking spray.
Insert metal blade into bowl of food processor.
Add yams, egg substitute, sugar, vanilla and 2 tablespoons flour to bowl; replace top and process until smooth, about 30 seconds.
Pour mixture into prepared dish.
In a small bowl, combine 3 tablespoons flour, brown sugar and granola; mix well.
Add yogurt to crumb mixture and mix with hands until moist, but crumbly.
Sprinkle crumb mixture on top of potato casserole.
Bake in preheated oven 25-30 minutes, until golden brown.

Serves: 6

Nutrition per Serving		Exchanges
Calories	362	1 starch
Carbohydrate	80 grams	4 1/3 fruit
Cholesterol	0 milligrams	
Dietary Fiber	3 grams	
Fat	< 1 gram	
Protein	4 grams	
Sodium	65 milligrams	

Shopping List: 2 - 15 oz. cans orange-pineapple yams, 4 oz. egg substitute, sugar, vanilla, flour, brown sugar, fat-free granola, fat-free vanilla yogurt.

TRI-COLOR COLESLAW

AVERAGE - DO AHEAD

ingredients:
1 small head green cabbage
1 small head red cabbage
2 large carrots, peeled and halved
4 scallions
1/4 cup fat-free mayonnaise
2 tbsp. white vinegar
1 tbsp. Dijon mustard
1 tbsp. sugar
1/8 tsp. pepper

directions:
Insert thin slicing disc into food processor.
Cut 1-inch off the top of each cabbage; rinse well and drain.
Cut green and red cabbage into wedges that will fit feed tube of food processor.
Place cabbage in tube and process until all cabbage is sliced very thin; repeat process with scallions. Remove cabbage and scallions and place in large mixing bowl.
Insert shredding disc into food processor. Place carrots in feed tube and process until finely shredded. Add to cabbage mixture in mixing bowl.
Insert metal blade into food processor bowl. Add mayonnaise, vinegar, mustard, sugar and pepper to processor bowl; process until creamy and blended. Scrape bowl, if necessary, to blend all ingredients.
Pour dressing over cabbage mixture; toss and mix well. Cover and refrigerate several hours before serving.

Serves: 8

Nutrition per Serving

Calories	62
Carbohydrate	14 grams
Cholesterol	0 milligrams
Dietary Fiber	4 grams
Fat	< 1 gram
Protein	2 grams
Sodium	130 milligrams

Exchanges
2 1/2 vegetable

Shopping List: 1 green cabbage head, 1 red cabbage head, 2 carrots, scallions, 2 oz. fat-free mayonnaise, white vinegar, Dijon mustard, sugar, pepper.

BEAN CAKES

EASY - DO AHEAD

ingredients:
2 cups canned black beans
1 1/2 cups fat-free bread crumbs
1 tbsp. onion powder
1/2 tsp. garlic powder
1 tbsp. canned jalapeño peppers, chopped
1/3 cup egg substitute
2 tbsp. tomato paste
1/3 cup fat-free sour cream
1/3 cup garden-style salsa (Tostitos)

directions:
Preheat oven to 350 degrees. Lightly spray baking sheet with nonfat cooking spray.

Insert metal blade into bowl of food processor. Combine beans, bread crumbs, onion powder, garlic powder, peppers, egg substitute and tomato paste in bowl; replace top of food processor and process 30-40 seconds until blended and smooth. Form mixture into thick patties and place on baking sheet. Bake in preheated oven 35-40 minutes, until knife inserted in center comes out clean.

In a small bowl, combine sour cream and salsa; mix lightly. Top bean cakes with 1-2 tablespoons sour cream mixture, if desired.

Serves: 4

Nutrition per Serving		Exchanges
Calories	191	2 starch
Carbohydrate	33 grams	1 meat
Cholesterol	0 milligrams	
Dietary Fiber	4 grams	
Fat	< 1 gram	
Protein	12 grams	
Sodium	264 milligrams	

Shopping List: 28 oz. fat-free black beans, fat-free bread crumbs, onion powder, garlic powder, canned jalapeño peppers, 3 oz. egg substitute, tomato paste, 3 oz. fat-free sour cream, 3 oz. Tostito's garden-style salsa (or salsa of choice).

FABULOUS
FOOD PROCESSOR

VEGETABLE FRITTATA

AVERAGE

ingredients:
1 medium onion, peeled and quartered
1 small red bell pepper, cored and quartered
1 medium carrot, peeled and trimmed
1 small sweet potato, peeled
1 cup egg substitute
4 large egg whites
1/4 cup skim milk
1 tsp. dried parsley
1/4 tsp. pepper
3/4 cup fat-free shredded Cheddar cheese

directions:
Insert metal blade into food processor bowl.
Add onion and bell pepper; pulse several times until chopped in medium-sized pieces; remove. Set aside. Add potato to bowl; pulse just until chopped in medium-sized pieces. Remove potato; add to onion and pepper. Insert shredding disc into food processor; place carrot in feed tube and process until finely shredded. Lightly spray large nonstick skillet with nonfat cooking spray and heat over medium-high heat. Add onion, red pepper, carrot and potato to skillet and cook over medium heat 5 minutes, stirring frequently. Reduce heat to low, cover and simmer 15 to 20 minutes until potatoes are tender.
Sprinkle vegetables with parsley and pepper. Combine egg substitute, egg whites and milk in medium bowl and whisk until blended. Pour egg mixture over vegetables and mix lightly.
Cook over medium-low heat until eggs are set and cooked through. Sprinkle cheese on top, cover, and cook over low heat until cheese is melted.

Serves: 4

Nutrition per Serving		**Exchanges**
Calories	139	1 1/2 meat
Carbohydrate	17 grams	3 vegetable
Cholesterol	< 1 milligram	
Dietary Fiber	2 grams	
Fat	< 1 gram	
Protein	16 grams	
Sodium	364 milligrams	

Shopping List: 1 onion, 1 red bell pepper, 1 carrot, 1 sweet potato, 8 oz. egg substitute, whole eggs, 2 oz. skim milk, dried parsley, pepper, 3 oz. fat-free shredded Cheddar cheese.

BANANA CREAM PIE

EASY - DO AHEAD

ingredients:
- 1 1/2 cups Cornflake crumbs
- 2 tbsp. sugar
- 2 tbsp. brown sugar
- 1/4 cup reconstituted Butter Buds
- 2 large bananas, sliced
- 1 cup fat-free sour cream
- 1 cup skim milk
- 3 1/2 oz. instant banana pudding mix

directions: Preheat oven to 350 degrees. Lightly spray 9-inch pie pan with nonfat cooking spray.
Insert metal blade in food processor bowl. Add Cornflake crumbs, sugar and brown sugar to bowl; process until ingredients are mixed well.
Pour crumbs into pie pan; drizzle Butter Buds over crumbs and press lightly into pan.
Bake in preheated oven 10 minutes, until lightly browned. Remove from oven and cool completely. Arrange banana slices on bottom of pie plate, reserving several slices for top of pie.
With metal blade in food processor bowl, add sour cream, milk and pudding mix to bowl and process until creamy and smooth. Spoon mixture into crust; cover and refrigerate several hours.
Just before serving, top with remaining banana slices.

Serves: 6

Nutrition per Serving

Calories	254
Carbohydrate	54 grams
Cholesterol	1 milligram
Dietary Fiber	1 gram
Fat	< 1 gram
Protein	6 grams
Sodium	457 milligrams

Exchanges

2 starch
1 2/3 fruit

Shopping List: Cornflake crumbs, sugar, brown sugar, Butter Buds, 2 bananas, 8 oz. fat-free sour cream, 8 oz. skim milk, 3 1/2 oz. instant banana pudding mix.

BERRY FRUIT SOUFFLÉ

AVERAGE

ingredients: 1 cup strawberries, washed and hulled
1/2 cup blueberries, rinsed and drained
1/2 cup raspberries, rinsed and drained
2 tbsp. cornstarch
2 tbsp. skim milk
3 large egg whites
1/2 cup sugar

directions: Insert metal blade into bowl of food processor.
Add strawberries, blueberries and raspberries and
purée; set aside.
In a large bowl, combine cornstarch and milk and
mix until blended and thick.
Stir in puréed fruit and mix well.
Place egg whites in medium bowl. Beat with electric mixer until stiff; add sugar and beat until stiff
peaks form.
Fold egg whites into fruit mixture; carefully fold
mixture together until all ingredients are blended.
Preheat oven to 400 degrees. Arrange 6 custard
baking cups in large baking dish and fill baking
dish 1-inch deep with hot water. Divide berry
mixture among baking cups and bake in preheated oven 30 minutes. Serve immediately.

Serves: 6

Nutrition per Serving		Exchanges
Calories	100	1 2/3 fruit
Carbohydrate	23 grams	
Cholesterol	0 milligrams	
Dietary Fiber	2 grams	
Fat	< 1 gram	
Protein	1 gram	
Sodium	31 milligrams	

Shopping List: 1/2 pint strawberries, 1/4 pint blueberries, 1/4
pint raspberries, cornstarch, skim milk, whole eggs,
sugar.

CHOCOLATE CARAMEL CAKE

AVERAGE - DO AHEAD - FREEZE

ingredients:
1 cup flour
1/2 cup sugar
1 1/2 cups brown sugar, divided
1 cup fat-free caramel yogurt
1/4 cup egg substitute
3 tbsp. unsweetened cocoa powder
1/2 tsp. baking powder
1/2 tsp. baking soda
1/4 cup reconstituted Butter Buds
1/4 cup corn syrup
1/4 cup skim milk
2 cups powdered sugar

directions:
Preheat oven to 350 degrees. Lightly spray 8-inch baking dish with nonfat cooking spray.
Insert metal blade into bowl of food processor.
Combine flour, sugar, 3/4 cup brown sugar, yogurt, egg substitute, cocoa, baking powder and baking soda in food processor bowl; replace top. Process 20-30 seconds until batter is creamy and smooth. Pour batter into baking dish and bake in preheated oven 30-35 minutes, until knife inserted in center comes out clean. Cool completely.
Lightly spray small saucepan with nonfat cooking spray. Pour Butter Buds into saucepan; add remaining brown sugar, corn syrup and milk and mix well. Cook over medium heat until mixture comes to a boil; remove from heat and let cool 5-10 minutes at room temperature. Stir in powdered sugar; mix until blended smooth. Spread frosting over cooled chocolate cake.

Serves: 8

Nutrition per Serving		Exchanges
Calories	406	5 2/3 fruit
Carbohydrate	100 grams	1 starch
Cholesterol	1 milligram	
Dietary Fiber	< 1 gram	
Fat	< 1 gram	
Protein	4 grams	
Sodium	167 milligrams	

Shopping List: flour, sugar, brown sugar, 8 oz. fat-free caramel yogurt, 2 oz. egg substitute, unsweetened cocoa powder, baking powder, baking soda, Butter Buds, corn syrup, 2 oz. skim milk, powdered sugar.

FROZEN FRUIT POPS

EASY - DO AHEAD - FREEZE

ingredients: 3/4 cup frozen strawberries, sweetened
1/2 cup pine-orange-banana concentrate
1/2 cup water

directions: Insert metal blade into food processor bowl.
Combine all ingredients in bowl and process until
blended smooth.
Spoon mixture into 4 paper cups; insert wooden
stick, if desired.
Freeze 6-8 hours, or overnight; peel away paper
just before serving.

Serves: 4

Nutrition per Serving		Exchanges
Calories	82	1 1/3 fruit
Carbohydrate	21 grams	
Cholesterol	0 milligrams	
Dietary Fiber	1 gram	
Fat	< 1 gram	
Protein	1 gram	
Sodium	1 milligram	

Shopping List: frozen sweetened strawberries, pine-orange- banana concentrate.

FROZEN STRAWBERRY CREME

EASY - DO AHEAD - FREEZE

ingredients:
2 cups unsweetened frozen strawberries
2 tbsp. sugar
2 tbsp. honey
3 tbsp. strawberry preserves
2/3 cup fat-free ricotta cheese
1/3 cup fat-free sour cream
1/3 cup nonfat dry milk
3/4 tsp. vanilla

directions:
Insert metal blade into bowl of food processor. Combine all ingredients in bowl and replace top. Process mixture until blended smooth and creamy. Spoon into freezer container and freeze 30-45 minutes. If mixture is frozen longer, let thaw at room temperature 10-15 minutes until soft.
Top with fresh strawberries just before serving, if desired.

Serves: 6

FABULOUS FOOD PROCESSOR

Nutrition per Serving		Exchanges
Calories	126	1 meat
Carbohydrate	26 grams	1 2/3 fruit
Cholesterol	5 milligrams	
Dietary Fiber	1 gram	
Fat	< 1 gram	
Protein	6 grams	
Sodium	85 milligrams	

Shopping List: 16 oz. frozen unsweetened strawberries, sugar, honey, strawberry preserves, 5 oz. fat-free ricotta cheese, 3 oz. fat-free sour cream, nonfat dry milk, vanilla.

PIE CRUST

EASY - DO AHEAD

ingredients: 2 cups fat-free granola
1 tbsp. apple butter
1 tbsp. sugar
2 tbsp. egg substitute

directions: Insert metal blade into bowl of food processor. Combine all ingredients in food processor bowl and process 15-20 seconds, until ingredients are mixed well.

Preheat oven to 350 degrees. Lightly spray 8- or 9-inch pie plate with nonfat cooking spray.

Press granola mixture into pie plate and bake in preheated oven 15 minutes, until lightly browned. Let pie crust cool while preparing filling, and bake as directed.

Serves: 8

Nutrition per Serving		Exchanges
Calories	81	1 1/3 fruit
Carbohydrate	20 grams	
Cholesterol	0 milligrams	
Dietary Fiber	2 grams	
Protein	1 gram	
Sodium	4 milligrams	

Shopping List: fat-free granola, apple butter, sugar, 1 oz. egg substitute.

PINEAPPLE SPONGE CAKE
EASY - DO AHEAD

ingredients:
2 cups flour
1 3/4 cups sugar, divided
1/2 cup bown sugar
1 tsp. baking soda
20 oz. pineapple chunks in juice
1/2 cup egg substitute
1 tsp. pineapple extract
1/4 cup powdered sugar, optional

directions:
Insert metal blade into food processor bowl. Pour pineapple chunks into bowl and pulse several times until pineapple is crushed; remove and set aside. Combine flour, 1 cup sugar, brown sugar, baking soda, egg substitute, and pineapple extract in food processor bowl and process until ingredients are blended smooth. Pour crushed pineapple back into bowl; pulse several times until batter is blended. Preheat oven to 350 degrees. Lightly spray 9x13 inch baking dish with nonfat cooking spray. Pour batter into dish and bake in preheated oven 45 -55 minutes, until knife inserted in center comes out clean. Cool cake 10-15 minutes. Sprinkle with powdered sugar, if desired.

Serves: 12

FABULOUS FOOD PROCESSOR

Nutrition per Serving
Calories	256
Carbohydrate	62 grams
Cholesterol	0 milligrams
Dietary Fiber	1 gram
Fat	< 1 gram
Protein	3 grams
Sodium	45 milligrams

Exchanges
1 starch
3 fruit

Shopping List: 1/2 lb. flour, sugar, brown sugar, baking soda, 20 oz. pineapple chunks in juice, 4 oz. egg substitute, pineapple extract, powdered sugar (optional).

ZUCCHINI COOKIES

AVERAGE - DO AHEAD - FREEZE

ingredients:
1 medium zucchini
1/4 cup reconstituted Butter Buds
1/4 cup corn syrup
1/4 cup egg substitute
1 tsp. vanilla
2 cups flour
1/2 tsp. baking soda
1/2 cup baking powder
1 tsp. cinnamon
3/4 cup raisins
1/2 cup reduced-fat chocolate chips
3/4 cup fat-free granola

directions:
Preheat oven to 350 degrees. Lightly spray cookie sheets with nonfat cooking spray.
Insert shredding disc into food processor; replace top. Cut off ends of zucchini and feed through tube; if zucchini is too thick, cut vertically in half. Place zucchini in feed tube and process until shredded. Remove zucchini from bowl and set aside.
Insert the metal blade into bowl of food processor. Add Butter Buds, corn syrup, egg substitute, vanilla, flour, baking soda, baking powder and cinnamon to bowl of food processor; process 20-30 seconds, until creamy and smooth.
Spoon batter over shredded zucchini; top with chocolate chips, raisins and granola; mix until ingredients are blended.
Drop dough by rounded tablespoons on cookie sheet; bake in preheated oven 12-15 minutes, until golden brown.

Serves: 36

Nutrition per Serving

Calories	63	
Carbohydrate	14 grams	
Cholesterol	0 milligrams	
Dietary Fiber	< 1 gram	
Fat	< 1 gram	
Protein	1 gram	
Sodium	30 milligrams	

Exchanges
2/3 starch

Shopping List: 1 zucchini, Butter Buds, 2 oz. corn syrup, 2 oz. egg substitute, flour, baking soda, baking powder, cinnamon, raisins, reduced-fat chocolate chips, fat-free granola, vanilla.

RECIPES FOR

FAT FREE LIVING TOASTER OVEN

by Jyl Steinback

TIPS FOR TOASTER OVEN COOKING

The toaster oven is a great appliance when cooking or baking for 1-2 people as it will not use as much electricity or heat up the kitchen as a larger oven would. The dimensions of the toaster oven may vary according to the model you purchase. The size of the oven will determine the types of bakeware you can use in your toaster oven. The insides of the standard toaster oven are 11" x 7 1/2" x 3". Here are some cooking tips for the most successful toaster oven recipes:

-Line baking tray with foil to prevent dripping or stains on tray.

-Do Not use throw-away muffin pans or trays when baking cookies, breads, muffins, etc. These do not allow even cooking as well as teflon-coated pans.

-Pans that work: 6-cup muffin pan, 12-cup mini muffin pan, medium loaf pan (8 1/2" x 4 1/2 x 2 1/2"), mini loaf pan (5 3/4" x 3" x 2 1/4"), 1 1/2-quart rectangular baking dish.

-When baking sweet bread (i.e. Blueberry-Banana Loaf, Pineapple Pumpkin Bread) do not fill loaf pan(s) more than half full. If the bread rises too high, the top will burn and the bread will be undercooked. The toaster oven can hold either 1 medium or 3 mini loaf pans.

CRAB DEVILS

EASY - DO AHEAD

ingredients:	3/4 cup fat-free canned crabmeat, drained
	1/4 cup fat-free mayonnaise
	2 tbsp. fat-free Parmesan cheese
	1/8 tsp. Worcestershire sauce
	1/8 tsp. onion powder
	2 drops Tabasco sauce
	6 fat-free crackers
directions:	Combine crabmeat, mayonnaise, Parmesan cheese, Worcestershire sauce, onion powder and Tabasco sauce and mix until blended.
	Spread crab mixture onto crackers; arrange in single layer on toaster oven baking tray.
	Sprinkle crackers with extra Parmesan cheese, if desired; bake in 400 degree toaster oven 4-7 minutes, until lightly browned and bubbly.

Serves: 2

Nutrition per Serving		Exchanges
Calories	123	1 starch
Carbohydrate	13 grams	2 meat
Cholesterol	77 milligrams	
Dietary Fiber	0 grams	
Fat	< 1 gram	
Protein	15 grams	
Sodium	670 milligrams	

Shopping List: 6 ounces canned crabmeat, 2 ounces fat-free mayonnaise, Parmesan cheese, Worcestershire sauce, onion powder, Tabasco sauce, fat-free crackers.

HOT ARTICHOKE DIP

EASY - DO AHEAD

ingredients: 10 oz. frozen artichokes, thawed and chopped
1/2 cup fat-free mayonnaise
1/2 cup fat-free Parmesan cheese
1 1/2 tsp. minced garlic

directions: Combine all the ingredients in an ovenproof dish for the toaster oven.
Bake in 350 degree toaster oven for 20-25 minutes, until mixture is hot and bubbly. Sprinkle with extra Parmesan cheese, if desired, and serve with fat-free crackers or vegetables.

Serves: 4

Nutrition per Serving
Calories	104
Carbohydrate	21 grams
Cholesterol	0 milligrams
Dietary Fiber	1 gram
Fat	< 1 gram
Protein	5 grams
Sodium	303 milligrams

Exchanges
1/2 starch
2 vegetable

Shopping List: 10 ounces frozen artichokes, 4 ounces fat-free mayonnaise, 2 ounces fat-free Parmesan cheese, minced garlic.

TREMENDOUS TOASTER OVEN

147

HOT BEAN DIP

EASY - DO AHEAD

ingredients: 1 cup fat-free refried beans
1/2 cup fat-free shredded Cheddar cheese, divided
1/4 cup chopped tomatoes
1 tbsp. chopped onion
1 tbsp. diced green chilies

directions: Lightly spray glass baking dish for the toaster oven with nonfat cooking spray. Combine beans, 1/4 cup cheese, tomatoes, onion and chilies in baking dish and mix well.
Sprinkle top with remaining cheese. Bake in 350 degree toaster oven 20-25 minutes, until mixture is bubbly and cheese is melted. Serve with fat-free tortilla or pita chips.

Serves: 4

Nutrition per Serving		Exchanges
Calories	94	1 starch
Carbohydrate	14 grams	1/2 meat
Cholesterol	0 milligrams	
Dietary Fiber	2 grams	
Fat	< 1 gram	
Protein	8 grams	
Sodium	457 milligrams	

Shopping List: 8 ounces fat-free refried beans, 2 ounces fat-free shredded Cheddar cheese, 1 small tomato, 1 small onion, diced green chilies.

ONION CHEESE PUFFS

EASY - DO AHEAD

ingredients:
1/3 cup fat-free mayonnaise
1/3 cup fat-free Parmesan cheese
1 tsp. onion powder
3/4 tsp. skim milk
6 fat-free crackers

directions:
In a small bowl, combine mayonnaise, Parmesan cheese, onion powder and milk; mix until smooth. Lightly spray toaster oven baking tray or foil with nonfat cooking spray.
Arrange crackers in a single layer; top with mayonnaise mixture and bake in 350 degree toaster oven 5-10 minutes, until lightly browned.

Serves: 2

Nutrition per Serving		Exchanges
Calories	108	1 starch
Carbohydrate	18 grams	1 vegetable
Cholesterol	12 milligrams	
Dietary Fiber	1 gram	
Fat	< 1 gram	
Protein	6 grams	
Sodium	512 milligrams	

Shopping List: 3 ounces fat-free mayonnaise, fat-free Parmesan cheese, onion powder, skim milk, fat-free crackers.

TREMENDOUS TOASTER OVEN

PITA CHIPS

EASY - DO AHEAD

---

ingredients: 1 fat-free pita pocket
1 tsp. garlic powder
1 tsp. onion powder
1/2 tsp. paprika

directions: Split pita pocket in half; cut each half into 8 wedges. Lightly spray foil or baking tray for toaster oven with nonfat cooking spray. Arrange pita wedges in a single layer; lightly spray pitas with nonfat cooking spray and immediately sprinkle with garlic powder, onion powder and paprika.
Bake in 350 degree toaster oven 10-15 minutes until crisp. Turn chips over halfway through baking.
Cool completely and store in airtight container.

Serves: 2

Nutrition per Serving		Exchanges
Calories	62	2/3 starch
Carbohydrate	12 grams	
Cholesterol	0 milligrams	
Dietary Fiber	< 1 gram	
Fat	< 1 gram	
Dietary Fiber	2 grams	
Sodium	109 milligrams	

Shopping List: Fat-free pita pocket, garlic powder, onion powder, paprika.

POTATO SKINS

EASY - DO AHEAD

ingredients:　1 large baking potato
1/2 cup fat-free shredded Cheddar cheese
1 tsp. Bac-Os (optional), not in analysis

directions:　Pierce potato with fork in several places. Bake in 450 degree toaster oven 1 hour, until potato is tender and cooked through. Remove from oven and let cool 5-10 minutes, until easy to handle. Cut potato in half. Scoop out pulp, leaving 1/4 - inch around sides. Lightly spray toaster oven baking tray or foil with nonfat cooking spray and place potato skins on top. Sprinkle skins with 1/4 cup cheese and 1/2 teaspoon Bac-Os, if desired. Bake in 450 degree toaster oven until cheese is melted and lightly browned. Serve with fat-free Ranch dressing, fat-free sour cream, or low-calorie Bar-B-Q sauce.

Serves: 1

Nutrition per Serving		Exchanges
Calories	235	2 1/3 starch
Carbohydrate	38 grams	2 meat
Cholesterol	0 milligrams	
Dietary Fiber	4 grams	
Fat	< 1 gram	
Protein	19 grams	
Sodium	568 milligrams	

Shopping List: 1 large baking potato, 2 ounces fat-free shredded Cheddar cheese, Bac-Os (optional).

TREMENDOUS TOASTER OVEN

APPLE BANANA BERRY BREAD

EASY - DO AHEAD - FREEZE

ingredients:
1 cup flour
1/4 cup brown sugar
1/2 tsp. baking powder
1/2 tsp. baking soda
1/4 cup lite applesauce
2 tbsp. orange juice
1/4 cup mashed bananas
1/2 tsp. vanilla
1/2 cup cranberries

directions: Lightly spray medium loaf pan with nonfat cooking spray.
In a medium bowl, combine flour, brown sugar, baking powder and baking soda and mix until blended. Add applesauce, orange juice, banana and vanilla and mix until dry ingredients are moistened and blended.
Fold in cranberries.
Spread batter into loaf pan and bake in 375 degree toaster oven 40 to 45 minutes, until knife inserted in center comes out clean.

Serves: 6

Nutrition per Serving		Exchanges
Calories	136	2/3 starch
Carbohydrate	31 grams	1 1/3 fruit
Cholesterol	0 milligrams	
Dietary Fiber	1 gram	
Fat	< 1 gram	
Protein	2 grams	
Sodium	100 milligrams	

Shopping List: Flour, brown sugar, baking powder, baking soda, 4 ounces lite applesauce, 1 ounce orange juice, 1 small banana, vanilla, 1/4 pint cranberries.

BREAKFAST SWEET ROLL

EASY

ingredients: 2 tbsp. fat-free cottage cheese
1/2 tsp. cinnamon
1 tsp. sugar
1 bagel or bialy

directions: Cut bialy or bagel in half and toast on lightest setting.
Place toasted bialys on foil and top each half with 1 tablespoon cottage cheese and sprinkle with 1/2 teaspoon sugar and 1/4 teaspoon cinnamon; swirl sugar-cinnamon lightly into cottage cheese. Bake in 350 degree toaster oven 5-7 minutes, until heated through.

Serves: 2

Nutrition per Serving		Exchanges
Calories	93	1 1/4 starch
Carbohydrate	18 grams	
Cholesterol	< 1 milligram	
Dietary Fiber	1 gram	
Fat	< 1 gram	
Protein	4 grams	
Sodium	111 milligrams	

Shopping List: 1 bagel or bialy, cinnamon, sugar, 1 ounce fat-free cottage cheese.

CARROT-ZUCCHINI TEA LOAF

EASY - DO AHEAD - FREEZE

ingredients: 3 tbsp. egg substitute
2 tbsp. unsweetened applesauce
2 tbsp. corn syrup
1/2 cup brown sugar
1 tsp. vanilla
3/8 cup shredded zucchini
3/8 cup shredded carrots
1 cup flour
1/4 tsp. baking soda
1/8 tsp. baking powder
1/2 tsp. cinnamon
1/4 tsp. pumpkin pie spice

directions: Lightly spray 1 medium loaf pan with nonfat cooking spray.
In medium bowl, combine egg substitute, applesauce, corn syrup, brown sugar and vanilla and mix until blended smooth. Add flour, baking soda, baking powder, cinnamon and pumpkin pie spice to egg mixture; mix until dry ingredients are moistened. Fold in zucchini and carrots and mix lightly. Spread batter into loaf pan and bake in 375 degree toaster oven for 45 minutes, until knife inserted in center comes out clean.
Cool 5 minutes; invert onto serving plate.

Serves: 6

Nutrition per Serving		Exchanges
Calories	175	1 starch
Carbohydrate	41 grams	1 1/2 fruit
Cholesterol	0 milligrams	
Dietary Fiber	1 gram	
Fat	< 1 gram	
Protein	3 grams	
Sodium	58 milligrams	

Shopping List: Egg substitute, unsweetened applesauce, corn syrup, brown sugar, vanilla, flour, baking soda, baking powder, cinnamon, pumpkin pie spice, zucchini, carrot.

154

GARLIC CHEESE BREAD

EASY - DO AHEAD

ingredients: 4 slices fat-free French bread
1/2 cup fat-free shredded Mozzarella cheese
2 slices fat-free American cheese, cut in half
2 tsp. garlic powder
1 1/4 tbsp. Butter Buds

directions: Lightly spray toaster oven baking tray or foil with nonfat cooking spray.
Arrange bread in a single layer; sprinkle with garlic powder and Butter Buds.
Sprinkle 2 tablespoons Mozzarella and 1/2 slice American cheese on each bread slice.
Bake in 400 degree toaster oven 3-5 minutes, until cheese is melted and lightly browned.

Serves: 4

TREMENDOUS TOASTER OVEN

Nutrition per Serving

Calories	136
Carbohydrate	18 grams
Cholesterol	0 milligrams
Dietary Fiber	1 gram
Protein	12 grams
Sodium	365 milligrams

Exchanges

1 1/3 starch
1 meat

Shopping List: Fat-free French bread, 2 ounces fat-free shredded Mozzarella cheese, fat-free American cheese slices, garlic powder, Butter Buds.

155

PINEAPPLE PUMPKIN BREAD

EASY - DO AHEAD - FREEZE

ingredients: 1 1/2 cups flour
1/3 cup brown sugar
1 tsp. baking powder
3/4 tsp. pumpkin pie spice
1/4 cup crushed pineapple in juice
1/2 cup canned pumpkin, mashed
2 tbsp. egg substitute

directions: Lightly spray 3 mini loaf pans with nonfat cooking spray.
In a medium bowl, combine flour, brown sugar, baking powder and pumpkin pie spice and mix until blended.
Add pineapple, pumpkin and egg substitute and mix until dry ingredients are moistened and batter is smooth.
Divide batter between loaf pans and bake in 375 degree toaster oven 35-40 minutes, until knife inserted in center comes out clean.

Serves: 9

Nutrition per Serving		Exchanges
Calories	116	2/3 starch
Carbohydrate	26 grams	1 fruit
Cholesterol	0 milligrams	
Dietary Fiber	1 gram	
Fat	< 1 gram	
Protein	2 grams	
Sodium	41 milligrams	

Shopping List: Flour, brown sugar, 4 ounces crushed pineapple, canned pumpkin, egg substitute, baking powder, pumpkin pie spice.

RASPBERRY CRUMBLE MUFFINS

EASY - DO AHEAD - FREEZE

---

ingredients:
1 cup flour
1/4 cup + 1 tbsp. brown sugar, divided
1 1/2 tsp. baking powder
1/2 tsp. vanilla
1/4 cup fat-free vanilla yogurt
2 tbsp. skim milk
1 1/2 tbsp. mixed berry applesauce
2 tbsp. egg substitute
1/3 cup raspberries
1/4 tsp. cinnamon

directions:
Lightly spray muffin cups with nonfat cooking spray. In medium bowl, combine yogurt, vanilla, milk, applesauce, egg substitute and 1/4 cup brown sugar; mix until blended smooth. Add flour and baking powder; mix until dry ingredients are moistened. Fold in raspberries.
In a small bowl, combine 1 tablespoon brown sugar and cinnamon and mix well.
Fill muffin cups with batter and sprinkle with cinnamon-sugar mixture.
Bake in 400 degree toaster oven 15-20 minutes, until tops of muffins spring back.

Serves: 6

Nutrition per Serving		**Exchanges**
Calories	133	1 starch
Carbohydrate	30 grams	1 fruit
Cholesterol	0 milligrams	
Dietary Fiber	1 gram	
Fat	< 1 gram	
Protein	3 grams	
Sodium	96 milligrams	

Shopping List: Flour, brown sugar, baking powder, cinnamon, vanilla, 2 ounces fat-free vanilla yogurt, skim milk, mixed berry applesauce, egg substitute, fresh or frozen raspberries.

TREMENDOUS TOASTER OVEN

BAKED COD

EASY

ingredients: 8 oz. cod fillets, cut in half
1/4 tsp. pepper
3/4 cup sliced mushrooms
1 tbsp. fresh parsley, minced
2 tbsp. dry white wine
2 tsp. Worcestershire sauce

directions: Lightly spray toaster oven baking dish with nonfat cooking spray.
Arrange sole fillets in a single layer in the bottom of dish and sprinkle with pepper.
Cover with sliced mushrooms and sprinkle with parsley.
In a small cup, combine wine and Worcestershire sauce and mix well; pour evenly over fish.
Bake in 400 degree toaster oven 12-15 minutes, until fish is cooked through and flakes easily.

Serves: 2

Nutrition per Serving		**Exchanges**
Calories	127	3 meat
Carbohydrate	4 grams	1 vegetable
Cholesterol	49 milligrams	
Dietary Fiber	< 1 gram	
Fat	< 1 gram	
Protein	21 grams	
Sodium	113 milligrams	

Shopping List: 8 ounces cod fillets, 1/4 pound mushrooms, fresh parsley, white wine, Worcestershire sauce, pepper.

CHEDDAR MACARONI LOAF

EASY - DO AHEAD - FREEZE

ingredients:
4 oz. macaroni, cooked and drained
1 cup skim milk, scalded
6 tbsp. egg substitute
1 cup fat-free bread crumbs
1 1/2 cups fat-free shredded Cheddar cheese
2 tbsp. chopped scallions
1 tbsp. parsley
1/8 tsp. pepper
1 1/4 cups fat-free pasta sauce

directions:
Lightly spray 2 mini loaf pans or 1 medium loaf pan with nonfat cooking spray.

In a medium bowl, combine macaroni, milk, egg substitute, bread crumbs, cheese, scallions, parsley and pepper and mix well. Divide mixture between loaf pans and bake 45-55 minutes until center is firm.

Let casserole stand at room temperature 5 minutes; invert onto plates. Heat pasta sauce in saucepan or microwave; spoon sauce over loaves just before serving.

Serves: 4

TREMENDOUS TOASTER OVEN

Nutrition per Serving
Calories	256
Carbohydrate	38 grams
Cholesterol	1 milligram
Dietary Fiber	1 gram
Fat	< 1 gram
Protein	21 grams
Sodium	749 milligrams

Exchanges
2 starch
1 vegetable
2 meat

Shopping List: 1/4 pound macaroni, 8 ounces skim milk, 3 ounces egg substitute, fat-free bread crumbs, 6 ounces fat-free shredded Cheddar cheese, 2 green onions, fresh parsley, pepper, 10 ounces fat-free pasta sauce.

159

CHEESE ENCHILADAS

EASY - DO AHEAD

ingredients: 4 fat-free corn or flour tortillas (burrito size)
1/2 cup fat-free ricotta cheese
1 tbsp. chopped green onion
1/4 tsp. coriander
1/3 tsp. ground cumin
1/4 tsp. chili powder
1/8 tsp. cayenne pepper
1 tsp. lemon juice
1/2 cup fat-free Mozzarella cheese

directions: Lightly spray toaster oven baking dish with nonfat cooking spray.
Wrap tortillas in aluminum foil and warm in 350 degree toaster oven for 10 minutes, or until warm and soft. Remove the tortillas, set aside, and increase toaster oven temperature to 375 degrees.
In a small bowl, combine ricotta cheese, green onion, coriander, cumin, chili powder, cayenne pepper and lemon juice and mix well.
Spread 2 tablespoons of the cheese mixture in the center of each tortilla and fold 1 side over the filling. Place tortillas in baking pan; cover with foil and bake 20 minutes. Uncover pan, sprinkle enchiladas with Mozzarella cheese and bake 5 minutes, or until the cheese is melted.
Serve immediately.

Serves: 4

Nutrition per Serving		Exchanges
Calories	208	2 1/3 starch
Carbohydrate	35 grams	1 meat
Cholesterol	5 milligrams	
Dietary Fiber	3 grams	
Fat	< 1 gram	
Protein	15 grams	
Sodium	623 milligrams	

Shopping List: Fat-free corn or flour burrito-size tortillas, 4 ounces fat-free ricotta cheese, 2 ounces fat-free shredded Mozzarella cheese, green onion, coriander, ground cumin, chili powder, cayenne pepper, lemon juice.

DELECTABLE FISH FILLETS

EASY

ingredients: 1/2 lb. cod fillet
1 medium onion, sliced
2 tbsp. fat-free mayonnaise
1 1/2 tsp. Worcestershire sauce
1 1/2 tsp. lemon juice
1 tbsp. fat-free Parmesan cheese
1 1/2 tsp. chopped fresh parsley

directions: Lightly spray toaster oven baking tray with nonfat cooking spray.
Arrange sliced onions on tray and bake in 350 degree toaster oven 12-15 minutes, until tender and lightly browned.
Cut fish in half and place on top of onion slices.
In a small bowl, combine mayonnaise, Worcestershire sauce, lemon juice, Parmesan cheese and parsley and mix well.
Spread mixture on top of fish and bake in 350 degree toaster oven 30-35 minutes, until fish flakes easily with a fork.

Serves: 2

Nutrition per Serving		Exchanges
Calories	131	2 3/4 meat
Carbohydrate	8 grams	1/2 starch
Cholesterol	49 milligrams	
Dietary fiber	1 gram	
Fat	< 1 gram	
Protein	22 grams	
Sodium	228 milligrams	

Shopping List: 1/2 pound cod fillet, 1 medium onion, fat-free mayonnaise, Worcestershire sauce, lemon juice, fat-free Parmesan cheese, fresh parsley.

TREMENDOUS TOASTER OVEN

EGGPLANT CASSEROLE

EASY - DO AHEAD

ingredients: 1/2 small eggplant
1 medium tomato, sliced thin
1 cup diced green pepper
1/2 cup chopped onion
1/4 tsp. garlic powder
1/4 tsp. onion powder
1/8 tsp. pepper
3/4 cup fat-free shredded Cheddar cheese

directions: Lightly spray toaster oven baking dish with nonfat cooking spray.
Arrange a layer of eggplant slices in bottom of dish; top with half the tomatoes, green peppers and onions. Sprinkle with 1/8 teaspoon onion powder, 1/8 teaspoon garlic powder and pepper. Sprinkle 1/4 cup cheese on top. Repeat layers, ending with cheese.
Cover with foil and bake in 400 degree toaster oven 25-30 minutes.
Uncover casserole, reduce heat to 350 degrees and cook 15-20 minutes, until eggplant is tender and sauce is thick and lightly browned.

Serves: 2

Nutrition per Serving		Exchanges
Calories	159	5 vegetable
Carbohydrate	24 grams	1 meat
Cholesterol	0 milligrams	
Dietary Fiber	2 grams	
Fat	< 1 gram	
Protein	15 grams	
Sodium	433 milligrams	

Shopping List: Small eggplant, 1 tomato, 1 green bell pepper, 1 small onion, garlic powder, onion powder, pepper, 3 ounces fat-free shredded Cheddar cheese.

GRILLED HOAGIE SANDWICH

EASY - DO AHEAD

ingredients:	2 slices fat-free bread
	2 tbsp. fat-free shredded Cheddar cheese
	2 tsp. fat-free mayonnaise
	1 tsp. honey mustard
	2 oz. fat-free deli-sliced turkey
	1 slice tomato
	1 slice onion
	1 slice green bell pepper
directions:	Place 1 slice bread on toaster oven baking tray. In a small bowl, combine cheese, mayonnaise and honey mustard and mix until blended. Spread cheese mixture on bread slice. Top with turkey slices, tomato, onion and green pepper. Cover with top slice of bread. Wrap sandwich completely in foil. Place foil packet in 350 degree toaster oven and bake 10-15 minutes, until cheese is melted and sandwich is heated through.

TREMENDOUS TOASTER OVEN

Serves: 1

Nutrition per Serving		Exchanges
Calories	212	2 starch
Carbohydrate	29 grams	1 1/2 meat
Cholesterol	20 milligrams	
Dietary Fiber	1 gram	
Fat	< 1 gram	
Protein	17 grams	
Sodium	1056 milligrams	

Shopping List: Fat-free bread, fat-free shredded Cheddar cheese, fat-free mayonnaise, honey mustard, 2 ounces fat-free deli turkey slices, small tomato, small onion, small green bell pepper.

OVEN-BAKED SEAFOOD SALAD

AVERAGE - DO AHEAD

ingredients:	2 oz. fat-free lobster
	4 oz. crabmeat, drained
	1/3 cup sliced water chestnuts
	2 tbsp. sliced mushrooms
	1/3 cup chopped celery
	2 tbsp. chopped green bell pepper
	1 hard-cooked egg white, chopped
	1/3 cup fat-free mayonnaise
	2 tsp. fat-free chicken broth, heated
	1/4 tsp. Worcestershire sauce

directions: Lightly spray baking dish for toaster oven with nonfat cooking spray.

Combine lobster, crabmeat, water chestnuts, mushrooms, celery, green pepper and egg white in medium bowl.

In separate bowl, combine mayonnaise, chicken broth and Worcestershire sauce and mix until blended.

Pour mayonnaise dressing over seafood mixture and mix well.

Spoon seafood mixture into casserole and bake in 350 degree toaster oven 40-45 minutes, until hot and bubbly around the edges.

Serves: 2

Nutrition per Serving		**Exchanges**
Calories	126	3 vegetable
Carbohydrate	14 grams	1 meat
Cholesterol	71 milligrams	
Dietary Fiber	1 gram	
Fat	< 1 gram	
Protein	16 grams	
Sodium	835 milligrams	

Shopping List: 2 ounces fat-free lobster, 4 ounces canned crabmeat, sliced water chestnuts, mushrooms, celery, small green bell pepper, egg, fat-free mayonnaise, fat-free chicken broth, Worcestershire sauce.

SEAFOOD RICE CASSEROLE

EASY - DO AHEAD

ingredients: 2/3 cup fat-free cooked rice
2 tbsp. chopped green bell pepper
1/3 cup chopped celery
2 tbsp. chopped onion
1/4 cup canned, sliced water chestnuts
1/2 cup canned crabmeat
2 oz. fat-free lobster flakes
1/3 cup fat-free mayonnaise
1/3 cup tomato juice without salt
1/8 tsp. pepper
1/3 cup fat-free shredded Cheddar cheese

directions: Lightly spray baking dish for the toaster oven with nonfat cooking spray.
Combine all ingredients except cheese in a medium bowl and mix well. Spread mixture into casserole and top with cheese.
Bake in 350 degree toaster oven 25-30 minutes, until cheese is melted and casserole is heated through.

Serves: 2

Nutrition per Serving		Exchanges
Calories	185	1 starch
Carbohydrate	28 grams	2 1/2 vegetable
Cholesterol	39 milligrams	1 meat
Dietary Fiber	1 gram	
Fat	< 1 gram	
Protein	16 grams	
Sodium	833 milligrams	

Shopping List: Fat-free rice, green bell pepper, celery, frozen chopped onions, canned sliced water chestnuts, 4 ounces canned crabmeat, 2 ounces fat-free lobster flakes, fat-free mayonnaise, tomato juice without salt, pepper, fat-free shredded Cheddar cheese.

TREMENDOUS TOASTER OVEN

SWISS CHEESE TOMATO BAKE

EASY

ingredients:
1 cup fat-free croutons
1 medium tomato, sliced
1 cup fat-free shredded Swiss cheese
1/4 cup egg substitute
3/4 cup skim milk
1/4 tsp. paprika
1/4 tsp. dry mustard

directions:
Lightly spray toaster oven baking dish with nonfat cooking spray.
Arrange croutons on bottom of dish. Top with tomato slices and sprinkle with cheese.
In a small bowl, combine egg substitute, milk, paprika and mustard; mix until blended.
Pour egg mixture over cheese.
Bake in 350 degree toaster oven 35-40 minutes, until casserole is puffy and lightly browned.
Serve immediately.

Serves: 4

Nutrition per Serving		Exchanges
Calories	100	1/2 starch
Carbohydrate	13 grams	1 vegetable
Cholesterol	1 milligram	1 meat
Dietary Fiber	< 1 gram	
Fat	< 1 gram	
Protein	8 grams	
Sodium	339 milligrams	

Shopping List: Fat-free croutons, 1 medium tomato, 4 ounces fat-free Swiss cheese, 2 ounces egg substitute, 6 ounces skim milk, paprika, dry mustard.

TUNA RICE CASSEROLE

EASY - DO AHEAD

ingredients: 6 oz. fat-free tuna
3/4 cup fat-free cooked rice
1/4 cup fat-free shredded Cheddar cheese
2 tbsp. fat-free shredded Mozzarella cheese
3/4 cup evaporated skim milk
1/2 cup egg substitute

directions: Lightly spray toaster oven baking dish with nonfat cooking spray.
In a medium bowl, combine tuna, rice, Cheddar cheese and Mozzarella cheese; mix well.
In a small bowl, combine egg substitute and milk; mix until blended smooth.
Fold into tuna mixture and mix lightly. Spoon into baking dish and bake in 350 degree toaster oven 30-45 minutes, until knife inserted in center comes out clean.

Serves: 2

Nutrition per Serving		Exchanges
Calories	300	1 1/3 starch
Carbohydrate	26 grams	5 meat
Cholesterol	19 milligrams	1 vegetable
Dietary Fiber	0 grams	
Fat	< 1 gram	
Protein	44 grams	
Sodium	660 milligrams	

Shopping List: 6 ounces fat-free tuna, fat-free rice, 1 ounce fat-free shredded Cheddar cheese, fat-free shredded Mozzarella cheese, 6 ounces evaporated skim milk, 4 ounces egg substitute.

BROCCOLI-CHEESE CASSEROLE

EASY - DO AHEAD

ingredients: 10 oz. frozen chopped broccoli, thawed and
drained
1 cup fat-free cooked rice
1/2 cup fat-free shredded Cheddar cheese

directions: Lightly spray toaster oven baking dish with nonfat
cooking spray.
Combine broccoli, rice and cheese in dish and mix
well.
Bake in 350 degree toaster oven 20-25 minutes,
until cheese is melted and casserole is heated
through.

Serves: 2

Nutrition per Serving

Calories	166	
Carbohydrate	27 grams	
Cholesterol	0 milligrams	
Dietary Fiber	6 grams	
Fat	< 1 gram	
Protein	14 grams	
Sodium	316 milligrams	

Exchanges
1 starch
2 vegetable
1 meat

Shopping List: 10 ounces frozen chopped broccoli, fat-free rice
(3/4 cup), 2 ounces fat-free shredded Cheddar
cheese.

FRENCH FRIES
EASY - DO AHEAD

ingredients: 1 large baking potato, sliced
1 tsp. garlic powder
1 tbsp. fat-free Parmesan cheese (optional), not
in analysis

directions: Lightly spray toaster oven tray or foil with nonfat cooking spray.
Arrange potato slices in a single layer; lightly spray with nonfat cooking spray and immediately sprinkle with garlic powder and Parmesan cheese, if desired.
Bake in 450 degree toaster oven 20-25 minutes, until lightly browned and crisp.
Turn potatoes halfway through cooking.

Serves: 1

Nutrition per Serving		Exchanges
Calories	154	2 starch
Carbohydrate	36	
Cholesterol	0 milligrams	
Dietary Fiber	4 grams	
Fat	< 1 gram	
Protein	4 grams	
Sodium	9 milligrams	

Shopping List: 1 large baking potato, garlic powder, fat-free Parmesan cheese (optional).

TREMENDOUS
TOASTER OVEN

PINEAPPLE SWEET POTATOES

EASY - DO AHEAD

ingredients: 8 oz. canned sweet potatoes, mashed
6 tbsp. egg substitute
1/4 cup brown sugar
2 tbsp. corn flake crumbs
8 oz. crushed pineapple in juice

directions: Lightly spray toaster oven baking dish with nonfat cooking spray.
Combine mashed sweet potatoes, egg substitute, sugar and pineapple in baking dish and mix until blended.
Sprinkle top with corn flake crumbs and bake in 350 degree toaster oven 40-45 minutes, until heated through.

Serves: 2

Nutrition per Serving

Calories	332
Carbohydrate	78 grams
Cholesterol	0 milligrams
Dietary Fiber	3 grams
Fat	< 1 gram
Protein	6 grams
Sodium	206 milligrams

Exchanges

2 starch
3 fruit

Shopping List: 8-ounce can sweet potatoes, 3 ounces egg substitute, brown sugar, corn flake crumbs, 8-ounce can crushed pineapple in juice.

POTATO KUGEL

EASY - DO AHEAD

ingredients: 2 large baking potatoes, peeled and grated
1/2 cup chopped onion
1/2 cup shredded carrot
1/3 cup egg substitute
1/4 tsp. pepper
2 tbsp. matzo meal

directions: Lightly spray toaster oven baking dish with nonfat cooking spray.
Combine potatoes, onion and carrot in baking dish; add egg substitute and pepper and toss until well mixed.
Stir in matzo meal and mix until blended.
Bake in 400 degree toaster oven 20-25 minutes. Reduce oven temperature to 350 degrees and bake 25-30 minutes until lightly browned.

Serves: 2

Nutrition per Serving		Exchanges
Calories	217	2 1/2 starch
Carbohydrate	47 grams	1 vegetable
Cholesterol	0 milligrams	
Dietary Fiber	6 grams	
Fat	< 1 gram	
Protein	7 grams	
Sodium	59 milligrams	

Shopping List: 2 large baking potatoes, 1 small onion, 1 carrot (or packaged shredded carrots), egg substitute, pepper, matzo meal.

TREMENDOUS TOASTER OVEN

STUFFED TOMATOES

EASY

ingredients:
1 large tomato, cut in half
1/4 cup fat-free sour cream
4 tsp. chopped green bell pepper
4 tsp. chopped green onion
1 tsp. flour
1/2 tsp. sugar
2 tbsp. fat-free shredded Monterey Jack cheese
2 tbsp. fat-free shredded Cheddar cheese

directions:
Lightly spray toaster oven baking tray or foil with nonfat cooking spray.
Carefully remove seeds and juice of tomato and drain upside down on paper towels. Place tomato halves on baking tray.
In a small bowl, combine sour cream, peppers, onions, flour and sugar; mix until blended.
Spoon half the mixture into each tomato cup.
Bake in 450 degree toaster oven 3-5 minutes, until bubbly and lightly browned.
Sprinkle tomatoes with cheeses and continue baking 5-7 minutes, until cheese is melted and lightly browned.

Serves: 2

Nutrition per Serving

Calories	76
Carbohydrate	8 grams
Cholesterol	0 milligrams
Dietary Fiber	1 gram
Fat	< 1 gram
Protein	7 grams
Sodium	169 milligrams

Exchanges
1 meat
1 1/2 vegetable

Shopping List: 1 large tomato, 2 ounces fat-free sour cream, green bell pepper, green onions, flour, sugar, fat-free shredded Monterey Jack cheese, fat-free shredded Cheddar cheese.

SUPER STUFFED POTATO

EASY - DO AHEAD

ingredients: 1 large baking potato
1/4 cup fat-free sour cream
1/4 cup fat-free shredded Cheddar cheese
1/3 cup chopped, cooked spinach

directions: Pierce potato several times with a fork and bake in 450 degree toaster oven 1 hour. Remove from oven and let cool at room temperature 5 minutes until easy to handle.
Lightly spray baking tray or foil with nonfat cooking spray.
Cut potato in half; scoop out pulp, leaving a 1/4-inch shell and place shells on baking tray.
In a small bowl, combine potato pulp, sour cream and spinach; mix until blended.
Spoon potato mixture back into shells and top with Cheddar cheese.
Bake in 400 degree toaster oven 8-10 minutes, until cheese is melted and lightly browned.

Serves: 1

Nutrition per Serving

Calories	227
Carbohydrate	36 grams
Cholesterol	0 milligrams
Dietary Fiber	4 grams
Fat	< 1 gram
Protein	15 grams
Sodium	323 milligrams

Exchanges
2 starch
1 vegetable
1 meat

Shopping List: 1 large baking potato, 2 ounces fat-free sour cream, 1 ounce fat-free shredded Cheddar cheese, frozen chopped spinach.

BAKED APPLES

EASY

ingredients: 2 large apples
              2 1/4 tsp. lemon juice
              1/4 cup raisins
              1/4 tsp. cinnamon
              6 tbsp. maple syrup
              2 1/4 tsp. water

directions: Line toaster oven baking tray with foil and lightly
              spray with nonfat cooking spray.
              Core apples and peel a 1-inch strip around the top;
              place apples on tray.
              Brush the tops and insides of each apple with
              lemon juice.
              In a small bowl, combine raisins and cinnamon.
              Fill the center of each apple with raisin mixture.
              Pour 3 tablespoons syrup over each apple and add
              water to the bottom of the baking tray.
              Bake in 300 degree toaster oven 30-45 minutes,
              until apples are tender.
              Spoon sauce over apples several times while cook-
              ing.

              Serves: 2

Nutrition per Serving   **Exchanges**
Calories   302   5 fruit
Carbohydrate   81 grams
Cholesterol   0 milligrams
Dietary Fiber   6 grams
Fat   < 1 gram
Protein   1 gram
Sodium   65 milligrams

Shopping List: 2 apples, lemon juice, raisins, cinnamon, maple
              syrup.

CARROT CAKE
EASY - DO AHEAD - FREEZE

ingredients:
1 cup flour
1 tsp. cinnamon
1/2 cup applesauce
1/2 cup egg substitute
1 1/2 cups shredded carrots
1 cup sugar
1/2 tsp. baking soda
1/2 tsp. baking powder
1/4 cup fat-free cream cheese, softened
1/2 cup powdered sugar
1/2 tsp. vanilla
3/4 tsp. skim milk

directions:
Lightly spray 8 1/4 x 5 1/4 x 1-inch baking trays with nonfat cooking spray.

In a medium bowl, combine flour, sugar, baking soda, baking powder and cinnamon; mix well until blended.

Add egg substitute and applesauce and mix until dry ingredients are moistened. Fold in carrots.

Spread batter into baking tray and bake in 375 degree toaster oven 40-45 minutes, until knife inserted in center comes out clean. Let cool 10 minutes at room temperature; invert onto plate and cool completely.

In medium bowl, combine cream cheese, powdered sugar, vanilla and milk; beat until blended smooth and creamy. Spread frosting over cakes; refrigerate if not serving immediately.

Serves: 10

Nutrition per Serving		Exchanges
Calories	165	1 1/2 fruit
Carbohydrate	39 grams	1 starch
Cholesterol	0 milligrams	
Dietary Fiber	1 gram	
Fat	< 1 gram	
Protein	3 grams	
Sodium	120 milligrams	

Shopping List: Flour, cinnamon, baking soda, baking powder, 1/2 pound sugar, 1/2 pound powdered sugar, 4 ounces egg substitute, 4 ounces applesauce, packaged shredded carrots, 4 ounces fat-free cream cheese, skim milk, vanilla.

TREMENDOUS TOASTER OVEN

CHERRY PIE CRUMBLE

EASY - DO AHEAD

ingredients:
1 cup lite cherry pie filling
1 1/2 tbsp. multi-grain oatmeal
1 1/2 tbsp. flour
1 1/4 tbsp. brown sugar
1/4 tsp. cinnamon
1 1/2 tsp. fat-free vanilla yogurt

directions:
Lightly spray toaster oven baking dish with nonfat cooking spray.
Spread cherry pie filling into dish.
In a small bowl, combine oatmeal, flour, brown sugar and cinnamon and mix until blended; cut yogurt into mixture until crumbly.
Sprinkle crumbs over pie filling and bake in 350 degree toaster oven 30-35 minutes, until top is lightly browned.

Serves: 2

Nutrition per Serving

Calories	203
Carbohydrate	50 grams
Cholesterol	0 milligrams
Dietary Fiber	1 gram
Fat	< 1 gram
Protein	1 gram
Sodium	111 milligrams

Exchanges
3 1/3 fruit

Shopping List: Lite cherry pie filling, Quaker multi-grain oatmeal, flour, brown sugar, cinnamon, fat-free vanilla or cherry yogurt.

CHOCO-BANANA BROWNIES

EASY - DO AHEAD - FREEZE

ingredients:
1/2 cup flour
1/4 cup unsweetened cocoa powder
1/4 cup sugar
1/4 cup brown sugar
1 large banana, mashed
2 1/2 tbsp. + 1 tsp. egg substitute
1/2 tsp. vanilla

directions:
Lightly spray toaster oven baking dish with nonfat cooking spray.
In a large bowl, combine flour, cocoa, sugar and brown sugar; mix until blended.
Stir in banana, egg substitute and vanilla; blend until smooth.
Spread batter into prepared pan and bake in 350 degree toaster oven 25-30 minutes, until knife inserted in center comes out clean.
Cool to room temperature; cut into squares.

Serves: 6 cookies

Nutrition per Serving		Exchanges
Calories	133	2/3 starch
Carbohydrate	33 grams	1 1/3 fruit
Cholesterol	0 milligrams	
Dietary Fiber	< 1 gram	
Fat	< 1 gram	
Protein	2 grams	
Sodium	7 milligrams	

Shopping List: Flour, unsweetened cocoa powder, sugar, brown sugar, 1 large banana, egg substitute, vanilla.

GINGERSNAPS
EASY - DO AHEAD - FREEZE

ingredients:
1/2 cup brown sugar
2 tbsp. egg substitute
1/4 cup dark molasses
1 1/2 tbsp. Lighter Bake
1 tbsp. orange juice
1 cup flour
1 tsp. baking soda
1/2 tsp. cloves
1/2 tsp. cinnamon
1/2 tsp. ginger

directions:
In a medium bowl, combine brown sugar, egg substitute, molasses, Lighter Bake and orange juice and mix until blended creamy and smooth.
Add flour, baking soda, cloves, cinnamon and ginger and mix until dry ingredients are moistened and blended.
Lightly spray toaster oven baking tray or foil with nonfat cooking spray.
Drop dough by rounded tablespoons; sprinkle with sugar, if desired, and bake in 350 degree toaster oven 10-12 minutes, until lightly browned. Refrigerate or freeze unused batter 1-2 weeks and make cookies as needed.

Serves: 12 cookies

TREMENDOUS TOASTER OVEN

Nutrition per Serving

Calories	93
Carbohydrate	22 grams
Cholesterol	0 milligrams
Dietary Fiber	0 grams
Fat	< 1 gram
Protein	1 gram
Sodium	79 milligrams

Exchanges
1/2 starch
1 fruit

Shopping List: Brown sugar, 1 ounce egg substitute, 2 ounces dark molasses, Lighter Bake, orange juice, flour, baking soda, cloves, cinnamon, ginger.

PUMPKIN COOKIES

EASY - DO AHEAD - FREEZE

ingredients:
1/4 cup canned pumpkin, mashed
6 tbsp. brown sugar
2 tbsp. maple syrup
2 tbsp. egg substitute
1 1/4 cups flour
1/2 tsp. baking soda
1/2 tsp. pumpkin pie spice
1 tbsp. cinnamon
2 tbsp. sugar

directions:
Lightly spray toaster oven baking tray or foil with nonfat cooking spray.

In a medium bowl, combine pumpkin, brown sugar, maple syrup and egg substitute and mix until blended smooth.

Add flour, baking soda and pumpkin pie spice and mix until dry ingredients are moistened and blended.

In a small cup, combine cinnamon and sugar.

Drop batter by tablespoons onto baking tray and sprinkle with cinnamon-sugar. Bake in 350 degree toaster oven 10-12 minutes, until lightly browned. Refrigerate or freeze unused batter 1-2 weeks.

Serves: 12 cookies

TREMENDOUS TOASTER OVEN

Nutrition per Serving

Calories	93
Carbohydrate	22 grams
Cholesterol	0 milligrams
Dietary Fiber	< 1 gram
Fat	< 1 gram
Protein	1 gram
Sodium	41 milligrams

Exchanges

1/3 starch
1 fruit

Shopping List: Canned pumpkin, brown sugar, maple syrup, egg substitute, flour, baking soda, pumpkin pie spice, cinnamon, sugar.

SNICKERDOODLES

EASY - DO AHEAD - FREEZE

ingredients: 1 tbsp. fat-free margarine
1 tbsp. Lighter Bake
8 tbsp. sugar, divided
6 tbsp. brown sugar
1 1/2 tsp. vanilla
2 tbsp. egg substitute
1 1/2 cups flour
1/4 tsp. baking soda
1/2 tsp. baking powder
1 tbsp. cinnamon

directions: In medium bowl, combine margarine, Lighter Bake, 6 tablespoons sugar, brown sugar, vanilla and egg substitute; mix until creamy and smooth.
Add flour, baking soda and baking powder and mix until dry ingredients are moistened and blended.
Lightly spray plastic wrap with nonfat cooking spray; wrap dough in plastic wrap and refrigerate 1-2 hours.
In a small cup, combine cinnamon and 2 tablespoons sugar and mix well.
Shape batter into 1-inch balls and roll in cinnamon-sugar mixture to coat.
Place on baking tray and slightly flatten.
Bake in 350 degree toaster oven 10-15 minutes, until lightly browned. Centers of cookies will still be soft when removed from oven.
Refrigerate or freeze unused batter 1-2 weeks.

Serves: 12 cookies

Nutrition per Serving		Exchanges
Calories	120	2/3 starch
Carbohydrate	28 grams	1 fruit
Cholesterol	0 milligrams	
Dietary Fiber	< 1 gram	
Fat	< 1 gram	
Protein	2 grams	
Sodium	42 milligrams	

Shopping List: Fat-free margarine, Lighter Bake, sugar, brown sugar, vanilla, egg substitute, flour, baking soda, baking powder, cinnamon.

RECIPES FOR

FAT FREE LIVING® PIZZA

by Jyl Steinback

- Calzones
- Favorite Pizza Dishes
- Dessert Pizzas

PIZZA

Simple Add-ons for Pizza:
> bottled roasted red peppers
> sun-dried tomatoes
> artichoke hearts
> shrimp, scallops
> tuna
> Italian pickled peppers
> canned pickled jalapeños
> fat-free smoked sausage (Butterball)
> fat-free turkey bacon

- gather ingredients from your local supermarket salad bar to create your own pizza - chopped onions, artichokes, peppers, tomatoes, mushrooms, pineapple, chopped olives, etc.
- prepare simple cheese and tomato pizzas - freeze - top with fresh vegetables and bake for quick meal.

Save 13-25 grams of fat by preparing your own fat-free pizzas!
A Pizza Hut medium cheese Pan pizza = 13 grams fat, 20 grams with meat, 25 grams with pepperoni.

- Avoid soggy pizza - in order to get the crispiest crust, get plenty of heat directly on the crust. Bake pizza on pan with holes or thin, black baking sheet (black absorbs the heat). Great pizza from baking directly on rack - place foil or baking sheet on bottom of oven to catch "drips".
- If you are baking frozen pizzas, top pizza just before baking; do not let pizza thaw or you will end up with a soggy crust.

Pizza dough recipe equivalents:
> 16" thin crust = 8 slices
> 14" medium = 6 slices
> 12" thick = 6 slices
> 8" double crust = 4 slices
> 9x13" rectangular = 8 slices
> 4 large calzones = 8"
> 6 medium calzones = 6"
> 8 mini pizzas or calzones = 4"

Pizza crust substitutes:

    bagel

    frozen bread dough (thaw and rise)

    egg roll wrappers - lightly spray with cooking spray and bake until crisp

    English muffins

    flour tortilla

    French bread

    Italian bread - cut in half horizontally, toast lightly before adding topping

    pita bread

CRISPY THIN PIZZA CRUST

EASY - DO AHEAD

ingredients:　　1 1/2 cups flour
1/4 tsp. salt
1/2 tsp. garlic powder
1/2 tsp. onion powder
3/4 tsp. Italian seasoning
1/2 cup water

directions:　　Combine all ingredients in a medium bowl and mix well. Knead dough several minutes and form dough into ball. Lightly spray large nonstick skillet with nonfat cooking spray and heat over medium-high heat. Tear dough into 6 equal pieces; roll on lightly floured surface until very thin. Place crust in hot skillet and cook 1-2 minutes per side until lightly browned. Remove from skillet and top with sauce, cheese, or other toppings as desired. Bake in preheated oven 5-8 minutes.

Serves: 6

Nutrition per Serving		Exchanges
Calories	116	1 1/2 starch
Carbohydrate	24 grams	
Cholesterol	0 milligrams	
Dietary Fiber	1 gram	
Fat	< 1 gram	
Protein	3 grams	
Sodium	90 milligrams	

Shopping List: flour, salt, garlic powder, onion powder, Italian seasoning.

DEEP-DISH PIZZA CRUST

AVERAGE - DO AHEAD

ingredients:
1 1/3 tbsp. yeast
1/3 cup nonfat dry milk powder
3/4 cup warm water
1/4 cup sugar
2 3/4 cups flour, divided
1/4 cup egg substitute
1/2 tsp. salt
1 tsp. cornmeal

directions:
Dough can be prepared in bread machine on dough cycle. Roll into crust and bake according to recipe directions.

Pour water into large mixing bowl; sprinkle yeast and milk powder into water and mix until dissolved. Add sugar, 1 1/2 cups flour and egg substitute to yeast mixture and mix well. Cover bowl with clean towel or plastic wrap and let rise 30 minutes. Add 1 1/4 cups flour and salt to dough mixture and mix until dough forms into a ball. Add additional flour as needed; knead dough 4-5 minutes on lightly floured surface. Lightly spray bowl with nonfat cooking spray; roll dough around the bowl, cover with a towel, and let rise 45 minutes.

Lightly spray 9x13-inch baking dish with nonfat cooking spray; sprinkle with cornmeal. Punch dough down and knead lightly on floured surface. Press dough into baking dish and up sides. Preheat oven to 400°. Bake crust 5 minutes, until lightly browned. Top dough with sauce, cheese, and other toppings. Bake according to recipe directions.

Serves: 6

Nutrition per Serving		Exchanges
Calories	261	3 1/3 starch
Carbohydrate	55 grams	
Cholesterol	1 milligram	
Dietary Fiber	2 grams	
Fat	< 1 gram	
Protein	9 grams	
Sodium	214 milligrams	

Shopping List: yeast, nonfat dry milk powder, flour, sugar, salt, cornmeal, 2 ounces egg substitute.

SWEET PIZZA CRUST

AVERAGE - DO AHEAD - FREEZE

ingredients:
1 1/4 cups warm water
1 package active dry yeast
1/2 cup brown sugar
1/4 cup sugar
3 cups bread flour
1 tsp. salt
2 tbsp. reconstituted Butter Buds

directions: Dough can be prepared in bread machine on dough cycle. Roll into crust and bake according to recipe directions.

Combine warm water, yeast and a pinch of sugar in a small bowl; cover with a towel and let stand at room temperature 10 minutes. Combine 2 3/4 cups flour, brown sugar, sugar, salt and Butter Buds in a large bowl and mix well; make a well in the center of flour mixture. Pour yeast mixture into flour mixture and mix until dry ingredients are moistened and blended. Turn dough onto lightly floured surface; knead dough until it becomes smooth and elastic. Form dough into a ball. Lightly spray a medium bowl with nonfat cooking spray; place dough in bowl and roll to coat with spray. Cover with a towel and let rise in a warm place 1 hour. Punch dough down, cover and let rise 40 minutes.

Preheat oven to 400 degrees. Lightly spray pizza pan with nonfat cooking spray. Prick crust with a fork in several places. Bake in preheated oven 6-8 minutes until lightly browned. Great for berry pizzas, dessert pizzas, etc.

Serves: 6

Nutrition per Serving		Exchanges
Calories	304	2 starch
Carbohydrate	70 grams	2 1/2 fruit
Cholesterol	1 milligram	
Dietary Fiber	2 grams	
Fat	< 1 gram	
Protein	7 grams	
Sodium	39 milligrams	

Shopping List: 1 package active dry yeast, brown sugar, sugar, bread flour, salt, Butter Buds.

WHOLE WHEAT PIZZA CRUST

AVERAGE - DO AHEAD - FREEZE

ingredients:
1 cup warm water
1 package active dry yeast
3/4 tsp. brown sugar
1 tsp. salt
1 1/2 cups whole wheat flour
1 3/4 cups bread flour

directions: Dough can be prepared in bread machine on dough cycle. Roll into crust and bake according to recipe directions.

Pour warm water into a small bowl. Sprinkle yeast and brown sugar into water and stir until completely dissolved. Cover bowl with a clean towel and let sit 10 minutes until it becomes foamy. Combine bread flour, whole wheat flour, and salt in a large bowl and mix well. Pour yeast mixture into center of flour mixture and mix until soft dough forms. Turn dough onto lightly floured surface and knead until smooth and elastic. Spray large bowl with nonfat cooking spray; place dough in bowl and roll to coat. Cover bowl with clean towel and let dough rise in a warm place about 1 hour or until doubled in size. Punch dough down; cover and let rise 40 minutes. Pat and stretch dough on lightly floured surface to fit pizza pan. Preheat oven to 400 degrees. Prick crust in several places with a fork and bake 5-6 minutes until crust begins to brown. Top crust according to recipe directions. Use this crust in any of your favorite pizza recipes.

Serves: 6

Nutrition per Serving		Exchanges
Calories	240	3 starch
Carbohydrate	48 grams	
Cholesterol	0 milligrams	
Dietary Fiber	5 gram	
Fat	< 1 gram	
Protein	8 grams	
Sodium	359 milligrams	

Shopping List: 1 package active dry yeast, brown sugar, salt, whole wheat flour, bread flour.

CHUNKY ITALIAN TOMATO SAUCE

EASY - DO AHEAD - FREEZE

ingredients:
2 tbsp. fat-free chicken broth
1 tsp. minced garlic
3/4 cup chopped onions
15 oz. can crushed tomatoes
6 oz. can tomato paste
1 tsp. Italian seasoning
1 bay leaf
1/4 tsp. fennel seed
1/2 tsp. sugar
1/8 tsp. pepper

directions:
Pour chicken broth into medium saucepan and heat over medium-high heat. Add garlic and onions to saucepan and cook, stirring frequently, until onions are tender and soft. Add remaining ingredients to saucepan and bring to a boil over high heat. Reduce heat to low; simmer, uncovered, 30-35 minutes until sauce thickens. Remove bay leaf from sauce. Cover and refrigerate or freeze if not using immediately. This sauce can be used in any recipe calling for fat-free pizza sauce and Simple Pizza Sauce.

Serves: 12

Nutrition per Serving		Exchanges
Calories	27	1 vegetable
Carbohydrate	6 grams	
Cholesterol	0 milligrams	
Dietary Fiber	1 gram	
Fat	< 1 gram	
Protein	1 gram	
Sodium	108 milligrams	

Shopping List: 15-ounce can crushed tomatoes, 6-ounce can tomato paste, 8-ounce package chopped onions or 1 large onion, minced garlic, Italian seasoning, bay leaf, fennel seeds, sugar, pepper, fat-free chicken broth.

PEPPER-CHEESE SAUCE

EASY - DO AHEAD

ingredients:
32 oz. frozen pepper strips
1 tbsp. onion powder
1/2 tsp. garlic powder
1/2 tsp. ground cumin
1/4 tsp. red pepper flakes
1/4 tsp. chili powder
1 1/2 cups fat-free ricotta cheese

directions:
Lightly spray large nonstick skillet with nonfat cooking spray and heat over medium-high heat. Add frozen peppers to skillet and cook, stirring frequently, 3-5 minutes until peppers are soft. Sprinkle onion powder, garlic powder, cumin, pepper flakes and chili powder over vegetables; cook 1-2 minutes, stirring frequently, until spices are blended. Remove from heat and cool 15-20 minutes. Combine ricotta cheese and pepper mixture in food processor or blender and process until creamy and smooth. Cover and refrigerate until ready to use. Sauce will keep in refrigerator 1-2 weeks. This sauce can be used in any of your favorite pizza recipes. It is especially good with vegetables or chicken.

Serves: 12

Nutrition per Serving		**Exchanges**
Calories	46	1/2 milk
Carbohydrate	5 grams	
Cholesterol	5 milligrams	
Dietary Fiber	1 gram	
Fat	< 1 gram	
Protein	5 grams	
Sodium	63 milligrams	

Shopping List: 12 ounces fat-free ricotta cheese, 2 16-ounce packages frozen pepper strips, onion powder, garlic powder, ground cumin, red pepper flakes, chili powder.

SIMPLE PIZZA SAUCE

EASY - DO AHEAD - FREEZE

ingredients: 2 cups tomato sauce
3/4 cup tomato paste
1/2 tsp. onion powder
2 tsp. garlic powder
1 1/2 tsp. oregano
1 tsp. thyme
1 tsp. sage
1 tsp. rosemary
1 tsp. basil leaves

directions: Combine all ingredients in a bowl, blender, or food processor and blend until smooth. Spread over pizza dough and bake as directed.

You can make several batches of sauce and freeze for several months. Lightly spray large muffin pan with nonfat cooking spray. Pour 1/2-3/4 cup sauce into each cup; cover with freezer-safe wrap and freeze. Remove from muffin cups; wrap in individual packages (or baggies) and freeze until ready to use. When ready to use, remove the required amount from freezer, thaw, and use as needed.

Serves: 6

Nutrition per Serving		Exchanges
Calories	65	3 vegetable
Carbohydrate	14 grams	
Cholesterol	0 milligrams	
Dietary Fiber	3 grams	
Fat	< 1 gram	
Protein	3 grams	
Sodium	281 milligrams	

Shopping List: 16 ounces tomato sauce, 6 ounces tomato paste, onion powder, garlic powder, oregano, thyme, sage, rosemary, basil.

PERFECT PIZZAS

WHITE CREAM SAUCE

EASY - DO AHEAD

ingredients: 1 1/2 cups fat-free ricotta cheese
1/2 tsp. onion powder
1/2 tsp. garlic salt
2 tsp. minced garlic

directions: Combine all ingredients in a food processor or blender and blend until smooth. Spread on pizza crust; top pizza with chicken, seafood, or vegetables and bake according to directions.

Serves: 6

<u>**Nutrition per Serving**</u>

Calories	47
Carbohydrate	3 grams
Cholesterol	10 milligrams
Dietary Fiber	0 grams
Fat	< 1 gram
Protein	9 grams
Sodium	291 milligrams

<u>**Exchanges**</u>
1/2 milk

Shopping List: 12 ounces fat-free ricotta cheese, onion powder, garlic salt, minced garlic.

ARTICHOKE-SHRIMP PIZZA

AVERAGE - DO AHEAD

ingredients: 1--14-inch fat-free pizza crust
1 cup cooked shrimp, chopped
10 oz. frozen artichokes, thawed, drained and chopped
3/4 tsp. dried oregano
1 cup Simple Pizza Sauce*
1 1/2 cups fat-free mozzarella cheese, finely shredded
2 tbsp. reduced-fat feta cheese

directions: Preheat oven to 475 degrees. Lightly spray 14-inch pizza pan with nonfat cooking spray. Prepare pizza crust according to directions; stretch and roll dough to fit pizza pan. Prepare Simple Pizza Sauce according to directions. Spread pizza sauce onto crust. Sprinkle 1 cup mozzarella cheese over sauce. Arrange shrimp and artichokes on top and sprinkle with oregano. Sprinkle remaining mozzarella cheese and feta cheese over top and bake in preheated oven 12-15 minutes, until crust is lightly browned and cheese is completely melted.

*You can substitute 1 cup (any brand) fat-free pizza sauce, if desired.

Serves: 6

Nutrition per Serving		Exchanges
Calories	269	2 starch
Carbohydrate	40 grams	2 vegetable
Cholesterol	46 milligrams	2 meat
Dietary Fiber	2 grams	
Fat	< 1 gram	
Protein	22 grams	
Sodium	596 milligrams	

Shopping List: 6-8 ounces cooked shrimp (small), 10 ounces frozen artichokes, 6 ounces fat-free finely shredded mozzarella cheese, 1/2 ounce low-fat feta cheese, dried oregano - ingredients for Simple Pizza Sauce and fat-free pizza crust.

PERFECT PIZZAS

BACON-CHEESEBURGER PIZZA

AVERAGE - DO AHEAD - FREEZE

ingredients:
1 fat-free deep-dish pizza crust
3 cups frozen Harvest Burger beef crumbles
1 tbsp. onion flakes
1 1/4 cups fat-free pizza sauce
2 medium tomatoes, sliced thin
6 slices turkey bacon, cooked and drained
1 3/4 cups fat-free shredded pizza cheese

directions:
Preheat oven to 450 degrees. Lightly spray 9x13-inch baking dish with nonfat cooking spray. Prepare pizza crust according to directions; stretch and roll dough to fit baking dish. Press dough into dish, slightly building up the edges. Prick crust in several places with a fork. Bake crust in preheated oven 8-10 minutes until lightly browned.

Spread pizza sauce over baked crust. Scatter beef crumbles over sauce; sprinkle with onion flakes. Arrange tomato slices and bacon over top. Sprinkle generously with cheese. Bake in oven 10-12 minutes, until cheese is completely melted and pizza is cooked through.

Serves: 8

Nutrition per Serving
Calories	309
Carbohydrate	50 grams
Cholesterol	16 milligrams
Dietary Fiber	4 grams
Fat	< 1 gram
Protein	27 grams
Sodium	855 milligrams

Exchanges
3 starch
2 vegetable
1 1/3 meat

Shopping List: 10 ounces frozen Harvest Burger beef crumbles, 10 ounces fat-free pizza sauce, 2 medium tomatoes, fat-free turkey bacon, 7 ounces fat-free shredded pizza cheese, onion flakes - ingredients for fat-free deep-dish pizza crust.

BASIC CHEESE AND TOMATO PIZZA

EASY - DO AHEAD - FREEZE

ingredients:
1 fat-free pizza crust
28 oz. can crushed tomatoes, drained
1 tsp. Italian seasoning
2 tbsp. tomato paste
1/4 tsp. black pepper
1 1/2 cups fat-free mozzarella cheese, finely shredded
1/4 cup fat-free Parmesan cheese

directions:
Preheat oven to 425 degrees. Lightly spray 14-inch pizza pan with nonfat cooking spray. Prepare pizza dough; stretch and roll dough on lightly floured surface to fit pizza pan. Prick in several places with a fork and bake in preheated oven 5-6 minutes until lightly browned. Remove from oven. Combine tomatoes, Italian seasoning, tomato paste, and pepper in a medium bowl; mix well. Spread tomato mixture over crust; sprinkle mozzarella and Parmesan cheese on top. Bake 15-18 minutes, until cheese is melted and crust is lightly browned.

Serves: 6

Nutrition per Serving
Calories	235
Carbohydrate	40 grams
Cholesterol	0 milligrams
Dietary Fiber	2 grams
Fat	< 1 gram
Protein	16 grams
Sodium	750 milligrams

Exchanges
2 starch
2 vegetable
1 meat

Shopping List: 28-ounce can crushed tomatoes, tomato paste, 6 ounces fat-free finely shredded mozzarella cheese, 1 ounce fat-free Parmesan cheese, Italian seasoning, black pepper, ingredients for fat-free pizza crust.

BROCCOLI PIZZA WITH WHITE CREAM SAUCE

AVERAGE - DO AHEAD - FREEZE

ingredients:
1--14-inch fat-free pizza crust
3 cups frozen broccoli flowerets, thawed and drained
1 cup fat-free White Cream Sauce*
1/2 cup sliced red bell pepper
1 1/2 cups fat-free mozzarella cheese, finely shredded
1/4 cup fat-free Parmesan cheese

directions:
Preheat oven to 475 degrees. Lightly spray 14-inch pizza pan with nonfat cooking spray. Prepare pizza crust according to directions; stretch, roll and press into pizza pan. Bake crust in preheated oven 5-6 minutes.

Prepare White Cream Sauce* according to directions. Spread sauce over crust. Arrange broccoli and red peppers over sauce. Sprinkle mozzarella and Parmesan cheese over top. Bake in preheated oven 12-15 minutes, until crust is lightly browned and cheese is melted.

Serves: 6

Nutrition per Serving		Exchanges
Calories	245	2 starch
Carbohydrate	36 grams	1 vegetable
Cholesterol	7 milligrams	2 meat
Dietary Fiber	2 grams	
Fat	< 1 gram	
Protein	22 grams	
Sodium	630 milligrams	

Shopping List: 3--10-ounce packages frozen broccoli flowerets, 1 red bell pepper, 6 ounces fat-free finely shredded mozzarella cheese, 1 ounce fat-free Parmesan cheese - ingredients for White Cream Sauce* (see recipe, page 9), and 1--14-inch fat-free pizza crust.

CHICKEN-VEGETABLE PIZZA

AVERAGE - DO AHEAD

ingredients:
1 fat-free deep-dish pizza crust
2 tbsp. fat-free chicken broth
1 lb. fat-free chicken tenders
1 tsp. garlic powder
1 1/2 tsp. onion powder
2 tsp. dried basil
2 cups fat-free pizza sauce
1 medium yellow bell pepper, sliced thin
1 medium red bell pepper, sliced thin
1 cup sliced mushrooms
1 medium red onion, sliced thin
1/3 cup fat-free Parmesan cheese
2 cups fat-free shredded pizza cheese

directions:
Preheat oven to 425 degrees. Lightly spray deep-dish pizza pan with nonfat cooking spray. Prepare pizza dough and press into pan. Prick several times with fork; bake in preheated oven 10-12 minutes until lightly browned.

Lightly spray large nonstick skillet with nonfat cooking spray; pour chicken broth into skillet and heat over medium-high heat. Add chicken tenders; sprinkle with garlic powder, onion powder, and basil. Cook over medium heat, stirring frequently, 8-10 minutes until chicken is no longer pink. Remove chicken from skillet and cut into bite-size pieces. Pour pizza sauce over crust. Sprinkle half the pizza cheese over sauce. Top with chicken, yellow and red peppers, mushrooms, and sliced onion. Sprinkle with remaining pizza cheese and Parmesan cheese. Bake in preheated oven 10-12 minutes until cheese is completely melted.

Serves: 6

Nutrition per Serving		Exchanges
Calories	358	2 starch
Carbohydrate	49 grams	4 vegetable
Cholesterol	37 milligrams	3 meat
Dietary Fiber	4 grams	
Fat	< 1 gram	
Protein	38 grams	
Sodium	840 milligrams	

Shopping List: 1 pound fat-free chicken tenders, 16 ounces fat-free pizza sauce, 1 yellow bell pepper, 1 red bell pepper, 4 ounces sliced mushrooms, 1 red onion, 8 ounces fat-free shredded pizza cheese, fat-free Parmesan cheese, fat-free chicken broth, garlic powder, onion powder, dried basil, 1 fat-free pizza crust.

HOT AND SPICY MEXICAN PIZZA

EASY - DO AHEAD

ingredients:
1 fat-free pizza crust
15 oz. fat-free spicy refried beans
1/2 cup chunky-style salsa, divided
1 tsp. ground cumin
1/8 tsp. cayenne pepper
1 tsp. garlic powder
1 1/2 cups fat-free shredded Mexican cheese
1/2 cup chopped green onions
1/2 cup chopped red bell pepper
1 cup fat-free sour cream

directions: Preheat oven to 425 degrees. Lightly spray 14-inch pizza pan with nonfat cooking spray. Prepare pizza crust and press into pan. Prick crust with fork and bake in preheated oven 7-10 minutes until lightly browned. Combine beans, 3 tablespoons salsa, cumin, cayenne pepper, and garlic powder in a medium bowl and mix until blended. Spread bean mixture over hot crust. Sprinkle cheese over beans; top with green onions and bell pepper. Bake 10-12 minutes until cheese is completely melted. Combine sour cream and remaining salsa in a small bowl; mix well. Serve with pizza, if desired.

Serves: 6

Nutrition per Serving		**Exchanges**
Calories	297	2 starch
Carbohydrate	49 grams	4 vegetable
Cholesterol	1 milligram	1 meat
Dietary Fiber	3 grams	
Fat	< 1 gram	
Protein	21 grams	
Sodium	786 milligrams	

Shopping List: 15 ounces fat-free spicy refried beans, 6 ounces fat-free shredded Mexican cheese, 4 ounces fat-free chunky salsa, 1 small red bell pepper, green onions, 8 ounces fat-free sour cream, ground cumin, cayenne pepper, garlic powder, 1 fat-free pizza crust.

ITALIAN SHRIMP PIZZA

EASY - DO AHEAD

ingredients:
1 fat-free pizza crust
3/4 lb. frozen fat-free shrimp, thawed
1 tsp. minced garlic
6 tbsp. fat-free Italian salad dressing, divided
1/4 tsp. pepper
1/4 cup fat-free Parmesan cheese

directions:
Combine 1/4 cup Italian salad dressing, garlic, and pepper in a small cup; blend well. Place shrimp in a shallow baking dish; pour Italian dressing mixture over shrimp and toss until shrimp are coated. Cover with plastic wrap and refrigerate 30 minutes. Preheat oven to 450 degrees. Lightly spray pizza pan with nonfat cooking spray. Prepare pizza crust and press into pizza pan. Bake crust 5-6 minutes; remove from oven. Remove shrimp from marinade with a slotted spoon and arrange on pizza crust. Sprinkle with Parmesan cheese and bake 10-12 minutes, until shrimp turn pink and crust is lightly browned.

Serves: 6

Nutrition per Serving		Exchanges
Calories	213	2 2/3 starch
Carbohydrate	40 grams	
Cholesterol	7 milligrams	
Dietary Fiber	1 gram	
Fat	< 1 gram	
Protein	11 grams	
Sodium	642 milligrams	

Shopping List: 3/4 pound fat-free shrimp, 3 ounces fat-free Italian salad dressing, 1 ounce fat-free Parmesan cheese, minced garlic, pepper, 1 fat-free pizza crust.

RATATOUILLE PIZZA ON DEEP-DISH CRUST

DIFFICULT - DO AHEAD

ingredients:
1 fat-free deep-dish pizza crust
3/4 lb. eggplant
2 tbsp. vegetable broth
28 oz. can chopped tomatoes, drained
1 tbsp. onion flakes
1 1/2 tsp. minced garlic
1 tsp. Italian seasoning
1/2 tsp. sugar
1/8 tsp. pepper
1 medium zucchini, sliced thin
1 medium yellow squash, sliced thin
1 red onion, sliced thin
1 1/4 cups fat-free mozzarella cheese, finely
 shredded
2 tbsp. reduced-fat feta cheese

directions: Preheat oven to 400 degrees. Lightly spray 14-inch pizza pan with nonfat cooking spray. Prepare deep-dish pizza crust; stretch and roll dough on lightly floured surface and press into pan. Cut eggplant in half; chop 1/2 the eggplant and set aside. Thinly slice the remaining eggplant and set aside. Lightly spray a large nonstick skillet with nonfat cooking spray; add vegetable broth and heat over medium-high heat. Add chopped eggplant, chopped tomatoes, onion flakes, garlic, Italian seasoning, sugar and pepper; cook over medium-low heat 15-20 minutes until all the liquid has evaporated. Drain off any remaining liquid. Using the back of a spoon, press the eggplant-tomato mixture into a spreading consistency. Spread over pizza crust. Arrange zucchini, squash, and onion slices over sauce. Lightly spray the vegetables with cooking spray; sprinkle with mozzarella and feta cheese. Bake in preheated oven 15-18 minutes, until crust is lightly browned, cheese is completely melted and vegetables are heated through.

Serves: 8

Nutrition per Serving		Exchanges
Calories	277	2 starch
Carbohydrate	53 grams	5 vegetable
Cholesterol	1 milligram	
Dietary Fiber	5 grams	
Fat	< 1 gram	
Protein	14 grams	
Sodium	404 milligrams	

Shopping List: 3/4 pound eggplant, 28-ounce can chopped tomatoes, 1 zucchini, 1 yellow squash, 1 red onion, 1 ounce reduced-fat feta cheese, 5 ounces fat-free finely shredded mozzarella cheese, onion flakes, minced garlic, Italian seasoning, sugar, pepper, vegetable broth, 1 deep-dish pizza crust.

SHRIMP AND MUSHROOM PIZZA

EASY - DO AHEAD

ingredients:
1 fat-free thin pizza crust
1 cup frozen chopped spinach, chopped and drained
3/4 lb. cooked fat-free shrimp
1/2 cup sliced mushrooms
1/2 cup shiitake mushrooms
1 1/2 cups fat-free mozzarella cheese, finely shredded
1 1/2 cups White Cream Sauce*

directions:
Preheat oven to 400 degrees. Lightly spray 14-inch pizza pan wit nonfat cooking spray. Prepare pizza crust; stretch and roll dough to fit pizza pan. Press into pan; prick several places. Bake in preheated oven 5-6 minutes. Spread White Cream Sauce on crust; top with spinach and mushrooms. Sprinkle pizza with cheese. Bake 12-15 minutes until crust is lightly browned and cheese is completely melted.

Serves: 6

Nutrition per Serving		Exchanges
Calories	302	2 starch
Carbohydrate	44 grams	3 vegetable
Cholesterol	17 milligrams	2 meat
Dietary Fiber	2 grams	
Fat	< 1 gram	
Protein	30 grams	
Sodium	1,076 milligrams	

Shopping List: 10 ounces frozen chopped spinach, 3/4 pound cooked shrimp, white mushrooms, shiitake mushrooms, 6 ounces fat-free finely shredded mozzarella cheese - ingredients for White Cream Sauce (see recipe, page 9) and fat-free thin pizza crust.

FRENCH BREAD PIZZA BITES

EASY - DO AHEAD

ingredients:
1--16-inch loaf fat-free French bread
1/4 cup Butter Buds, reconstituted
3/4 tsp. Italian seasoning
1/8 tsp. pepper
1/2 lb. fat-free pastrami, sliced
3/4 cup tomato paste
1 1/2 tsp. onion powder
1/3 cup chili sauce
1/4 cup chopped green and red bell peppers
1 cup chopped tomatoes
2 tbsp. chopped black olives
1 1/2 cups fat-free finely shredded mozzarella cheese
1/3 cup fat-free Parmesan cheese

directions:
Preheat oven to 400 degrees. Line baking sheet with foil and lightly spray with nonfat cooking spray. Cut bread in half horizontally. In a small bowl, combine Butter Buds, Italian seasoning, and pepper; mix well. Brush butter mixture over cut sides of bread and place, buttered-side up, on baking sheet. Arrange pastrami slices on bread. Combine tomato paste, onion powder, chili sauce, bell peppers, tomatoes and olives in a small bowl; mix well. Spread sauce over pastrami. Bake bread in preheated oven 15-18 minutes. Sprinkle mozzarella and Parmesan cheese on top; bake 5-6 minutes until cheese is melted and lightly browned. Slice each bread loaf into 8 pieces and serve.

Serves: 6

Nutrition per Serving		Exchanges
Calories	261	2 starch
Carbohydrate	38 grams	2 vegetable
Cholesterol	14 milligrams	1 1/2 meat
Dietary Fiber	3 grams	
Fat	< 1 gram	
Protein	22 grams	
Sodium	1,494 milligrams	

Shopping List: 1--16-inch loaf fat-free French bread, Butter Buds, 1/2 pound fat-free pastrami, 6 ounces tomato paste, 3 ounces chili sauce, 1 small red bell pepper, 1 small green bell pepper, 4-ounce can chopped black olives, 6 ounces fat-free finely shredded mozzarella cheese, 1 large tomato, fat-free Parmesan cheese, onion powder, pepper, Italian seasoning.

PINEAPPLE-PEPPER PIZZA

AVERAGE - DO AHEAD

ingredients:
1 lb. fat-free frozen bread dough, thawed
3/4 cup fat-free pizza sauce
1 tsp. garlic powder
1 1/2 tsp. Italian seasoning
3/4 lb. frozen Harvest Burger beef crumbles
2 cups crushed pineapple, drained
1 medium green bell pepper, sliced
1/2 cup chopped green onions
2 1/2 cups fat-free shredded mozzarella cheese
1/4 cup fat-free Parmesan cheese

directions: Preheat oven to 475 degrees. Lightly spray 14-inch pizza pan with nonfat cooking spray. Roll and stretch dough on lightly floured surface to fit 14-inch pizza pan. Prick dough several times with fork. Bake in preheated oven 10-12 minutes. Remove from oven. Combine pizza sauce, garlic powder, Italian seasoning, and beef crumbles in a medium saucepan and heat over low heat until beef is warm, about 5 minutes. Spread sauce on pizza crust. Arrange pineapple, green pepper, and onions on sauce; top with mozzarella and Parmesan cheese. Bake pizza in preheated oven 12-15 minutes, until crust is lightly browned and cheese is completely melted.

Serves: 6

Nutrition per Serving		Exchanges
Calories	437	1 fruit
Carbohydrate	67 grams	3 starch
Cholesterol	0 milligrams	1 vegetable
Dietary Fiber	6 grams	3 1/2 meat
Fat	< 1 gram	
Protein	36 grams	
Sodium	1,057 milligrams	

Shopping List: 1 pound fat-free frozen bread dough, 8 ounces fat-free pizza sauce, 3/4 pound frozen Harvest Burger beef crumbles, 16 ounces crushed pineapple in juice, 1 green bell pepper, green onions, 10 ounces fat-free shredded mozzarella cheese, 1 ounce fat-free Parmesan cheese, garlic powder, Italian seasoning.

TUNA-CHEESE PIZZA BREAD

EASY - DO AHEAD

ingredients:
1--1 lb. loaf Italian bread
3--6 oz. cans fat-free tuna, drained
1 1/2 cups fat-free cream cheese, softened
1 1/2 cups fat-free Cheddar cheese, finely shredded
2 cups chopped celery
1 tbsp. onion powder
3/4 tsp. pepper

directions:
Preheat broiler on high heat. Line baking sheet with foil and lightly spray with nonfat cooking spray. Cut bread loaf in half horizontally; place on baking sheet and toast lightly under broiler. Watch carefully! Remove from oven. Turn oven to bake and temperature to 400 degrees. Combine tuna, cream cheese, Cheddar cheese, celery, onion powder, and pepper in a large bowl and mix until all ingredients are blended. Spread tuna mixture on bread and bake 12-15 minutes until cheese is melted and lightly browned.

Serves: 6

Nutrition per Serving		Exchanges
Calories	429	3 starch
Carbohydrate	51 grams	1 vegetable
Cholesterol	15 milligrams	5 meat
Dietary Fiber	3 grams	
Fat	< 1 gram	
Protein	49 grams	
Sodium	1,402 milligrams	

Shopping List: 1 loaf Italian bread, 3--6-ounce cans fat-free tuna, 12 ounces fat-free cream cheese, 6 ounces fat-free finely shredded Cheddar cheese, 1 pound celery, onion powder, pepper.

LOTS 'O ONIONS PIZZA

EASY - DO AHEAD

ingredients: 12--5-inch lahvosh crackers
1 tsp. dried rosemary
2 cups sliced onions
3/4 cup fat-free mozzarella cheese, finely
shredded

directions: Lightly spray large nonstick skillet with nonfat
cooking spray and heat over medium-high heat.
Add onions and rosemary to skillet and cook 10-12
minutes until tender and lightly browned. Remove onions from skillet and set aside.

Preheat oven to 400 degrees. Line baking sheet(s)
with foil and lightly spray with nonfat cooking
spray. Arrange crackers in a single layer on baking
sheet(s). Lightly spray crackers with nonfat cooking spray. Sprinkle with mozzarella cheese. Divide onions among crackers and arrange on top.
Bake in preheated oven 5-6 minutes until cheese is
completely melted.

Serves: 6

Nutrition per Serving		Exchanges
Calories	99	1/2 starch
Carbohydrate	16 grams	2 vegetable
Cholesterol	0 milligrams	
Dietary Fiber	1 gram	
Fat	< 1 gram	
Protein	7 grams	
Sodium	178 milligrams	

Shopping List: 5-inch lahvosh crackers, 2 large onions, 3 ounces
fat-free finely shredded mozzarella cheese, dried
rosemary.

PERFECT
PIZZAS

CHILI-CHEESE TORTILLA PIZZA

EASY - DO AHEAD

ingredients:
6 fat-free flour tortillas
3/4 cup fat-free pizza sauce
3/4 cup fat-free mozzarella cheese, finely shredded
3/4 cup fat-free Cheddar cheese, finely shredded
2 tbsp. chopped green chilies
2 tbsp. chopped black olives

directions:
Lightly spray large nonstick skillet with nonfat cooking spray. Spread 1/2 of each tortilla with 2 tablespoons pizza sauce; top with 1 teaspoon chilies and 1 teaspoon olives. Sprinkle cheese over top. Fold tortilla in half. Heat skillet over medium-high heat. Add tortillas 2-3 at a time and cook 2 minutes until bottom of tortilla begins to brown. Carefully flip tortilla with spatula and cook 2-3 minutes until cheese is completely melted and tortilla is lightly browned. Cut into wedges and serve.

Serves: 6

Nutrition per Serving		Exchanges
Calories	173	1 2/3 starch
Carbohydrate	29 grams	1 vegetable
Cholesterol	0 milligrams	1/2 meat
Dietary Fiber	3 grams	
Fat	< 1 gram	
Protein	13 grams	
Sodium	673 milligrams	

Shopping List: fat-free flour tortillas, 6 ounces fat-free pizza sauce, 3 ounces fat-free finely shredded mozzarella cheese, 3 ounces fat-free finely shredded Cheddar cheese, 4-ounce can chopped green chilies, 4-ounce can chopped black olives.

VEGETARIAN PIZZA ROUNDS

EASY - DO AHEAD

ingredients:
12 large lahvosh crackers
1 tbsp. vegetable broth
10 ounces frozen cut asparagus, thawed
1 medium yellow squash, sliced thin
1 cup sliced mushrooms
1 tsp. garlic powder
1 tbsp. onion powder
1 cup chopped tomatoes
1 1/2 cups fat-free mozzarella cheese, finely shredded
3/4 cup fat-free Parmesan cheese

directions:
Preheat oven to 400 degrees. Line baking sheet(s) with foil and lightly spray with nonfat cooking spray. Arrange lahvosh crackers in a single layer on baking sheet(s). Lightly spray large nonstick skillet with nonfat cooking spray. Pour vegetable broth into skillet and heat over medium-high heat. Add asparagus, squash and mushrooms to skillet; sprinkle with onion and garlic powder; stir-fry 2-3 minutes until tender-crisp. Divide vegetable mixture evenly and arrange on crackers; top with chopped tomato. Sprinkle mozzarella and Parmesan cheese over top. Bake in preheated oven 8 to 10 minutes until cheese is completely melted and pizzas are heated through.

Serves: 6 (2 crackers per serving)

Nutrition per Serving		Exchanges
Calories	166	1/2 starch
Carbohydrate	22 grams	3 vegetable
Cholesterol	0 milligrams	1 1/2 meat
Dietary Fiber	1 gram	
Fat	< 1 gram	
Protein	18 grams	
Sodium	436 milligrams	

Shopping List: 1 package large lahvosh crackers, 1 large tomato, 10 ounces frozen cut asparagus, 1 medium yellow squash, 4 ounces sliced mushrooms, 6 ounces fat-free finely shredded mozzarella cheese, 3 ounces fat-free Parmesan cheese, garlic powder, onion powder, vegetable broth.

CREAMY VEGETABLE PITA PIZZA

EASY - DO AHEAD

ingredients:
6 whole pita pockets
1 1/2 cups fat-free cottage cheese
1 1/2 cups fat-free shredded Cheddar cheese
2 cups shredded carrots
1/2 cup chopped celery
1/4 cup chopped green onions
1 1/2 tsp. dill
1/2 tsp. garlic powder
1/4 tsp. cayenne pepper
1/4 tsp. pepper
fat-free Parmesan cheese (optional)

directions:
Preheat oven to 400 degrees. Line baking sheet(s) with foil and lightly spray with nonfat cooking spray. Arrange pitas on baking sheet in a single layer and bake 7-8 minutes until lightly browned. Remove from oven. Combine cottage cheese, Cheddar cheese, carrots, celery and green onions in a large bowl and mix until all ingredients are blended. Combine dill, garlic powder, cayenne, and pepper in a small cup and mix well; sprinkle over cheese mixture and blend well. Spread cheese sauce over hot pitas and bake 4-6 minutes until cheese topping is bubbly and lightly browned. Sprinkle with Parmesan cheese, if desired.

Serves: 6

Nutrition per Serving
Calories	180
Carbohydrate	28 grams
Cholesterol	1 milligram
Dietary Fiber	2 grams
Fat	< 1 gram
Protein	14 grams
Sodium	564 milligrams

Exchanges
1 starch
3 vegetable
1 meat

Shopping List: fat-free pita pockets, 12 ounces fat-free cottage cheese, 6 ounces fat-free finely shredded Cheddar cheese, 8-ounce package shredded carrots (or 3-4 carrots), 1/4 pound celery, green onions, dill, garlic powder, cayenne pepper, pepper, fat-free Parmesan cheese (optional).

KID'S CREATE-A-MONSTER PIZZA

EASY - DO AHEAD - FREEZE

ingredients:
6 fat-free pita pockets
3/4 cup fat-free pizza sauce
1 1/2 cups fat-free shredded pizza sauce
3 black olives, cut in half
1 medium zucchini, cut in 12 slices
1 small green bell pepper, sliced thin
1 small red bell pepper, sliced thin

directions:
Preheat oven to 400 degrees. Line baking sheet(s) with foil and lightly spray with nonfat cooking spray. Arrange pita pockets on baking sheet in a single layer. Spread 2 tablespoons pizza sauce on each pita pocket. Sprinkle cheese over top. To make a monster pizza: use 2 zucchini for eyes, 2 green pepper slices for eyebrows, 1/2 olive for nose, red bell slice for mouth. Add additional ingredients (tomatoes, broccoli, cauliflower, mushrooms, etc.) to create any "face" you want. Bake in preheated oven 8-10 minutes until pita is lightly browned and cheese is melted.

Serves: 6

Nutrition per Serving		Exchanges
Calories	180	1 1/2 starch
Carbohydrate	29 grams	1 vegetable
Cholesterol	0 milligrams	1 meat
Dietary Fiber	2 grams	
Fat	< 1 gram	
Protein	14 grams	
Sodium	502 milligrams	

Shopping List: fat-free pita pockets, 6 ounces fat-free pizza sauce, 6 ounces fat-free shredded pizza cheese, black olives, 1 zucchini, 1 green bell pepper, 1 red bell pepper.

STUFFED PITA POCKET PIZZA

AVERAGE - DO AHEAD - FREEZE

ingredients:
6 fat-free pita pockets
1 1/4 cups fat-free pizza sauce
16 ounces frozen Italian mixed vegetables
2 1/2 oz. jar sliced mushrooms, drained
2 tbsp. sliced olives, drained
1 1/2 tsp. garlic powder
1 tsp. Italian seasoning
2 cups fat-free mozzarella cheese, finely
shredded
1/4 cup fat-free Parmesan cheese

directions:
Preheat oven to 425 degrees. Line baking sheet with foil and lightly spray with nonfat cooking spray. Cut pita pockets in half, but do not cut all the way through. Lightly spray nonstick skillet with nonfat cooking spray and heat over medium-high heat. Add mixed vegetables, olives, and mushrooms to skillet; sprinkle vegetables with garlic powder and Italian seasoning; cook 5-6 minutes until tender-crisp. (Or, combine vegetables in microwave-safe dish and sprinkle with seasonings; cover with plastic wrap and microwave on High 5-6 minutes until tender-crisp.) Spread 2 tablespoons pizza sauce inside each pita pocket. Stuff with cooked vegetables and sprinkle with mozzarella cheese. Arrange on baking sheet and bake in preheated oven 8-10 minutes until cheese is melted. Remove from oven and sprinkle inside of pita with Parmesan cheese; bake an additional 5-6 minutes until cheese is completely melted and pita is lightly browned.

Serves: 6

Nutrition per Serving

Calories	248
Carbohydrate	37 grams
Cholesterol	0 milligrams
Dietary Fiber	6 grams
Fat	< 1 gram
Protein	21 grams
Sodium	809 milligrams

Exchanges
2 starch
1 vegetable
2 meat

Shopping List: fat-free pita pockets, 10 ounces fat-free pizza sauce, 16 ounces frozen Italian mixed vegetables, 2 1/2-ounce jar sliced mushrooms, 2 1/2-ounce can sliced olives, 8 ounces fat-free finely shredded mozzarella cheese, 1 ounce fat-free Parmesan cheese, garlic powder, Italian seasoning.

CHICKEN TACO PIZZA

EASY - DO AHEAD

ingredients: 6 fat-free flour tortillas
1 1/2 cups fat-free chicken tenders, cooked and shredded
1 1/2 tsp. taco seasoning mix
1 1/2 cups fat-free Cheddar cheese, finely shredded
1 1/2 tbsp. chopped jalapeño peppers
3/4 cup chopped tomatoes
3/4 cup fat-free taco sauce

directions: Preheat oven to 425 degrees. Line baking sheet with foil and lightly spray with nonfat cooking spray. Arrange tortillas in a single layer on baking sheet(s). Spread each tortilla with 1-2 tablespoons taco sauce just to coat. Combine chicken and taco seasoning in a small bowl and toss until chicken is coated. Scatter chicken over sauce. Sprinkle peppers, tomatoes, and cheese over chicken. Bake in preheated oven 5-7 minutes, until cheese is melted and tortilla is lightly browned. Serve with additional taco sauce, if desired.

Serves: 6

Nutrition per Serving		Exchanges
Calories	230	1 starch
Carbohydrate	30 grams	3 vegetable
Cholesterol	28 milligrams	2 1/2 meat
Dietary Fiber	2 grams	
Fat	< 1 gram	
Protein	26 grams	
Sodium	996 milligrams	

Shopping List: fat-free flour tortillas, 1 1/4 pounds fat-free chicken tenders, taco seasoning mix, 6 ounces fat-free finely shredded Cheddar cheese, canned jalapeño peppers, 1 medium tomato, 6 ounces fat-free taco sauce.

PERFECT PIZZAS

SPINACH-CHEESE CALZONE

EASY - DO AHEAD - FREEZE

ingredients: 1 pound fat-free frozen bread dough, thawed
1 cup fat-free ricotta cheese
16 ounces frozen chopped spinach, thawed and drained
1/2 cup fat-free Parmesan cheese
1 1/2 tsp. onion powder
1 tsp. garlic powder
1 tsp. dried basil
1/4 tsp. pepper
1 tbsp. skim milk

directions: Preheat oven to 375 degrees. Lightly spray 14-inch pizza pan with nonfat cooking spray. Divide bread dough in half; roll each half into 14-inch circle. Pat and dry spinach with paper towels to remove all the water. Combine ricotta cheese, spinach, Parmesan cheese, onion powder, garlic powder, basil, and pepper in a medium bowl; mix well. Spread filling on half of each circle, leaving a 1-inch edge. Lightly moisten edges of dough with water; fold dough and press with fork to seal edges. Prick the top of each calzone with fork in several places. Brush top of calzones lightly with milk. Bake in preheated oven 30-35 minutes, until bread is lightly browned and cooked through.

Serves: 6

Nutrition per Serving		Exchanges
Calories	289	3 vegetable
Carbohydrate	52 grams	2 starch
Cholesterol	7 milligrams	1/2 milk
Dietary Fiber	4 grams	
Fat	< 1 gram	
Protein	19 grams	
Sodium	549 milligrams	

Shopping List: 1 pound fat-frozen bread dough, 8 ounces fat-free ricotta cheese, 16 ounces frozen chopped spinach, 2 ounces fat-free Parmesan cheese, onion powder, garlic powder, basil, pepper, skim milk.

TURKEY-CHEESE CALZONE
AVERAGE - DO AHEAD - FREEZE

ingredients:
2 fat-free pizza crusts
1 lb. fat-free ground turkey
1 tbsp. onion powder
1 tsp. Italian seasoning
28 oz. can Italian-style stewed tomatoes
16 oz. frozen chopped broccoli, thawed and drained
1 cup fat-free mozzarella cheese, finely shredded
1 cup fat-free Cheddar cheese, finely shredded
1/2 cup fat-free Parmesan cheese
1 1/2 tbsp. skim milk
1 1/2 cups fat-free pizza sauce, optional

directions: Preheat oven to 425 degrees. Line baking sheet with foil and lightly spray with nonfat cooking spray. Lightly spray large nonstick skillet with nonfat cooking spray and heat over medium-high heat. Add turkey, onion powder and Italian seasoning; cook, stirring frequently, until turkey is browned and cooked through. Add tomatoes and broccoli; increase heat to high and bring to a boil. Reduce heat; simmer, uncovered, 12-15 minutes until most of the liquid is absorbed. Remove from heat. Roll each crust on lightly floured surface into 10x15-inch rectangle. Cut dough into 8 squares. Divide filling among pizza dough squares. Sprinkle each square with mozzarella and Cheddar cheese. Lightly moisten edges of dough with water; fold dough over and seal well with tines of fork. Arrange calzones on baking sheet(s) and prick tops with tines of fork. Lightly brush tops with skim milk. Bake in preheated oven 10 minutes. Remove from oven and carefully flip calzones. Bake an additional 5-6 minutes until lightly browned. Pour pizza sauce into microwave-safe dish or saucepan; heat until warmed through and serve with calzones, if desired.

Serves: 6

Nutrition per Serving (without sauce)		Exchanges
Calories	484	4 vegetable
Carbohydrate	78 grams	4 starch
Cholesterol	27 milligrams	2 meat
Dietary Fiber	3 grams	
Fat	< 1 gram	
Protein	36 grams	
Sodium	1,929 milligrams	

Shopping List: 1 pound fat-free ground turkey, 28-ounce can Italian-style stewed tomatoes, 16 ounces frozen chopped broccoli, 4 ounces fat-free finely shredded mozzarella cheese, 4 ounces fat-free finely shredded Cheddar cheese, 2 ounces fat-free Parmesan cheese, 12 ounces fat-free pizza sauce (optional), skim milk, Italian seasoning, onion powder, 2 fat-free pizza crusts.

PERFECT PIZZAS

BANANA-BERRY BROWNIE PIZZA

EASY - DO AHEAD

ingredients:
18 oz. package fat-free brownie mix*
1/2 cup hot water
3/4 cup fat-free cream cheese
1/4 cup sugar
1/4 cup egg substitute
1 tsp. vanilla
2 medium bananas, sliced
2 cups sliced strawberries
2 tbsp. lite chocolate syrup

directions:
Preheat oven to 350 degrees. Lightly spray 12-inch pizza pan with nonfat cooking spray. Combine brownie mix and hot water in a large bowl and mix until blended smooth. Spread batter into prepared pan and bake in preheated oven 20-25 minutes, until knife inserted in center comes out clean. Combine cream cheese, sugar, egg substitute, and vanilla in a medium bowl and blend until smooth. Spread mixture over hot crust and bake 8-10 minutes until cheese is set. Remove from oven and let cool completely. Lightly spray plastic wrap with nonfat cooking spray; cover brownie pizza and refrigerate overnight. Just before serving, arrange bananas and strawberries over cheese topping; drizzle with chocolate syrup. Cut into wedges and serve.

*Be sure to choose a brownie mix that only requires water as additional ingredient (i.e. Krusteaz).

Serves: 6

Nutrition per Serving
Calories	437
Carbohydrate	99 grams
Cholesterol	0 milligrams
Dietary Fiber	3 grams
Fat	< 1 gram
Protein	8 grams
Sodium	698 milligrams

Exchanges
2 starch
4 1/2 fruit

Shopping List: 18-ounce package fat-free brownie mix*, 6 ounces fat-free cream cheese, sugar, 2 ounces egg substitute, 2 bananas, 1 pint strawberries, lite chocolate syrup, vanilla.

BERRY CHEESE PIZZA PIE

EASY - DO AHEAD

ingredients: 1 Sweet Pizza Dough*
1 cup fat-free ricotta cheese
1/3 cup sugar, divided
1/2 tsp. vanilla
1/2 tsp. almond extract
1/2 tsp. orange juice
1 cup blueberries
1 cup raspberries
1 cup sliced strawberries
1 tbsp. powdered sugar

directions: Prepare Sweet Pizza Dough according to directions. Preheat oven to 400 degrees. Stretch and roll dough to fit 13-inch pizza pan; press into pan and prick with fork in several places. Sprinkle 1-2 tablespoons sugar over dough and bake in preheated oven 6-8 minutes until lightly browned. Remove from oven and cool completely.

Combine ricotta cheese, sugar, vanilla, almond extract, and orange juice in a small bowl and mix until blended smooth. Spread filling over cooled crust. Top with fresh berries; sprinkle with powdered sugar. Cut into wedges and serve.

Serves: 12

Nutrition per Serving		Exchanges
Calories	206	1/2 milk
Carbohydrate	46 grams	1 starch
Cholesterol	3 milligrams	1 1/3 fruit
Dietary Fiber	2 grams	
Fat	< 1 gram	
Protein	7 grams	
Sodium	236 milligrams	

Shopping List: 8 ounces fat-free ricotta cheese, sugar, 1/2 pint blueberries, 1/2 pint raspberries, 1/2 pint strawberries, vanilla, almond extract, orange juice, powdered sugar - Sweet Pizza Dough* (see recipe, page 3).

PERFECT PIZZAS

213

CHOCOLATE-CHOCOLATE CHIP PIZZA

AVERAGE - DO AHEAD

ingredients:
3/4 cup fat-free cream cheese, softened
3/4 cup Butter Buds, reconstituted, divided
1/4 cup sugar
1/4 cup egg substitute
1/3 cup brown sugar
2 tsp. vanilla, divided
1 1/2 cups flour
1/2 tsp. baking soda
2 tbsp. reduced-fat chocolate chips
2 1/3 cups powdered sugar
1/4 cup unsweetened cocoa powder
2 tbsp. boiling water
colored sprinkles

directions: Preheat oven to 350 degrees. Lightly spray 14-inch pizza pan with nonfat cooking spray. Combine cream cheese, 1/2 cup Butter Buds, sugar, brown sugar, egg substitute, and 1 teaspoon vanilla in a medium bowl and blend until smooth. Add flour and baking soda; mix until all ingredients are blended. Fold in chocolate chips. Spread cookie dough into pizza pan. Bake in preheated oven, 20-25 minutes until lightly browned and cooked through. Cool completely.

Combine powdered sugar, cocoa, 1/4 cup Butter Buds, water and 1 teaspoon vanilla in a medium bowl; mix until blended smooth. Beat with electric mixer on low to medium speed until fluffy. Spread frosting over cooled cookie pizza. Sprinkle colored sprinkles over top. Cut into wedges and serve.

Serves: 12

Nutrition per Serving		Exchanges
Calories	205	1 starch
Carbohydrate	46 grams	2 fruit
Cholesterol	0 milligrams	
Dietary Fiber	< 1 gram	
Fat	< 1 gram	
Protein	4 grams	
Sodium	229 milligrams	

Shopping List: 6 ounces fat-free cream cheese, Butter Buds, sugar, brown sugar, 2 ounces egg substitute, 1 pound powdered sugar, unsweetened cocoa powder, vanilla, baking soda, flour, reduced-fat chocolate chips.

PEACH MELBA
DESSERT PIZZA

AVERAGE - DO AHEAD

ingredients:
1 fat-free thin pizza crust
1 cup fat-free ricotta cheese
1/3 cup sugar
1/2 tsp. almond extract
1/4 tsp. vanilla
1 1/2 cups raspberry-peach slices in juice
3/4 cup raspberries

directions: Preheat oven to 400 degrees. Lightly spray 14-inch pizza pan with nonfat cooking spray. Prepare pizza crust and press into pizza pan. Prick with fork in several places and bake in preheated oven 6-8 minutes. Remove from oven and cool 10 minutes. Drain peaches and reserve 1 tablespoon juice; set aside. Arrange peach slices and raspberries on crust. Combine ricotta cheese, sugar, almond extract, vanilla and reserved peach juice in a medium bowl; mix until blended. Pour sauce over fruit and bake in preheated oven 10-15 minutes until crust is lightly browned.

Serves: 6

Nutrition per Serving

Calories	233
Carbohydrate	47 grams
Cholesterol	7 milligrams
Dietary Fiber	2 grams
Fat	< 1 gram
Protein	10 grams
Sodium	260 milligrams

Exchanges
1 milk
1 starch
1 fruit

Shopping List: 8 ounces fat-free ricotta cheese, 16 ounces raspberry-flavored peach slices, 1/2 pint raspberries, sugar, almond extract, vanilla, 1 fat-free pizza crust.

TROPICAL DESSERT PIZZA

AVERAGE - DO AHEAD

ingredients:
1 large banana, peeled and sliced
3/4 cup pineapple tidbits in juice
2 kiwi fruit, sliced thin
3/4 cup sliced strawberries
1 tbsp. cornstarch
1/2 cup pineapple juice
1/2 cup orange juice
3 tbsp. sugar
1 fat-free thin pizza crust

directions:
Preheat oven to 475 degrees. Lightly spray 14-inch pizza pan with nonfat cooking spray. Prepare pizza crust and press into pan. Prick crust with fork in several places and bake in preheated oven 5-6 minutes until lightly browned. Remove crust from oven and cool slightly. Arrange fruit on crust. Combine cornstarch, pineapple juice, orange juice, and sugar in a medium saucepan; mix well. Cook over medium heat, stirring constantly, until mixture becomes thick. Remove from heat. Pour sauce over fruit and bake pizza 10-15 minutes until lightly browned.

Serves: 6

Nutrition per Serving		Exchanges
Calories	244	2 starch
Carbohydrate	56 grams	1 1/2 fruit
Cholesterol	0 milligrams	
Dietary Fiber	3 grams	
Fat	< 1 gram	
Protein	5 grams	
Sodium	181 milligrams	

Shopping List: 4 ounces pineapple juice, 4 ounces orange juice, 1 banana, 8 ounces pineapple tidbits in juice, 2 kiwi fruit, 1/2 pint strawberries, sugar, cornstarch, fat-free thin pizza crust.

RECIPES FOR

Fat Free Living
Kids Cookbook

by Jyl Steinback

- Food Kids Love
- Super Snacks
- Simple, Fun & Delicious

KIDS COOKING TIPS

In order to enjoy your cooking experience and create some delicious delights, follow the steps to safe cooking.

- Before you start cooking, make sure an adult is close by to help with instructions or preparations. Although you may be able to operate any electrical appliances, it is always safer to have an adult nearby.
- Choose your recipe and read it all the way through. Make sure to ask any questions BEFORE you start preparing the recipe.
- Wear comfortable clothes or an apron...just in case!
- When you are ready to begin, wash your hands in warm, soapy water; rinse and dry on a clean towel.
- Organize all the ingredients and utensils you need to prepare your recipe. Line ingredients up in the order you will use them; this way you cannot leave anything out! Put the ingredient away as soon as you are finished with it so you don't accidentally put it in twice.
- Make sure you have potholders nearby for removing pans from a hot oven or stove.
- When you are cooking on the stove, be sure to turn the pot handle toward the center of the stove and not over another hot burner.
- Turn the oven or stove off immediately when you are finished cooking.
- Thoroughly clean work surface and utensils after preparing meat, fish, or poultry; do not cut any other foods on the same surface before it has been cleaned.
- A time-saving trick is to clean up as you go along; don't wait until you have a sink full of dirty pots, pans, dishes, bowls, etc. You will enjoy your cooking experience much more if the clean-up isn't an exhausting chore!

KEEN
KIDS

BAGEL CRISPS
WITH FRUITY CREAM
CHEESE SPREAD

EASY - DO AHEAD - FREEZE

ingredients: 6 fat-free bagels
1 cup fat-free cream cheese, softened
1/4 cup apricot preserves or any fruit you like
(blackberries, strawberries, etc.)

directions: Preheat oven to 400 degree. Slice each bagel into
three or four thin slices. Arrange slices on baking
sheet and bake 8 minutes; turn slices over and bake
5-8 minutes until crisp. Combine cream cheese
and preserves in food processor or blender; process until blended creamy and smooth. Dip bagel
chips into cheese mixture or spread with knife.

Serves: 6

Nutrition per Serving		Exchanges
Calories	249	2 starch
Carbohydrate	52 grams	1 1/3 fruit
Cholesterol	0 milligrams	1/2 meat
Dietary Fiber	2 grams	
Fat	< 1 gram	
Protein	11 grams	
Sodium	536 milligrams	

Shopping List: 1/2 dozen fat-free bagels, 8 ounces fat-free cream
cheese, 2 ounces apricot preserves.

BLUEBERRY MUFFINS

EASY - DO AHEAD - FREEZE

ingredients:
3 cups flour, divided
1 Tbsp. baking powder
1/2 cup sugar, divided
3/4 cup brown sugar, divided
1/2 cup mixed berry applesauce
1/2 cup egg substitute
1 cup + 1 Tbsp. fat-free blueberry yogurt
1 tsp. vanilla
1 cup frozen blueberries

directions:
Preheat oven to 350 degrees. Lightly spray muffin pan with nonfat cooking spray. Combine 2 1/4 cups flour, baking powder, 1/4 cup sugar and 1/2 cup brown sugar in a large mixing bowl and blend well. Add applesauce, egg substitute, 1 cup yogurt and vanilla to flour mixture and blend until smooth. Fold in blueberries. In a small bowl, combine 3/4 cup flour, 1/4 cup sugar and 1/4 cup brown sugar; mix well. Gradually add 1 tablespoon yogurt to flour mixture and blend just until crumbly. Fill muffin cups with blueberry batter; sprinkle crumb topping on top and bake in preheated oven 20-25 minutes, until knife inserted in center comes out clean.

Serves: 12

Nutrition per Serving		Exchanges
Calories	224	1 2/3 starch
Carbohydrate	51 grams	1 2/3 fruit
Cholesterol	< 1 milligram	
Dietary Fiber	1 gram	
Fat	< 1 gram	
Protein	5 grams	
Sodium	113 milligrams	

Shopping List: flour, sugar, brown sugar, 4 ounces mixed berry applesauce, 4 ounces egg substitute, 9 ounces fat-free blueberry yogurt, 6 ounces frozen blueberries, baking powder, vanilla.

KEEN KIDS

CRAISIN MUFFIN SNACKS

EASY - DO AHEAD - FREEZE

ingredients: 1 1/4 cups flour
1 cup multi-grain oatmeal
1 tbsp. baking powder
1/2 cup + 2 tbsp. sugar, divided
1/4 cup brown sugar
1/2 cup egg substitute
1/2 cup whole berry cranberry sauce
1 cup fat-free vanilla yogurt
1 tsp. vanilla
1 cup Craisins

directions: Preheat oven to 350 degrees. Lightly spray muffin pan with nonfat cooking spray.
In a large bowl, combine flour, oatmeal, baking powder, 1/2 cup sugar and brown sugar; mix until blended. Add egg substitute, cranberry sauce, yogurt and vanilla to flour mixture; blend until dry ingredients are moistened. Fold in Craisins and mix lightly. Fill muffin cups with batter; sprinkle tops with remaining sugar. Bake in pre heated oven 20-25 minutes, until knife inserted in center comes out clean.

Serves: 12

Nutrition per Serving		Exchanges
Calories	187	1 starch
Carbohydrate	44 grams	2 fruit
Cholesterol	0 milligrams	
Dietary Fiber	2 grams	
Fat	< 1 gram	
Protein	4 grams	
Sodium	114 milligrams	

Shopping List: flour, multi-grain oatmeal, baking powder, sugar, brown sugar, 4 ounces egg substitute, 4 ounces whole berry cranberry sauce, 8 ounces fat-free vanilla yogurt, vanilla, Craisins.

FRENCH TOAST CASSEROLE

EASY - DO AHEAD

ingredients: 12 slices fat-free white bread, crusts removed
1 cup egg substitute
2 large egg whites
1 1/2 cups skim milk
1 1/2 tsp. almond extract
1 1/2 tsp. vanilla
1 1/2 tsp. cinnamon
3/4 tsp. nutmeg
2 tbsp. sugar
2 tbsp. brown sugar

directions: Lightly spray a 9x13-inch baking dish with nonfat cooking spray.
Arrange bread in bottom of baking dish.
Combine remaining ingredients in food processor or blender and process until all ingredients are blended. Pour liquid mixture over bread; cover with plastic wrap and refrigerate 1 hour or overnight.
Preheat oven to 350 degrees. Bake casserole 25-30 minutes, until lightly browned and puffy.
Serve with powdered sugar, cinnamon-sugar, jelly, or syrup.

Serves: 8

KEEN KIDS

Nutrition per Serving

Calories	192
Carbohydrate	36 grams
Cholesterol	1 milligram
Dietary Fiber	1 gram
Fat	< 1 gram
Protein	9 grams
Sodium	307 milligrams

Exchanges

2 starch
1/2 milk

Shopping List: 1 loaf fat-free white bread, 8 ounces egg substitute, eggs, 12 ounces skim milk, almond extract, vanilla, cinnamon, nutmeg, sugar, brown sugar.

PANCAKES

EASY - DO AHEAD - FREEZE

ingredients:
1 cup flour
1 tbsp. Butter Buds, reconstituted
1 cup egg substitute
4 large egg whites
2 tbsp. brown sugar
2 tbsp. sugar
1 cup skim milk
3/4 tsp. baking powder
3/4 tsp. vanilla

directions:
Combine flour, brown sugar, sugar and baking powder in a large bowl; mix well.

Combine egg substitute and egg whites in a medium bowl; beat until blended and frothy; add Butter Buds, milk and vanilla; blend until smooth. Add egg mixture to flour mixture and mix until ingredients are blended smooth.

Lightly spray large nonstick skillet with nonfat cooking spray and heat over medium-high heat. Scoop batter out of bowl with 1/4-cup measure and pour into hot skillet. Cook over medium heat until bubbles form on top; carefully flip over with spatula and cook until lightly browned. Remove from skillet and keep warm.

*Batter can also be prepared in food processor or blender, starting with eggs and liquid; add flour mixture at end.

Serves: 6

Nutrition per Serving		Exchanges
Calories	153	1 2/3 starch
Carbohydrate	28 grams	1/2 meat
Cholesterol	1 milligram	
Dietary Fiber	1 gram	
Fat	< 1 gram	
Protein	9 grams	
Sodium	168 milligrams	

Shopping List: flour, Butter Buds, 8 ounces egg substitute, eggs, brown sugar, sugar, 8 ounces skim milk, baking powder, vanilla.

CARROT-PINEAPPLE SURPRISE SALAD

EASY - DO AHEAD

ingredients: 4 cups shredded carrots
8 oz. crushed pineapple in juice, drained
3/4 cup dried mixed fruit, chopped
1 cup fat-free vanilla yogurt
1 tsp. orange juice
2 tbsp. powdered sugar

directions: Combine carrots, pineapple and dried fruit in a large bowl; mix well.
Combine yogurt, orange juice and powdered sugar in a small bowl; mix until blended smooth. Spoon dressing over carrot salad and mix until all ingredients are coated and mixed well. Cover with plastic wrap and refrigerate at least 1 hour before serving.

Serves: 8

Nutrition per Serving
Calories	95
Carbohydrate	23 grams
Cholesterol	< 1 milligram
Dietary Fiber	3 grams
Fat	< 1 gram
Protein	2 grams
Sodium	39 milligrams

Exchanges
1 fruit
1 1/2 vegetable

KEEN KIDS

Shopping List: 2 (8-ounce) packages shredded carrots, 8 ounces crushed pineapple in juice, dried mixed fruit, 8 ounces fat-free vanilla yogurt, orange juice, powdered sugar.

CHICKEN NOODLE SOUP

EASY - DO AHEAD - FREEZE

ingredients:
6 cups fat-free chicken broth
1 tbsp. onion powder
1 1/2 lb. fat-free chicken tenders, cooked and cubed
1 1/2 cups frozen carrot slices, thawed and drained
1 cup sliced celery
1/4 tsp. pepper
6 oz. yolk-free noodles

directions:
Combine chicken broth, onion powder, chicken, carrots, celery and pepper in a large saucepan. Bring to a boil over high heat; reduce heat to medium and cook, stirring occasionally, until carrots and celery are soft and tender (about 5-10 minutes).
Cook noodles according to package directions, rinse with hot water and drain well. Stir hot noodles into soup and mix well. Cook over medium heat 5 minutes.

Serves: 6

Nutrition per Serving

		Exchanges
Calories	234	1 starch
Carbohydrate	27 grams	2 vegetable
Cholesterol	71 milligrams	3 meat
Dietary Fiber	3 grams	
Fat	< 1 gram	
Protein	28 grams	
Sodium	632 milligrams	

Shopping List: 32 ounces fat-free chicken broth, 6 ounces yolk-free noodles, 1 1/2 pounds fat-free chicken tenders, 10 ounces frozen carrot slices, 2 stalks celery, onion powder, pepper.

VEGETABLE SOUP

EASY - DO AHEAD - FREEZE

ingredients: 6 oz. fat-free pasta
6 cups fat-free beef broth
1 1/2 tbsp. onion powder
16 oz. frozen mixed vegetables

directions: Cook pasta according to package directions and drain well.
Combine beef broth and onion powder in a Dutch oven or soup pot and bring to a boil over medium-high heat. Add vegetables and cook over medium-high. Stir in pasta and cook an additional 10-15 minutes until heated through.

Serves: 6

Nutrition per Serving		Exchanges
Calories	158	1 starch
Carbohydrate	32 grams	3 vegetable
Cholesterol	10 milligrams	
Dietary Fiber	4 grams	
Fat	< 1 gram	
Protein	6 grams	
Sodium	326 milligrams	

Shopping List: 6 ounces pasta, 3-14 1/2 ounce cans fat-free beef broth, onion powder, 16 ounces frozen mixed vegetables.

KEEN KIDS

ANGEL HAIR PASTA WITH TOMATO-CHEESE SAUCE

AVERAGE - DO AHEAD

ingredients:
4 cups fat-free angel hair pasta, cooked and drained
2 1/2 cups fat-free pasta sauce
1 1/4 tsp. onion powder
3/4 tsp. garlic powder
3 cups fat-free shredded Cheddar cheese
1/2 cup fat-free Parmesan cheese

directions:
Cook pasta according to package directions and drain well; set aside.
Preheat oven to 350 degrees. Lightly spray a 9x13-inch baking dish with nonfat cooking spray.
Pour pasta sauce into large bowl; sprinkle onion powder and garlic powder over top and mix well. Pour 1/2 cup pasta sauce evenly over bottom of dish. Top with 2 cups pasta; pour 1 cup sauce over top and sprinkle with 1 1/2 cups Cheddar cheese. Place remaining pasta over cheese; top with remaining pasta sauce and Cheddar cheese. Sprinkle Parmesan cheese over top and bake in preheated oven 30-35 minutes, until cheese is lightly browned and casserole is bubbly.

Serves: 6

Nutrition per Serving		Exchanges
Calories	272	2 2/3 starch
Carbohydrate	40 grams	2 meat
Cholesterol	0 milligrams	
Dietary Fiber	1 gram	
Fat	< 1 gram	
Protein	25 grams	
Sodium	920 milligrams	

Shopping List: fat-free angel hair pasta*, 24 ounces fat-free pasta sauce, onion powder, garlic powder, 12 ounces fat-free finely-shredded Cheddar cheese, 2 ounces fat-free Parmesan cheese.

*Tommaso angel hair pasta (1888TOMMASO)

CONFETTI CORN RICE

EASY - DO AHEAD

ingredients: 2 cups fat-free rice*
1 3/4 cups fat-free chicken broth
1 tbsp. onion powder
1 1/2 cups frozen corn kernels, thawed and
    drained
1 cup Tostitos garden salsa

directions: Lightly spray large nonstick skillet with nonfat cooking spray and heat over medium-high heat. Add rice to skillet and cook, stirring occasionally, 2-3 minutes. Pour broth into skillet; sprinkle with onion powder and mix well. Stir in salsa. Reduce heat to low; cover and simmer 10 minutes. Add corn to rice mixture and mix lightly; continue cooking until all liquid is absorbed.
This is great wrapped inside fat-free flour tortillas.

Serves: 4

Nutrition per Serving		Exchanges
Calories	366	3 starch
Carbohydrate	86 grams	5 vegetable
Cholesterol	0 milligrams	
Dietary Fiber	2 grams	
Fat	< 1 gram	
Protein	8 grams	
Sodium	358 milligrams	

Shopping List: fat-free rice (*do not use Minute Rice), 15 ounces fat-free chicken broth, onion powder, 10 ounces frozen corn kernels, 8 ounces Tostitos garden salsa.

GOOD OLD
MACARONI AND CHEESE
AVERAGE - DO AHEAD - FREEZE

ingredients:
10 oz. macaroni
1 1/2 cups skim milk, divided
1 tbsp. cornstarch
1 cup evaporated skim milk
1 tsp. onion powder
1/8 tsp. pepper
3 1/2 cups fat-free shredded Cheddar cheese
fat-free Parmesan cheese (opt.)

directions: Cook macaroni according to package directions; drain well and set aside. Lightly spray a 2-quart casserole with nonfat cooking spray and set aside. Lightly spray a large saucepan with nonfat cooking spray. Combine 2 tablespoons skim milk and cornstarch in a small cup and mix until blended smooth. Pour mixture into saucepan; add remaining skim milk, evaporated milk, onion powder and pepper; cook over medium heat, stirring frequently, until mixture comes to a boil and thickens. Cook and stir over medium heat, 1-2 minutes. Preheat oven to 350 degrees. Remove the saucepan from heat. Gradually add cheese to mixture and mix until completely melted. Add macaroni to cheese mixture and mix well. Spoon mixture into prepared casserole and bake in preheated oven 25-30 minutes until bubbly and heated through. Let stand at room temperature 5-10 minutes before serving. Sprinkle with Parmesan cheese, if desired.

Serves: 6

Nutrition per Serving		Exchanges
Calories	341	3 starch
Carbohydrate	49 grams	2 meat
Cholesterol	3 milligrams	1/2 milk
Dietary Fiber	< 1 gram	
Fat	< 1 gram	
Protein	30 grams	
Sodium	738 milligrams	

Shopping List: 10 ounces macaroni, 12 ounces skim milk, 8 ounces evaporated skim milk, 14 ounces fat-free shredded Cheddar cheese, onion powder, pepper, cornstarch, fat-free Parmesan cheese (optional).

SIMPLE SPAGHETTI

EASY - DO AHEAD - FREEZE

ingredients: 4 cups fat-free frozen beef crumbles - Harvest Burgers
1 tbsp. onion powder
1 tsp. garlic powder
2 cups water
3 cups fat-free pasta sauce
1 tsp. sugar
8 oz. spaghetti
1/2 cup fat-free Parmesan cheese

directions: Lightly spray Dutch oven with nonfat cooking spray and heat over medium-high heat.
Combine beef crumbles, onion powder, garlic powder, water, pasta sauce and sugar in a Dutch oven; mix well. Break spaghetti in Dutch oven and bring to a boil over medium-high heat, stirring frequently. Reduce heat to low, cover, and simmer 15-20 minutes, until spaghetti is tender and sauce is heated through. Just before serving, sprinkle spaghetti with Parmesan cheese.

Serves: 6

Nutrition per Serving		Exchanges
Calories	287	3 vegetable
Carbohydrate	46 grams	2 starch
Cholesterol	0 milligrams	1 1/2 meat
Dietary Fiber	3 grams	
Fat	< 1 gram	
Protein	23 grams	
Sodium	758 milligrams	

Shopping List: 12 ounces fat-free Harvest Burger beef crumbles, onion powder, garlic powder, 24 ounces fat-free pasta sauce (any flavor), sugar, 8 ounces spaghetti, 2 ounces fat-free Parmesan cheese.

KEEN KIDS

BACON-CHEESE
POTATO SKINS

EASY - DO AHEAD

ingredients: 6 medium baking potatoes
3/4 cup fat-free shredded Cheddar cheese
2 tbsp. bacon bits

directions: Wash and dry baking potatoes. Prick with fork in several places. Preheat oven to 450 degrees. Bake potatoes in oven 1 hour or until cooked through. Remove from oven and cook 15 minutes at room temperature. Cut potatoes in half; scoop out pulp, leaving 1/2-inch along edge. (Pulp can be used to make mashed potatoes, if desired.) Cut shells in half again. Line baking sheet with foil and lightly spray with nonfat cooking spray. Arrange potato shells on baking sheet. Sprinkle cheese into shells. Sprinkle 1 teaspoon bacon bits on top of cheese. Bake potato skins 12-15 minutes until cheese is lightly browned and skins are crisp.

Serves: 6

Nutrition per Serving		**Exchanges**
Calories	176	2 1/2 starch
Carbohydrate	35 grams	
Cholesterol	0 milligrams	
Dietary Fiber	4 grams	
Fat	< 1 gram	
Protein	8 grams	
Sodium	203 milligrams	

Shopping List: 6 baking potatoes, 3 ounces fat-free shredded Cheddar cheese, bacon bits

CHILI SLOPPY JOES

EASY - DO AHEAD - FREEZE

ingredients: 4 cups fat-free beef crumbles - Harvest Burgers
1 1/2 tbsp. onion powder
1 tsp. garlic powder
3/4 cup low-sodium ketchup
1/3 cup tomato sauce
2 tsp. chili powder

directions: Combine all ingredients in a large saucepan and bring to a boil over high heat. Reduce heat to low, cover, and simmer 15 minutes. Serve Sloppy Joes on fat-free bread or buns, baked potato or cooked pasta. Sprinkle with fat-free Cheddar cheese, if desired.

Serves: 6

Nutrition per Serving		Exchanges
Calories	110	1 1/2 meat
Carbohydrate	12 grams	2 vegetable
Cholesterol	0 milligrams	
Dietary Fiber	3 grams	
Fat	< 1 gram	
Protein	14 grams	
Sodium	540 milligrams	

Shopping List: 2 pounds Harvest Burgers frozen beef crumbles, onion powder, garlic powder, 6 ounces low-sodium ketchup, 3 ounces tomato sauce, chili powder.

KEEN KIDS

CORN DOG NUGGETS

AVERAGE - DO AHEAD - FREEZE

ingredients:
1 cup flour
1 cup yellow cornmeal
1 1/2 tsp. baking powder
2 tbsp. sugar
1/4 tsp. baking soda
1 tbsp. Butter Buds, reconstituted
3 tbsp. egg substitute
1/2 cup skim milk
6 fat-free hot dogs

directions:
Preheat oven to 375 degrees. Line baking sheet with foil and lightly spray with nonfat cooking spray. Combine flour, cornmeal, baking powder and baking soda in a large bowl; mix well. Add Butter Buds, egg substitute and skim milk to flour mixture and mix until dry ingredients are moistened and blended. Form dough into ball.
Cut each hot dog into 4 equal pieces. Wrap each piece with cornbread dough and seal at ends. Arrange nuggets in a single layer on baking sheets and bake in preheated oven 10-15 minutes, until lightly browned and cooked through.
Serve with mustard, ketchup, barbecue sauce, or fat-free cheese sauce.

Serves: 6

Nutrition per Serving		Exchanges
Calories	230	1/2 meat
Carbohydrate	43 grams	2 2/3 starch
Cholesterol	15 milligrams	
Dietary Fiber	2 grams	
Fat	< 1 gram	
Protein	11 grams	
Sodium	590 milligrams	

Shopping List: flour, yellow cornmeal, baking powder, baking soda, sugar, Butter Buds, egg substitute, skim milk, fat-free hot dogs.

COTTAGE FRIES

EASY - DO AHEAD - FREEZE

ingredients: 20 oz. pkg. Simply Potato potato slices
2 tbsp. garlic salt, divided
fat-free Parmesan cheese, optional

directions: Preheat oven to 400 degrees. Line baking sheet with foil and lightly spray with nonfat cooking spray. Spread potato slices on baking sheet in single layer, slightly overlapping, if necessary. Lightly spray potatoes with cooking spray; sprinkle with 1 tablespoon garlic salt and Parmesan cheese, if desired. Bake in preheated oven, 15 minutes. Remove from oven. Using a spatula, carefully flip potatoes over. Respray with cooking spray and sprinkle with remaining garlic salt. Bake an additional 20-25 minutes, until crisp and lightly browned.

Serves: 6

Nutrition per Serving

Calories	91	
Carbohydrate	21 grams	
Cholesterol	0 milligrams	
Dietary Fiber	2 grams	
Fat	< 1 gram	
Protein	2 grams	
Sodium	1,042 milligrams	

Exchanges

1 1/4 starch

Shopping List: 20-ounce package Simply Potatoes (potato slices), garlic salt.

KEEN KIDS

CRISPY "FRIED" ZUCCHINI STICKS

EASY - DO AHEAD - FREEZE

ingredients:
3 med. zucchini, sliced 1 1/2-inch thick
1 cup instant potato flakes
1/2 cup fat-free Parmesan cheese
1 tsp. garlic powder
1 tsp. onion powder
3 tbsp. reconstituted Butter Buds
1/2 cup egg substitute

directions:
Preheat oven to 400 degrees. Line baking sheet with foil and lightly spray with nonfat cooking spray. Combine instant potatoes, Parmesan cheese, garlic powder and onion powder in a shallow bowl; mix well. Pour egg substitute into shallow bowl and mix lightly. Place several zucchini slices in egg substitute and coat well; roll in potato mixture and coat on all sides. Arrange zucchini slices in a single layer on baking sheet(s). Drizzle zucchini with Butter Buds. Bake in preheated oven 12-15 minutes, until browned and crisp. Serve with fat-free Ranch dressing, fat-free honey-Dijon, or ketchup.

Serves: 6

Nutrition per Serving

Calories	83	
Carbohydrate	15 grams	
Cholesterol	0 milligrams	
Dietary Fiber	2 grams	
Fat	< 1 gram	
Protein	6 grams	
Sodium	139 milligrams	

Exchanges
1/3 starch
2 vegetable

Shopping List: 3 zucchini, instant potato flakes, 2 ounces fat-free Parmesan cheese, 4 ounces egg substitute, Butter Buds, garlic powder, onion powder.

GRILLED BACON-CHEESE SANDWICH

EASY - DO AHEAD

---

ingredients: 12 slices fat-free bread
12 slices fat-free American cheese slices
6 slices fat-free turkey bacon, cooked and
drained
mustard, ketchup, or barbecue sauce, optional

directions: Lightly spray nonstick skillet with nonfat cooking spray and heat over medium heat. To make sandwiches: lay 8 slices bread on flat surface (countertop). Place 2 slices cheese on bread; top with bacon and remaining bread slices. Lightly spray top of sandwich with cooking spray and place sprayed-side down in skillet. Cook over medium heat 2-3 minutes until bread is lightly browned on bottom. Using spatula, carefully flip sandwich over, and cook until cheese is melted and bread is lightly browned. Serve immediately, with mustard, ketchup or barbecue sauce, if desired.

Serves: 6

Nutrition per Serving		Exchanges
Calories	271	3 meat
Carbohydrate	34 grams	2 starch
Cholesterol	15 milligrams	
Dietary Fiber	2 grams	
Fat	< 1 gram	
Protein	25 grams	
Sodium	880 milligrams	

Shopping List: 1 loaf fat-free bread, 12 ounces fat-free American cheese slices, fat-free turkey bacon

OVEN-FRIED CHICKEN TENDERS

EASY - DO AHEAD - FREEZE

ingredients:
1 1/2 lb. fat-free chicken tenders
1/2 cup flour
1/2 tsp. onion powder
1/2 tsp. garlic powder
1/4 cup fat-free Parmesan cheese
1 1/2 cups cornflake crumbs
1/2 cup egg substitute

directions:
Preheat oven to 375 degrees. Line baking sheets with foil. Lightly spray with nonfat cooking spray. In a small bowl, combine flour, onion powder and garlic powder; mix well.
Combine Parmesan cheese and cornflake crumbs in pie plate; mix well.
Pour egg substitute into shallow dish.
Roll chicken tenders in flour mixture until coated on all sides; dip chicken in egg substitute and roll in cornflake crumb mixture until completely coated. Arrange chicken tenders in a single layer on prepared sheets, and bake in preheated oven 25-30 minutes, until golden brown and cooked through.

Serves: 6

Nutrition per Serving

Calories	239
Carbohydrate	26 grams
Cholesterol	71 milligrams
Dietary Fiber	< 1 gram
Protein	29 grams
Sodium	570 milligrams

Exchanges
1 2/3 starch
3 meat

Shopping List: 1 1/2 pounds fat-free chicken tenders, flour, onion powder, garlic powder, 1 ounce fat-free Parmesan cheese, cornflake crumbs, 4 ounces egg substitute.

SOFT TURKEY TACOS
EASY - DO AHEAD

ingredients:
1 lb. fat-free ground turkey
1 1/4 oz. taco seasoning mix
2 cups shredded lettuce
1 1/2 cups canned chopped tomatoes, drained
1 cup fat-free shredded Cheddar cheese
6 fat-free flour tortillas (8-inch)
3/4 cup fat-free salsa

directions:
Lightly spray large nonstick skillet with nonfat cooking spray and heat over medium-high heat. Add turkey to skillet and cook, stirring frequently, until turkey is cooked through and crumbled. Sprinkle taco seasoning mix over turkey and mix well. Pour 3/4 cup water into skillet and mix; bring to a boil over high heat. Immediately reduce heat to low, cover and simmer 10 minutes until heated through. Preheat oven to 350 degrees. Wrap tortillas in foil; warm in oven 3-5 minutes, just until heated and soft. Remove tortillas from oven. Spoon turkey mixture down center of tortilla; top with lettuce, tomatoes, cheese and salsa. Roll tortillas, or fold in half, and serve.

Serves: 6

KEEN KIDS

Nutrition per Serving
Calories	249
Carbohydrate	35 grams
Cholesterol	27 milligrams
Dietary Fiber	3 grams
Fat	< 1 gram
Protein	21 grams
Sodium	2113 milligrams

Exchanges
2 starch
1 vegetable
2 meat

Shopping List: 1 pound fat-free ground turkey, 1 1/4 ounce taco seasoning mix, 8-ounce package shredded lettuce, 16-ounce can chopped tomatoes, 4 ounces fat-free shredded Cheddar cheese, 8-inch fat-free tortillas, 6 ounces fat-free salsa.

CARAMEL CORN
EASY - DO AHEAD

ingredients: 6 cups air-popped popcorn
1/2 cup brown sugar
1/4 cup Butter Buds
2 tbsp. corn syrup
1/4 tsp. vanilla
1/4 tsp. baking soda

directions: Preheat oven to 200 degrees. Lightly spray a 9x13-inch baking dish with nonfat cooking spray. Place cooked popcorn in baking dish. Lightly spray medium saucepan with nonfat cooking spray; combine brown sugar, Butter Buds, corn syrup and vanilla in saucepan and cook over medium heat, stirring frequently, until mixture begins to boil. Cook, stirring frequently, 3-5 minutes until mixture thickens. Remove saucepan from heat; stir in baking soda and mix well. Pour caramel mixture over popcorn and mix well. Bake in preheated oven 15-20 minutes; cool completely and serve.

Serves: 6

Nutrition per Serving		**Exchanges**
Calories	118	2/3 fruit
Carbohydrate	28 grams	1 starch
Cholesterol	0 milligrams	
Dietary Fiber	< 1 gram	
Fat	< 1 gram	
Protein	1 gram	
Sodium	101 milligrams	

Shopping List: popcorn, brown sugar, Butter Buds, corn syrup, vanilla, baking soda.

CHUNKY CHERRY OATMEAL SNACK BARS

EASY - DO AHEAD - FREEZE

ingredients:
1 1/2 cups flour
3/4 cup multi-grain oatmeal
1 tsp. baking powder
1/2 cup + 1 1/2 tbsp. brown sugar
1/2 cup sugar
2 tbsp. fat-free cherry yogurt
1/2 cup mixed berry applesauce
1/4 cup egg substitute
1 1/2 tsp. vanilla
1 cup chunky cinnamon applesauce
3/4 cup dried cherries

directions:
Preheat oven to 350 degrees. Lightly spray a 9x13-inch baking dish with nonfat cooking spray. In a large bowl, combine sugar, 1/2 cup brown sugar, yogurt, berry applesauce, egg substitute and vanilla; blend until smooth. Add flour, oatmeal and baking powder to bowl; mix until ingredients are completely blended. Spread half the batter evenly into prepared baking dish. In a small bowl, combine chunky applesauce, 1 1/2 tablespoons brown sugar, and cherries; mix well. Spoon cherry filling over batter and spread evenly. Top with remaining batter, spreading evenly. Bake in preheated oven 25-30 minutes, until lightly browned and cooked through. Remove from oven and cool at room temperature 10-15 minutes. Cut into squares.

Serves: 16

Nutrition per Serving		Exchanges
Calories	140	1 starch
Carbohydrate	33 grams	1 fruit
Cholesterol	0 milligrams	
Dietary Fiber	1 gram	
Fat	< 1 gram	
Protein	2 grams	
Sodium	35 milligrams	

Shopping List: flour, multi-grain oatmeal, baking powder, brown sugar, sugar, fat-free cherry yogurt, 4 ounces mixed berry applesauce, 2 ounces egg substitute, vanilla, 8 ounces chunky cinnamon applesauce, dried cherries.

COLORFUL CRISPIE TREATS

EASY - DO AHEAD

ingredients: 3 tbsp. Butter Buds, reconstituted
1 tbsp. low-fat margarine
10 oz. marshmallows
6 cups Rice Krispies
1 cup Amazin' Fruit Gummy Bears or mini
jellybeans (40 large)

directions: Lightly spray 9x13-inch baking dish with nonfat cooking spray. Lightly spray Dutch oven with nonfat cooking spray. Add Butter Buds and margarine to pan and cook over low heat until margarine is melted. Add marshmallows and cook, stirring constantly, until marshmallows are completely melted. Remove pan from heat; stir in cereal and candies. Pat mixture into prepared baking dish and let stand at room temperature until completely set.

Serves: 24

Nutrition per Serving		Exchanges
Calories	78	1 1/3 fruit
Carbohydrate	20 grams	
Cholesterol	0 milligrams	
Dietary Fiber	0 grams	
Fat	< 1 gram	
Protein	1 gram	
Sodium	105 milligrams	

Shopping List: Butter Buds, low-fat margarine, 10 ounces marshmallows, Rice Krispies, Amazin' Fruit Gummy Bears or mini jellybeans.

FRUIT-FILLED FUN CONE

EASY - DO AHEAD

ingredients: 6 waffle bowls
1 cup sliced bananas
1 cup blueberries
3/4 cup mandarin oranges in juice, drained
1 cup sliced strawberries
3/4 cup grapes
2 tbsp. honey
2 tbsp. fat-free granola

directions: Combine all the fruit in a large bowl and toss until mixed. Sprinkle granola over fruit and mix lightly. Divide fruit filling among waffle bowls and fill almost to top. Drizzle 1 teaspoon honey over fruit and serve.

Serves: 6

Nutrition per Serving		Exchanges
Calories	143	2 1/2 fruit
Carbohydrate	36 grams	
Cholesterol	0 milligrams	
Dietary Fiber	2 grams	
Fat	< 1 gram	
Protein	1 gram	
Sodium	33 milligrams	

Shopping List: waffle bowls, 2 bananas, 1/2 pint blueberries, 8 ounces mandarin oranges in juice, 1/2 pint strawberries, 1/2 pound grapes, honey, fat-free granola.

KEEN KIDS

FRUIT KABOBS WITH HONEY YOGURT DIP

ingredients:
1/2 cup fat-free vanilla yogurt
1 tbsp. honey
1 tbsp. pine-orange banana juice (Dole)
1 large banana, cut into 8 slices
1 cup fresh strawberries, stems removed
1 cup pineapple chunks in juice, drained

directions:
Combine yogurt, honey and juice in a small bowl; mix until creamy and smooth. Refrigerate 1 hour before serving. Alternate bananas, strawberries and pineapple chunks on wooden skewers. Serve fruit kabobs with yogurt dip.

Serves: 4

Nutrition per Serving		Exchanges
Calories	108	1 2/3 fruit
Carbohydrate	27 grams	
Cholesterol	< 1 milligram	
Dietary Fiber	2 grams	
Fat	< 1 gram	
Protein	2 grams	
Sodium	20 milligrams	

Shopping List: 4 ounces fat-free vanilla yogurt, honey, pine-orange banana juice (Dole), 1 large banana, 1/2 pint strawberries, 8 ounces pineapple chunks in juice.

KEEN KIDS

MINI SNACK PIZZAS

EASY - DO AHEAD - FREEZE

ingredients: 8 fat-free crumpets
1 cup fat-free pasta sauce
2 tbsp. chopped black olives
1 cup fat-free Mozzarella cheese, finely
shredded

directions: Preheat oven to 425 degrees. Line baking sheet
with foil and lightly spray with nonfat cooking
spray. Toast crumpets in toaster oven or toaster
until lightly browned. Arrange crumpets in a single
layer on baking sheet. Top each crumpet with 2
tablespoons pasta sauce, 1 1/2 teaspoons olives
and 2 tablespoons cheese. Bake in preheated oven,
5-7 minutes, until cheese is completely melted.

Serves: 6

Nutrition per Serving		Exchanges
Calories	125	1 meat
Carbohydrate	19 grams	1 starch
Cholesterol	0 milligrams	1/2 vegetable
Dietary Fiber	1 gram	
Fat	< 1 gram	
Protein	9 grams	
Sodium	497 milligrams	

Shopping List: 12-ounce package fat-free crumpets, 8 ounces
fat-free pasta sauce, 4-ounce can chopped black
olives, 4 ounces fat-free Mozzarella cheese (finely
shredded).

KEEN KIDS

NACHOS

EASY

ingredients: 8 oz. fat-free pasteurized processed cheese
1 cup fat-free salsa, divided
1 1/2 tbsp. onion powder
48 low-fat tortilla chips
chopped green chilies, optional

directions: Lightly spray medium saucepan with nonfat cooking spray. Add cheese, 1/3 cup salsa and onion powder to pan and mix lightly. Cook cheese mixture, stirring constantly with a wooden spoon, over very low heat, until cheese is melted and ingredients are blended. Arrange tortilla chips on platter; spoon cheese sauce over top. Top nachos with chopped green chilies or salsa, if desired.

Serves: 6

Nutrition per Serving		Exchanges
Calories	194	1 meat
Carbohydrate	26 grams	1 starch
Cholesterol	1 milligram	2 vegetable
Dietary Fiber	1 gram	
Fat	< 1 gram	
Protein	13 grams	
Sodium	798 milligrams	

Shopping List: 8 ounces fat-free pasteurized processed cheese, 8 ounces fat-free salsa, onion powder, low-fat tortilla chips, chopped green chilies.

TROPICAL FRUIT
YOGURT POPSICLES

EASY - DO AHEAD - FREEZE

---

ingredients: 2 cups fat-free strawberry yogurt
1/2 cup crushed pineapple in juice, drained
6 ounces pine-orange banana concentrate,
thawed

directions: Combine all ingredients in a bowl and mix until blended. Pour mixture into paper cups and freeze 30-45 minutes until mixture thickens. Insert wooden sticks in center of cup. Freeze popsicles 4-6 hours until frozen solid. Peel paper from popsicle and serve.

Serves: 6

Nutrition per Serving		Exchanges
Calories	88	1/2 milk
Carbohydrate	19 grams	3/4 fruit
Cholesterol	2 milligrams	
Dietary Fiber	< 1 gram	
Fat	< 1 gram	
Protein	3 grams	
Sodium	48 milligrams	

KEEN KIDS

Shopping List: 16 ounces fat-free strawberry yogurt, 8 ounces crushed pineapple in juice, 6 ounces pine-orange banana concentrate.

CHOCOLATE CHIP COOKIES
EASY - DO AHEAD - FREEZE

ingredients:
1/4 cup Butter Buds, reconstituted
1/4 cup corn syrup
1/4 cup egg substitute
3/4 tsp. vanilla
1/2 cup sugar
1/2 cup brown sugar
1 3/4 cups flour
1/2 tsp. baking powder
1/4 tsp. baking soda
6 tbsp. reduced-fat chocolate chips

directions:
Preheat oven to 350 degrees. Lightly spray cookie sheet(s) with nonfat cooking spray.
Combine flour, baking powder, baking soda and sugar in a large mixing bowl; stir until all ingredients are blended.
Combine Butter Buds, corn syrup, egg substitute, vanilla and brown sugar in a food processor or blender, and process until mixture is creamy and smooth. Pour butter mixture into flour mixture and stir until all ingredients are blended. Fold in chocolate chips. Drop dough by rounded tablespoons onto cookie sheet and bake in preheated oven 10-15 minutes until lightly browned.

Serves: 24

Nutrition per Serving
Calories	93
Carbohydrate	21 grams
Cholesterol	0 milligrams
Dietary Fiber	< 1 gram
Fat	< 1 gram
Protein	1 gram
Sodium	37 milligrams

Exchanges
1 1/3 fruit

Shopping List: 2 ounces Butter Buds, 2 ounces corn syrup, 2 ounces egg substitute, vanilla, sugar, brown sugar, flour, baking powder, baking soda, reduced-fat chocolate chips.

CHOCOLATE CHIP GRAHAMWICHES

EASY - DO AHEAD - FREEZE

ingredients: 12 fat-free graham crackers
1 1/2 cups fat-free chocolate chips frozen
    yogurt, softened
3 tbsp. decors (colored sprinkles, etc.)

directions: Lay 6 graham cracker squares on flat surface. Spread 2-3 tablespoons frozen yogurt on each square. Top with remaining graham crackers. Pour decors in shallow dish; press sides of "sandwich" into decors to coat. Arrange sandwiches in a single layer on baking sheet and freeze 1-2 hours. Remove from freezer; wrap each sandwich in plastic wrap and freeze until firm.

Serves: 6

Nutrition per Serving		Exchanges
Calories	70	1 starch
Carbohydrate	15 grams	
Cholesterol	0 milligrams	
Dietary Fiber	1 gram	
Fat	< 1 gram	
Protein	3 grams	
Sodium	37 milligrams	

Shopping List: fat-free graham crackers, 12 ounces fat-free frozen chocolate chip yogurt, decors (sprinkles, colored sugar, etc.)

KEEN KIDS

CHOCOLATE CHOCOLATE CHIP BROWNIES

AVERAGE - DO AHEAD - FREEZE

ingredients:
1 cup flour
3/4 tsp. baking powder
1 cup brown sugar
3/4 cup sugar
3/4 cup unsweetened cocoa powder
3/4 cup + 2 tbsp. egg substitute
2/3 cup applesauce
1/4 cup fat-free vanilla yogurt
1 tsp. vanilla
7 tbsp. reduced-fat chocolate chips

directions:
Preheat oven to 350 degrees. Lightly spray a 9x13-inch baking dish with nonfat cooking spray.
In a large bowl, combine flour, baking powder, brown sugar, sugar and cocoa; mix until all ingredients are blended. Add egg substitute, applesauce, yogurt and vanilla; mix until dry ingredients are moistened and blended smooth. Fold in chocolate chips and mix well. Spread batter into prepared pan and bake in preheated oven, 25-30 minutes, until knife inserted in center comes out clean. Remove from oven and cool completely. Sprinkle with powdered sugar and cut into bars.

Serves: 36

Nutrition per Serving		Exchanges
Calories	72	1 fruit
Carbohydrate	17 grams	
Cholesterol	< 1 milligram	
Dietary Fiber	< 1 gram	
Fat	< 1 gram	
Protein	1 gram	
Sodium	18 milligrams	

Shopping List: brown sugar, sugar, unsweetened cocoa powder, flour, baking powder, 7 ounces egg substitute, vanilla, 5 ounces applesauce, 2 ounces fat-free vanilla yogurt, reduced-fat chocolate chips, powdered sugar.

GRANOLA RAISIN COOKIES

EASY - DO AHEAD - FREEZE

ingredients:
1 cup flour
3 cups fat-free granola
2 tsp. cinnamon
1 tsp. nutmeg
1 1/2 tbsp. baking powder
1/2 cup egg substitute
3/4 cup brown sugar
1/4 cup sugar
1 tbsp. cinnamon applesauce
1 tbsp. corn syrup
2 tbsp. vanilla
1/2 cup raisins
1/4 cup cinnamon-sugar blend

directions:
Preheat oven to 350 degrees. Line cookie sheets with foil and lightly spray with nonfat cooking spray.
In a large bowl, combine flour, granola, cinnamon, nutmeg and baking powder; mix well. Add egg substitute, brown sugar, sugar, applesauce, corn syrup and vanilla; mix until all ingredients are blended. Fold in raisins. Drop batter by rounded tablespoons onto cookie sheets and sprinkle with cinnamon-sugar blend; bake in preheated oven, 10-12 minutes, until lightly browned. Let cool 5 minutes; remove to wire rack or platter with spatula.

Serves: 24

KEEN KIDS

Nutrition per Serving

Calories	114	
Carbohydrate	27 grams	
Cholesterol	0 milligrams	
Dietary Fiber	1 gram	
Fat	< 1 gram	
Protein	2 grams	
Sodium	73 milligrams	

Exchanges
2/3 starch
1 fruit

Shopping List: 4 ounces egg substitute, brown sugar, sugar, cinnamon-applesauce, corn syrup, vanilla, flour, fat-free granola, baking powder, cinnamon, nutmeg, raisins, cinnamon-sugar blend.

VANILLA CUPCAKES

EASY - DO AHEAD - FREEZE

ingredients: 1 cup fat-free ricotta cheese
1/4 cups + 2 tbsp. egg substitute, divided
1 2/3 cup flour
1/2 tsp. baking powder
3/4 cup fat-free vanilla yogurt
1 1/4 cups sugar, divided
2 tsp. vanilla, divided
1/2 tsp. baking soda
1/2 cup lite applesauce

directions: Preheat oven to 350 degrees. Lightly spray muffin pan with nonfat cooking spray. Combine ricotta cheese, 1/4 cup sugar, 2 tablespoons egg substitute and 1 teaspoon vanilla in a medium mixing bowl and blend until smooth; set aside. You can combine these ingredients in a blender or food processor and process until smooth. Combine flour, 1 cup sugar, baking soda and baking powder in a large mixing bowl and mix well. Add 1/4 cup egg substitute, yogurt, applesauce and 1 teaspoon vanilla; mix until dry ingredients are moistened and batter is blended. Spoon half the batter into muffin cups. Spoon 1 1/2 tablespoons cheese filling over batter. Top with remaining batter. Bake in preheated oven 20-25 minutes, until knife inserted in center comes out clean. Remove cupcakes from oven and let cool 5-10 minutes at room temperature. Carefully remove cupcakes and place on wire rack or large platter.

Serves: 12

Nutrition per Serving

		Exchanges
Calories	168	1/2 milk
Carbohydrate	37 grams	1 starch
Cholesterol	4 milligrams	1 fruit
Dietary Fiber	1 gram	
Fat	< 1 gram	
Protein	6 grams	
Sodium	105 milligrams	

Shopping List: flour, sugar, 3 ounces egg substitute, 6 ounces fat-free vanilla yogurt, 4 ounces lite applesauce, 8 ounces fat-free ricotta cheese, baking soda, baking powder, vanilla.

CREAMY CHOCOLATE SHAKE

EASY

ingredients:
1 cup fat-free chocolate frozen yogurt
1 cup skim milk
2 tbsp. lite chocolate syrup
1 cup crushed ice

directions:
Combine all ingredients in a blender and process until creamy and smooth.

Serves: 2

Nutrition per Serving		Exchanges
Calories	154	1 milk
Carbohydrate	30 grams	1 fruit
Cholesterol	2 milligrams	
Dietary Fiber	< 1 gram	
Fat	< 1 gram	
Protein	8 grams	
Sodium	128 milligrams	

Shopping List: 8 ounces fat-free chocolate frozen yogurt, 8 ounces skim milk, 1 ounce lite chocolate syrup.

*To make a vanilla shake, substitute:
1 cup fat-free frozen vanilla yogurt and 1 tbsp. vanilla, and combine all ingredients.

KEEN KIDS

STRAWBERRY-BANANA PROTEIN SHAKE

EASY

---

ingredients:
1 cup cold skim milk
1/2 of 3 oz. package strawberry-banana
    sugar-free Jell-O
1/2 scoop protein powder
1 cup fat-free banana yogurt
6 ice cubes
1 large banana
3/4 cup frozen strawberries

directions:
Pour milk into blender or food processor. Add remaining ingredients and process until blended creamy and smooth.

Serves: 2

Nutrition per Serving

		Exchanges
Calories	253	1 milk
Carbohydrate	51 grams	1 starch
Cholesterol	5 milligrams	1 2/3 fruit
Dietary Fiber	3 grams	
Fat	< 1 gram	
Protein	13 grams	
Sodium	501 milligrams	

Shopping List: 8 ounces skim milk, 3 ounces sugar-free strawberry-banana Jell-O, protein powder*, 8 ounces fat-free banana yogurt, 1 large banana, 6 ounces frozen strawberries.

*Protein powder can be found in most supermarkets (in health food section) or health food stores. Shake can be prepared without protein powder, if desired.

FAT FREE LIVING® TREMENDOUS TEENS COOKBOOK

- Scrumptious Snacks
- Fabulous Fast Foods
- Tasty Treats

TEEN TIPS FOR
HEALTHY LIVING

Teenagers in today's society know far more about nutrition than teens 25 or 30 years ago. However, this does not mean they take advantage of such knowledge and often consume too much fat and too few nutrients. Teens require a healthy diet in order to perform well in school, athletics, or other extracurricular activities. Most teens run short on sleep, energy, and nutrients. Breakfast is a quick drive-thru or completely overlooked; lunch is whatever is available and appealing (usually French fries, sweets, soda), and dinner is hit or miss, depending on activity schedules. This leaves a lot of the pressure on parents to guide their teens in the right direction. Learning definitely begins at home where parents set the best example for healthy living. The recipes in this book were based on questionnaires given to teens (ages 12-18). Great ideas for fast food substitutions, quick breakfasts on the run, as well as sweet and satisfying snacks. These are recipes for healthy living, not DIET-ING. Here are a few tips to encourage your teens to start living healthy NOW -- the results will be a happy, healthy, energized teen!

- Teens are easily influenced by what they see, what they hear, and what others are doing. Learning to live healthy begins at home! Make it fun, challenging, and a family affair. Encourage your teen to participate in meal planning, shopping, and preparation. This puts some of the control in their hands!
- Teach teens how to read labels -- it may take awhile, but it soon becomes a game. Some of the foods they thought were so healthy are quite deceiving. My daughter picked up a bag of popcorn thinking this was a healthy choice and she quickly threw it back when she saw there were 18 GRAMS of FAT in a single serving bag!
- DO NOT BAN certain foods -- forbidden foods only become more desirable. I have seen kids who are denied certain foods at home and lose control when no one is watching.
- Teens tend to think about foods as "good" or "bad". There is no such thing! The answer is to teach CHOICES. There are mediocre, good, better, and best choices and the key is how they are consumed throughout the day. Let the teens take control of their own choices as you guide them in the right direction -- just don't PUSH!

- Keep healthy snacks on hand so they are less likely to reach for a mediocre choice. Fresh fruit, cut-up vegetables, frozen fruit bars, fat-free chips with salsa, bagels, sliced turkey and fat-free cheese -- the choices are endless.
- When your teen is craving a hot fudge sundae from Ben & Jerry's, you may want to suggest an alternative but don't forbid a sweet treat. Casually give them some nutrition facts such as: 4 ounces ice cream + 2 tablespoons hot fudge sauce + 2 tablespoons whipped cream = 426 calories, 24 grams of fat (48% calories from fat). Add 1 tablespoon chopped nuts and the nutritional value jumps to 481 calories and 29 grams of fat (51% calories from fat). Now would they still choose the splurge when they could have 4 ounces fat-free frozen yogurt or ice cream + 2 tablespoons lite chocolate syrup + 2 tablespoons fat-free Cool Whip = 263 calories, 0 grams of fat!
- Remember FAT-FREE does not mean CALORIE-FREE! A box of fat-free chocolate cookie snacks or a bag of fat-free pretzel nuggets can pack on an abundance of calories in a hurry. Encourage portion control.
- Encourage activity! Exercise should become a habit just as healthy eating habits. It's not always easy to get started, so encourage an activity they really enjoy. Most health clubs have reduced membership rates for teens. This is a great after-school activity where teens cans workout and socialize at the same time. They can have fun and reap the benefits of exercise without even trying too hard!

In today's fast-paced world we all get caught up in going for what's easy, quick and affordable. A bit of information + a bit of extra effort + a bit of physical activity = a healthy living habit!

CINNAMON RAISIN GRANOLA

EASY - DO AHEAD

ingredients: 1/2 cup corn syrup, divided
2 tbsp. orange juice
1 tsp. cinnamon
1 1/2 cups raisins
2 1/4 cups Quaker multi-grain oatmeal

directions: Preheat oven to 325 degrees. Line a baking sheet or jellyroll pan with foil and lightly spray with nonfat cooking spray. Combine 1/4 cup corn syrup, orange juice, cinnamon and raisins in a small saucepan and cook over medium heat, stirring frequently, until heated through. Spread oatmeal on baking sheet. Pour remaining corn syrup over oatmeal and toss lightly until coated. Bake in preheated oven, 15-20 minutes until lightly browned. Remove from oven; pour cooked fruit sauce over oatmeal and toss until coated. Spread mixture into even layer. Bake 20-25 minutes, stirring 3-4 times, until mixture is crisp and golden brown. Remove from oven and cool completely at room temperature; store in airtight container.

Substitute dried fruit for raisins or honey for corn syrup. Great in the morning mixed with 6 ounces fat-free flavored yogurt or sprinkle 1/4 cup over fat-free frozen yogurt for dessert.

Serves: 8

Nutrition per Serving		Exchanges
Calories	217	1 1/3 starch
Carbohydrate	54 grams	2 fruit
Cholesterol	0 milligrams	
Dietary Fiber	4 grams	
Fat	< 1 gram	
Protein	4 grams	
Sodium	24 milligrams	

Shopping List: 4 ounces corn syrup, orange juice, Quaker multi-grain oatmeal, raisins, cinnamon.

CREAMY DREAMY BANANA BOWL

EASY - DO AHEAD

ingredients: 2 large bananas, sliced
3/4 cup fat-free banana yogurt
1 1/2 tbsp. brown sugar
1/2 tsp. cinnamon
1/2 cup fat-free granola

directions: Combine yogurt, sugar and cinnamon in a medium bowl and mix until sugar is dissolved and ingredients are blended. Add bananas to yogurt mixture and toss until well coated. Sprinkle with fat-free granola and serve for breakfast, snack or dessert.

Serves: 4

Nutrition per Serving		Exchanges
Calories	124	2 fruit
Carbohydrate	30 grams	
Cholesterol	1 milligram	
Dietary Fiber	1 gram	
Fat	< 1 gram	
Protein	3 grams	
Sodium	30 milligrams	

Shopping List: 2 large bananas, 6 ounces fat-free banana yogurt, brown sugar, cinnamon, fat-free granola.

FRENCH TOAST STICKS

EASY - DO AHEAD - FREEZE

ingredients: 8 slices fat-free French bread, cut 1-inch thick
1/2 cup egg substitute
4 large egg whites
3 tbsp. skim milk
1 tbsp. vanilla extract
1 1/2 tsp. cinnamon
lite syrup, powdered sugar, or preserves

directions: Lightly spray large nonstick skillet with nonfat cooking spray and heat over medium-high heat. Cut bread into 1-inch-thick sticks, about 3 inches long. Combine egg substitute, egg whites, milk, vanilla and cinnamon in medium bowl; mix until completely blended. Dip bread sticks into egg mixture and coat well. Cook over medium heat until browned and crisp on all sides. Remove from skillet; wrap in foil and keep warm while preparing remaining bread sticks. Serve with lite syrup, powdered sugar, or fruit preserves.

Serves: 4

Nutrition per Serving		Exchanges
Calories	216	2 1/3 starch
Carbohydrate	37 grams	1 meat
Cholesterol	< 1 milligram	
Dietary Fiber	2 grams	
Fat	< 1 gram	
Protein	12 grams	
Sodium	405 milligrams	

Shopping List: 1/2 pound fat-free French bread, 4 ounces egg substitute, eggs, skim milk, vanilla, cinnamon (lite syrup, powdered sugar, or preserves).

TREMENDOUS TEENS

FRUITY PANCAKES

EASY - DO AHEAD - FREEZE

ingredients:
1 1/3 cups flour
2 tbsp. sugar
2 tsp. baking powder
1/4 cup egg substitute
1 cup fat-free vanilla yogurt
1/4 cup mixed berry applesauce
1/2 cup blueberries
3/4 cup sliced strawberries
1/2 cup sliced banana
2 tbsp. brown sugar

directions: Combine flour, sugar and baking powder in a medium bowl; mix well. Combine egg substitute, yogurt, and applesauce in separate bowl; mix until blended smooth and creamy. Add to flour mixture and stir just until dry ingredients are moistened. Combine blueberries, strawberries and banana in a small bowl and mix well. Add 1 cup fruit mixture to pancake batter and mix lightly. Preheat oven to 200 degrees. Line baking sheet with foil and set aside. Lightly spray large nonstick skillet with nonfat cooking spray and heat over medium-high heat. Using 1/4-cup measuring cup, pour batter into hot skillet. Cook 3-4 minutes until pancakes begin to brown on the bottom and bubble on the top. Carefully flip pancakes with spatula and cook until golden brown. Place cooked pancakes on baking sheet and keep warm in oven while preparing remaining batter. Combine remaining fruit and brown sugar in a food processor or blender; process until blended smooth. Serve fruit sauce with pancakes.

Serves: 4

Nutrition per Serving

		Exchanges
Calories	269	2 2/3 starch
Carbohydrate	58 grams	1 fruit
Cholesterol	1 milligram	
Dietary Fiber	3 grams	
Fat	< 1 gram	
Protein	8 grams	
Sodium	224 milligrams	

Shopping List: flour, 2 ounces egg substitute, 2 ounces mixed berry applesauce, 8 ounces fat-free vanilla yogurt, blueberries, strawberries, banana, baking powder, brown sugar.

TREMENDOUS TEENS

PITA POCKET
CHEESE OMELET
EASY - DO AHEAD

---

ingredients:

2 large egg whites
1 cup egg substitute
2 tbsp. skim milk
1/4 tsp. pepper
1/4 cup fat-free Cheddar cheese, finely shredded
2 fat-free pita pockets

directions:

Combine egg whites, egg substitute, milk and pepper in a medium bowl and whisk until blended and frothy. Lightly spray large nonstick skillet with nonfat cooking spray; heat over medium-high heat. Pour egg mixture into skillet and cook without stirring until eggs are set on bottom. Using spatula, lift eggs so the runny part flows underneath and cook until eggs are almost set. Sprinkle cheese on half the omelet; fold in half and cook over medium heat until cheese is completely melted. Wrap pitas in foil and heat in 350 degree oven 5-6 minutes, until soft and warm (or wrap in paper towels and heat in microwave 30-45 seconds). Carefully break omelet and stuff into pita pockets.

Add fat-free turkey, chicken, ham, or chopped vegetables to omelet when set; fold in half and cook until heated through.

Serves: 2

Nutrition per Serving

Calories	200
Carbohydrate	25 grams
Cholesterol	< 1 milligram
Dietary Fiber	1 gram
Fat	< 1 gram
Protein	22 grams
Sodium	578 milligrams

Exchanges

1 2/3 starch
2 meat

Shopping List: eggs, 8 ounces egg substitute, skim milk, 1 ounce fat-free finely-shredded Cheddar cheese, fat-free pita pockets, pepper.

CREATE A SHAKE

EASY

---

ingredients: 1 cup orange juice
1 medium banana
1 cup fat-free strawberry yogurt
3/4 cup frozen strawberries
ice

directions: Start with this basic shake recipe, then experiment with a variety of fruits, juices, milk and flavored yogurt. Some great combinations to try: pineapple juice, crushed pineapple, strawberry yogurt, frozen strawberries; apple juice, banana, frozen mixed berries, vanilla yogurt; skim milk, banana, lite chocolate syrup, frozen chocolate yogurt. Combine all ingredients in the blender or food processor and process until creamy and smooth.

Serves: 2

Nutrition per Serving		Exchanges
Calories	173	1/2 milk
Carbohydrate	38 grams	2 fruit
Cholesterol	3 milligrams	
Dietary Fiber	3 grams	
Fat	< 1 gram	
Protein	6 grams	
Sodium	73 milligrams	

Shopping List: 8 ounces fruit juice or skim milk, banana, fresh or frozen fruit of choice, 8 ounces fat-free flavored yogurt (refrigerated or frozen).

FROZEN FRUIT
YOGURT SHAKE
EASY - DO AHEAD

ingredients:
1/3 cup frozen blueberries
1/3 cup frozen strawberries
1/2 large banana, sliced
1 1/3 cups fat-free frozen vanilla yogurt
2 cups skim milk, ice cold
2 tbsp. sugar

directions: Combine all ingredients in food processor or blender and process until blended smooth. Top with fresh berries, if desired, and serve.

Serves: 2

Nutrition per Serving		Exchanges
Calories	299	2 2/3 fruit
Carbohydrate	60 grams	1 2/3 milk
Cholesterol	4 milligrams	
Dietary Fiber	2 grams	
Fat	< 1 gram	
Protein	14 grams	
Sodium	209 milligrams	

Shopping List: frozen blueberries, frozen strawberries, 1 banana, 12 ounces fat-free frozen vanilla yogurt, 16 ounces skim milk, sugar.

TREMENDOUS TEENS

CHICKEN-VEGETABLE SOUP WITH RICE

EASY - DO AHEAD - FREEZE

ingredients: 4 cups fat-free chicken broth
1 cup water
1/2 tsp. garlic powder
1/2 cup long-grain rice
1 pound fat-free chicken tenders
1/4 tsp. pepper
1 1/2 cups frozen mixed vegetables, thawed and
drained

directions: Combine chicken broth, water, and garlic powder in a medium saucepan; bring to a boil over high heat. Reduce heat to medium; add rice, cover, and simmer until rice is tender (10-15 minutes). Slice chicken into thin pieces; add chicken and vegetables to soup and cook over medium heat 5-7 minutes until chicken is no longer pink and is cooked through. Serve immediately, refrigerate and serve later, or freeze in individual serving sizes and pull out for a quick snack or meal. Heat in microwave or saucepan until heated through.

Serves: 4

Nutrition per Serving		Exchanges
Calories	238	3 vegetable
Carbohydrate	30 grams	1 starch
Cholesterol	71 milligrams	2 1/2 meat
Dietary Fiber	< 1 gram	
Fat	< 1 gram	
Protein	27 grams	
Sodium	585 milligrams	

Shopping List: 32 ounces fat-free chicken broth, long-grain rice, 1 pound fat-free chicken tenders, 16 ounces frozen mixed vegetables, garlic powder, pepper.

FRUITY COLESLAW
EASY - DO AHEAD

ingredients: 8 cups shredded broccoli slaw mix
16 ounces fruit cocktail in juice, drained
1/2 cup fat-free sour cream
1/2 cup fat-free yogurt
1 tbsp. lemon juice
1/2 cup sugar
1/4 cup vinegar

directions: Combine cabbage and drained fruit in large bowl; mix well. Combine remaining ingredients in food processor, blender, or bowl and mix until creamy and smooth. Pour over cabbage mixture and toss until ingredients are coated. Cover and refrigerate several hours before serving.

Serves: 4

Nutrition per Serving		Exchanges
Calories	220	2 fruit
Carbohydrate	51 grams	4 vegetable
Cholesterol	1 milligram	
Dietary Fiber	5 grams	
Fat	< 1 gram	
Protein	8 grams	
Sodium	83 milligrams	

Shopping List: 4 packages shredded broccoli slaw mix, 16 ounces fruit cocktail in juice, 4 ounces fat-free sour cream, 4 ounces fat-free yogurt, lemon juice, sugar, vinegar.

TREMENDOUS TEENS

PASTA VEGETABLE SALAD

EASY - DO AHEAD

ingredients: 8 ounces rotini pasta, cooked and drained
1 cup frozen broccoli flowerets, thawed and drained
1 cup frozen cauliflower flowerets, thawed and drained
3/4 cup cherry tomatoes
1/4 cup chopped red onions (optional)
1 tbsp. chopped black olives
1/2 cup chopped red bell pepper
1/2 cup fat-free creamy Italian salad dressing
1/4 cup fat-free Parmesan cheese

directions: Cook pasta according to package directions and drain well. Very lightly spray pasta with nonfat cooking spray and place in large mixing bowl. Add broccoli, cauliflower, tomatoes, onion, olives and bell pepper to pasta and mix well; sprinkle with Parmesan cheese. Pour salad dressing over top and toss until well coated. Cover with plastic wrap and refrigerate several hours before serving.

Add 12 ounces fat-free tuna or 3/4 pound fat-free cooked chicken tenders to pasta salad, if desired.

Serves: 4

Nutrition per Serving		Exchanges
Calories	153	1 starch
Carbohydrate	30 grams	3 vegetable
Cholesterol	0 milligrams	
Dietary Fiber	3 grams	
Fat	< 1 gram	
Protein	8 grams	
Sodium	263 milligrams	

Shopping List: 8-ounce package rotini pasta, cherry tomatoes, red onion, 4-ounce can black olives, red bell pepper, frozen broccoli flowerets, frozen cauliflower flowerets, 1 ounce fat-free Parmesan cheese, 4 ounces fat-free creamy Italian salad dressing.

SWEET AND SPICY TUNA SALAD

EASY - DO AHEAD

ingredients: 12 ounces fat-free tuna
2 tbsp. fat-free mayonnaise
1 tbsp. spicy mustard
1 cup chopped celery
1 cup chopped apple
1/2 cup chopped red bell pepper
8 ounces French bread, cut in half

directions: Cut bread in half horizontally. Combine mayonnaise and mustard in a small cup and mix until blended smooth. Combine tuna, celery, apple and red pepper in a medium bowl; mix well. Add mayonnaise mixture and blend well. Spread tuna mixture on half of bread; top with remaining bread and cut into four equal pieces.

Serves: 4

Nutrition per Serving		Exchanges
Calories	231	1/2 fruit
Carbohydrate	25 grams	1 vegetable
Cholesterol	15 milligrams	1 starch
Dietary Fiber	2 grams	
Fat	< 1 gram	2 1/2 meat
Protein	29 grams	
Sodium	585 milligrams	

Shopping List: 12 ounces fat-free tuna, fat-free mayonnaise, spicy mustard, celery, 1 apple, 1 red bell pepper, 1/2 pound fat-free French bread loaf.

TREMENDOUS TEENS

HOT TENDERS

EASY - DO AHEAD

ingredients:
1 lb. fat-free chicken tenders
3/4 cup red pepper sauce
1 tbsp. dry mustard
3 tbsp. vinegar

directions:
Preheat oven to 450 degrees. Line baking sheet with foil and lightly spray with nonfat cooking spray. Arrange chicken tenders on baking sheet in a single layer. Combine pepper sauce, mustard, and vinegar in a medium bowl and mix until blended. Brush half the sauce over chicken tenders, coating well. Bake in preheated oven 15 minutes; remove from oven and baste with remaining sauce. Bake 5-10 minutes until chicken is cooked through. Serve with celery sticks and fat-free ranch or blue cheese salad dressing.

Serves: 4

Nutrition per Serving
Calories	105
Carbohydrate	2 grams
Cholesterol	71 milligrams
Dietary Fiber	0 grams
Fat	< 1 gram
Protein	24 grams
Sodium	461 milligrams

Exchanges
3 1/3 meat

Shopping List: 1 pound fat-free chicken tenders, 6 ounces red pepper sauce, dry mustard, vinegar.

SESAME CHICKEN TENDERS

EASY - DO AHEAD - FREEZE

ingredients:
1 lb. fat-free chicken tenders
2 cups fat-free bread crumbs
2 tsp. sesame seeds
2 tsp. garlic powder
1 tbsp. onion powder
1/4 tsp. pepper
1/2 cup egg substitute

directions:
Preheat oven to 375 degrees. Line baking sheet with foil and lightly spray with nonfat cooking spray. Combine bread crumbs, sesame seeds, garlic powder, onion powder and pepper in a shallow dish; mix well. Pour egg substitute into shallow bowl. Dip chicken tenders in egg substitute and roll in bread crumb mixture until coated on all sides. Arrange in single layer on baking sheet and bake in preheated oven 15-20 minutes, until chicken is no longer pink and lightly browned. Dip tenders in low-sodium teriyaki sauce, fat-free honey mustard, or barbecue sauce.

Serves: 4

Nutrition per Serving		**Exchanges**
Calories	303	2 1/3 starch
Carbohydrate	35 grams	3 1/3 meat
Cholesterol	56 milligrams	
Dietary Fiber	< 1 gram	
Fat	< 1 gram	
Protein	33 grams	
Sodium	744 milligrams	

Shopping List: 1 pound fat-free chicken tenders, fat-free bread crumbs (or cracker crumbs), 4 ounces egg substitute, sesame seeds, garlic powder, onion powder, pepper.

SESAME TERIYAKI CHICKEN ON A STICK

EASY - DO AHEAD

ingredients:
1 pound fat-free chicken tenders
1/2 cup low-sodium teriyaki sauce
2 tsp. sesame seeds
2 cups fat-free cooked rice

directions:
Line baking sheet with foil and lightly spray with nonfat cooking spray. Soak wooden sticks or skewers with water. Thread chicken tenders on sticks and arrange on baking sheet. Pour teriyaki sauce over chicken and turn to coat on all sides; sprinkle with sesame seeds. Cover and refrigerate 1 hour. Preheat broiler on high heat. Cook chicken tenders 8-10 minutes, turning once, until no longer pink and cooked through. While chicken is cooking, prepare rice according to package directions (Minute Rice cooks quickest). Place 1/2 cup rice on each plate and top with skewered chicken. Serve with extra teriyaki sauce, if desired.

Serves: 4

Nutrition per Serving		Exchanges
Calories	286	2 1/2 starch
Carbohydrate	41 grams	2 2/3 meat
Cholesterol	71 milligrams	
Dietary Fiber	< 1 gram	
Protein	27 grams	
Sodium	913 milligrams	

Shopping List: 1 pound fat-free chicken tenders, 4 ounces low-sodium teriyaki sauce, fat-free rice, sesame seeds.

CHICKEN AND CHEESE NACHOS

EASY - DO AHEAD

ingredients:
4 cups fat-free tortilla chips
1/2 pound fat-free chicken tenders
3/4 tsp. garlic powder
3/4 tsp. onion powder
1/2 tsp. chili powder
1/4 cup chopped green chilies
2 cups fat-free Mexican cheese, finely shredded

directions:
Lightly spray large nonstick skillet with nonfat cooking spray and heat over medium-high heat. Add chicken to skillet and sprinkle on both sides with garlic powder, onion powder and chili powder. Cook chicken over medium-high heat, stirring occasionally, until chicken is no longer pink and is lightly browned. Remove from heat; cool slightly and shred chicken. Preheat oven to 450 degrees. Line baking sheet with foil and lightly spray with nonfat cooking spray. Arrange tortilla chips on baking sheet; sprinkle with chicken, chilies, and cheese. Bake in preheated oven 10-15 minutes, until cheese is completely melted and lightly browned.

Serves: 4

Nutrition per Serving
Calories	257
Carbohydrate	29 grams
Cholesterol	38 milligrams
Dietary Fiber	2 grams
Fat	< 1 gram
Protein	34 grams
Sodium	980 milligrams

Exchanges
1 2/3 starch
3 1/2 meat

Shopping List: fat-free tortilla chips, 1/2 pound fat-free chicken tenders, 8 ounces fat-free finely-shredded Mexican cheese, garlic powder, onion powder, chili powder, 4-ounce can chopped green chilies.

CHILI AND CHEESE SKINS

EASY - DO AHEAD

ingredients: 4 large baking potatoes
2 cups fat-free chili
1 cup fat-free Cheddar cheese, finely shredded
2 tbsp. chopped green chilies (optional)
2 tbsp. fat-free sour cream (optional)

directions: Preheat oven to 500 degrees. Wash potatoes; prick with fork in several places. Bake potatoes in preheated oven 1 hour, until tender and very crisp. Remove from oven and let cool 15 minutes; reduce oven temperature to 400 degrees. Cut potatoes in half, scoop out pulp and save for later (you can make some great fat-free mashed potatoes). Line baking sheet with foil and lightly spray with non-fat cooking spray. Arrange potato shells on baking sheet. Pour chili into microwave-safe bowl or sauce-pan and cook until heated through. Bake potato shells 5-6 minutes until insides are crisp. Serve skins with chili, cheese, and sour cream.

Serves: 4

Nutrition per Serving		Exchanges
Calories	271	2 1/3 starch
Carbohydrate	49 grams	3 vegetable
Cholesterol	0 milligrams	1/2 meat
Dietary Fiber	6 grams	
Fat	< 1 gram	
Protein	18 grams	
Sodium	573 milligrams	

Shopping List: 4 large baking potatoes, 16-ounce can fat-free chili, 4 ounces fat-free finely-shredded Cheddar cheese, green chilies (optional), fat-free sour cream (optional).

BEST TURKEY SANDWICH EVER!

EASY - DO AHEAD

ingredients:
3/4 cup fat-free mayonnaise
1/2 cup chopped celery
1 tsp. spicy mustard
4 lettuce leaves
1 small tomato, sliced thin
1/2 small red onion, sliced thin
1 pound fat-free deli-style turkey breast
1 medium red apple, sliced thin
4 whole bagels*

directions:
Combine mayonnaise, celery, and mustard in a small bowl; mix until blended. Toast bagels lightly. Spread bagels on both sides with mayonnaise mixture. Layer lettuce, tomato, onion, turkey and apples on bagels. Cut in half and serve.

*Substitute any fat-free bread, bialys, English muffins, fat-free flour tortillas, or other bread for bagels, if desired.

Serves: 4

Nutrition per Serving		Exchanges
Calories	406	1 fruit
Carbohydrate	68 grams	2 starch
Cholesterol	55 milligrams	3 1/2 vegetable
Dietary Fiber	5 grams	3 meat
Fat	< 1 gram	
Protein	33 grams	
Sodium	877 milligrams	

Shopping List: 6 ounces fat-free mayonnaise, 1 pound fat-free deli-style turkey breast, 1 red apple, 1 red onion, 1 tomato, lettuce, celery, spicy mustard, bagels (or bread of choice).

TREMENDOUS TEENS

GRILLED FISH SANDWICH

EASY - DO AHEAD

ingredients: 12 ounces cod fillets
4 ounces fat-free American cheese
1/4 cup fat-free tartar sauce
8 slices fat-free French bread

directions: Preheat broiler on high heat. Line baking sheet with foil and lightly spray with nonfat cooking spray. Arrange fish fillets on baking sheet and broil 5 to 6 minutes, turn fish over and broil 5-6 minutes, turn fish over and broil 5-6 minutes until fish flakes easily. Top each fillet with 1 ounce cheese and broil just until cheese melts. Lightly toast bread; spread four slices of bread with 1 tablespoon tartar sauce each. Place fish on bread and top with bread slices. Garnish with lettuce, tomatoes, onions, etc.

Serves: 4

Nutrition per Serving

Calories	291	
Carbohydrate	36 grams	
Cholesterol	37 milligrams	
Dietary Fiber	2 grams	
Fat	< 1 gram	
Protein	33 grams	
Sodium	678 milligrams	

Exchanges

2 starch
4 meat

Shopping List: 12 ounces cod fillets, 4 ounces fat-free American cheese, 2 ounces fat-free tartar sauce, 1/2 pound fat-free French bread.

TUNA BURGER DELUXE

EASY - DO AHEAD

ingredients: 12 ounces fat-free tuna, drained
1 cup fat-free mayonnaise
1/2 cup egg substitute
1/2 cup fat-free bread crumbs
3/4 cup finely-chopped celery
2 tsp. onion powder
1 1/2 tsp. lemon juice
toasted bagels, English muffins, or fat-free bread
lettuce leaves, tomato slices, bean sprouts
(optional)

directions: Combine mayonnaise, egg substitute, bread crumbs, celery, onion powder, lemon juice, and tuna in a medium bowl and mix until ingredients are blended. Form into patties and arrange on platter. Cover with plastic wrap and refrigerate at least 1 hour. Lightly spray large nonstick skillet with nonfat cooking spray and heat over medium heat. Add burgers to skillet and cook 3-4 minutes; carefully flip "burgers" and cook 3-4 minutes, until lightly browned and cooked through. Serve on toasted bagels, muffins or bread, with lettuce, tomato and bean sprouts, if desired.

Serves: 4

<u>Nutrition per Serving</u>		<u>Exchanges</u>
(without bread)		
Calories	186	2 1/2 vegetable
Carbohydrate	13 grams	3 1/2 meat
Cholesterol	15 milligrams	
Dietary Fiber	1 gram	
Fat	< 1 gram	
Protein	28 grams	
Sodium	812 milligrams	

Shopping List: 12 ounces fat-free tuna, 8 ounces fat-free mayonnaise, 4 ounces egg substitute, celery, fat-free bread crumbs (or cracker crumbs), onion powder, lemon juice, bread of choice, lettuce, tomato, bean sprouts (optional).

TREMENDOUS TEENS

VEGGIE TUNAWICH

EASY - DO AHEAD

ingredients: 4 fat-free sourdough English muffins*
3/4 cup shredded carrots
3/4 cup shredded cucumber
3/4 cup chopped celery
1/2 cup shredded jicama
12 ounces fat-free tuna, drained
1/4 cup fat-free mayonnaise
1 tbsp. sweet pickle relish

directions: Split English muffins in half and toast lightly. Combine remaining ingredients in a medium bowl and mix until ingredients are blended. Serve on toasted muffins with lettuce and sliced tomato, if desired.

*Substitute pita pockets, fat-free flour tortillas, fat-free bread, or bagels for English muffins.

Serves: 4

Nutrition per Serving
Calories	339
Carbohydrate	51 grams
Cholesterol	15 milligrams
Dietary Fiber	4 grams
Fat	< 1 gram
Protein	32 grams
Sodium	735 milligrams

Exchanges
2 starch
4 vegetable
2 1/2 meat

Shopping List: fat-free sourdough English muffins, packaged shredded carrots, 1 small cucumber, celery, 1 ounce jicama, 12 ounces fat-free tuna, 2 ounces fat-free mayonnaise, sweet pickle relish.

WHAT A BURGER!

EASY - DO AHEAD - FREEZE

ingredients: 1 pound fat-free ground turkey
4 large egg whites
1/2 cup A-1 steak sauce
1 cup cracker meal
2 tsp. garlic powder
1 1/2 tbsp. Worcestershire sauce

directions: Combine all the ingredients in a medium bowl and mix until completely blended. Form into patties and arrange on platter; cover with plastic wrap and refrigerate 2-3 hours. Lightly spray large non-stick skillet with nonfat cooking spray and heat over medium-high heat. Add burgers to skillet and cook 6-8 minutes per side, until browned and cooked through. Serve on fat-free bread rolls or buns with lettuce, tomatoes, red onions, sliced fat-free cheese, ketchup, barbecue sauce, mustard, etc.

Burgers can also be prepared on grill over medium-high heat. Be sure to spray grill with nonfat cooking spray. Flip burgers after 6 to 7 minutes and cook until browned on both sides.

Serves: 4

Nutrition per Serving		**Exchanges**
(burger only)		
Calories	187	1 starch
Carbohydrate	17 grams	3 meat
Cholesterol	41 milligrams	
Dietary Fiber	< 1 gram	
Fat	< 1 gram	
Protein	22 grams	
Sodium	1954 milligrams	

Shopping List: 1 pound fat-free ground turkey, eggs, 4 ounces A-1 steak sauce, cracker meal, garlic powder, Worcestershire sauce.

TREMENDOUS TEENS

ROCKIN' TACOS

EASY - DO AHEAD

ingredients:
1 tbsp. onion powder
1 tsp. garlic powder
2 cups fat-free black beans
1 tbsp. chili powder
1 1/2 cups frozen corn kernels, thawed and drained
4 ounces chopped green chilies
3/4 cup fat-free salsa
1 cup shredded lettuce
1/2 cup fat-free sour cream
1 cup chopped tomatoes
1 cup fat-free Cheddar cheese, finely shredded
4 fat-free flour or corn tortillas

directions: Lightly spray large nonstick skillet with nonfat cooking spray and heat over medium heat. Add beans to skillet; sprinkle with onion powder, garlic powder and chili powder; mix well. Add corn and green chilies to bean mixture and cook, stirring frequently, until heated through. Add salsa to skillet and cook over medium heat; reduce to low, cover and simmer 10-15 minutes. Warm flour or corn tortillas in oven; serve tacos with lettuce, sour cream, tomatoes and shredded cheese.

Serves: 4

Nutrition per Serving

		Exchanges
Calories	380	3 starch
Carbohydrate	70 grams	5 vegetable
Cholesterol	0 milligrams	1/2 meat
Dietary Fiber	9 grams	
Fat	< 1 gram	
Protein	25 grams	
Sodium	1276 milligrams	

Shopping List: 16 ounces fat-free black beans, 10 ounces frozen corn kernels, 4 ounces chopped green chilies, 6 ounces fat-free salsa, 4 ounces shredded lettuce, 1 large tomato, 4 ounces fat-free sour cream, 4 ounces fat-free finely-shredded Cheddar cheese, fat-free flour or corn tortillas, onion powder, garlic powder, chili powder.

TURKEY TACO PIE

EASY - DO AHEAD

ingredients: 12 ounces fat-free ground turkey
3 tbsp. taco seasoning mix, divided
1/3 cup tomato paste
1/4 + 1/3 cup water, divided
1/3 cup salsa
4 large fat-free flour tortillas
1 1/2 cups fat-free Mexican cheese, finely
shredded

ingredients: Preheat oven to 350 degrees. Lightly spray 8-inch baking dish with nonfat cooking spray. Lightly spray large nonstick skillet with nonfat cooking spray and heat over medium-high heat. Add turkey to skillet and cook, stirring frequently, until turkey is no longer pink and is cooked through; remove from heat and drain turkey. Reduce heat to medium and place skillet on stove. Add 2 tablespoons taco seasoning and 1/4 cup water to turkey; cook over low heat 10-15 minutes. Combine salsa, tomato paste, 1/3 cup water and 1 tablespoon taco seasoning in a medium bowl; mix until blended. Cut tortillas in quarters. Arrange tortillas in a single layer on the bottom of baking dish. Spread 1/3 cup salsa mixture on tortillas; top with 1/3 turkey mixture and top with 1/2 cup cheese. Repeat layers, ending with cheese on top. Lightly spray foil with nonfat cooking spray and cover dish tightly. Bake in preheated oven 20 minutes until cheese is melted. Remove foil and bake 5-7 minutes until lightly browned. Let stand at room temperature 5 minutes; cut into squares and serve with additional salsa, if desired.

Serves: 4

Nutrition per Serving		Exchanges
Calories	329	2 1/2 starch
Carbohydrate	43 grams	1 vegetable
Cholesterol	32 milligrams	3 meat
Dietary Fiber	3 grams	
Fat	< 1 gram	
Protein	32 grams	
Sodium	2306 milligrams	

Shopping List: 12 ounces fat-free ground turkey, 1 packet taco seasoning mix, tomato paste, fat-free salsa, fat-free flour tortillas, 6 ounces fat-free Mexican shredded cheese.

CHILI BEAN ROLL-UP

EASY - DO AHEAD

ingredients: 1 1/4 cups fat-free refried beans
1/2 cup fat-free salsa
1/2 tsp. chili powder
4 fat-free flour tortillas
1 cup shredded lettuce
1/2 cup fat-free shredded Mexican cheese
1/2 cup chopped tomatoes
1 tbsp. chopped green chiles

directions: Combine beans, salsa, and chili powder in a small saucepan. Cook over medium heat 4-5 minutes until beans are heated through. Spoon 1/4 cup bean mixture onto each tortilla. Top with cheese, lettuce, tomatoes, and chopped green chiles; roll tortillas up and serve with additional salsa.

Serves: 4

Nutrition per Serving
Calories	231
Carbohydrate	43 grams
Cholesterol	1 milligram
Dietary Fiber	5 grams
Fat	< 1 gram
Protein	14 grams
Sodium	974 milligrams

Exchanges
2 starch
2 vegetable
1 meat

Shopping List: 10 ounces fat-free refried beans, 4 ounces fat-free salsa, fat-free flour tortillas, 2 ounces fat-free Mexican cheese, 1 small tomato, 8-ounce package shredded lettuce, chili powder, chopped green chiles.

CRISPY "NO FRY" FRIES

EASY - DO AHEAD - FREEZE

ingredients: 6 medium potatoes
2 large egg whites
variety of spices: Cajun, Italian seasoning,
garlic powder, onion powder, fat-free
Parmesan cheese, taco seasoning

directions: Prick potatoes in several places with a fork. Cook in microwave on High, 25-30 minutes until tender and cooked through. Remove from oven and let cool 15 minutes. Preheat broiler on high heat. Line baking sheet with foil and lightly spray with non-fat cooking spray. Slice cooked potatoes into strips or wedges and arrange on baking sheet. Brush with egg whites; sprinkle with seasoning of choice. Broil 5-6 minutes; carefully flip fries and broil 5-6 minutes until golden brown and crisp. Serve with favorite dip.

Serves: 4

Nutrition per Serving		Exchanges
Calories	226	3 starch
Carbohydrate	51 grams	
Cholesterol	0 milligrams	
Dietary Fiber	6 grams	
Fat	< 1 gram	
Protein	6 grams	
Sodium	39 milligrams	

Shopping List: 6 potatoes, eggs, seasonings of choice.

TREMENDOUS TEENS

HASH BROWN POTATOES

EASY - DO AHEAD

ingredients:
1 1/2 cups chopped onions
1 1/2 cups chopped red bell pepper
1 1/2 tbsp. chopped green chilies
1/2 tsp. garlic powder
1/2 tsp. chili powder
1/4 tsp. pepper
2 cups red potatoes, cooked, peeled and cubed

directions:
Lightly spray large nonstick skillet with nonfat cooking spray and heat over medium-high heat. Add onions and red pepper to skillet and cook, stirring occasionally, 8-10 minutes until lightly browned. Add chilies, garlic powder, chili powder, and pepper; cook, stirring frequently, 1-2 minutes until heated through. Add potatoes and toss until ingredients are well mixed. Reduce heat to medium-low, cover, and cook 8-10 minutes until potatoes are browned and heated through.

Great with Pita Pocket Cheese Omelet!

Serves: 4

Nutrition per Serving		**Exchanges**
Calories	145	1 2/3 starch
Carbohydrate	33 grams	1 vegetable
Cholesterol	0 milligrams	
Dietary Fiber	5 grams	
Fat	< 1 gram	
Protein	3 grams	
Sodium	49 milligrams	

Shopping List: 1 large onion, 1 large red bell pepper, 4-ounce can chopped green chilies, red potatoes, garlic powder, chili powder, pepper.

CARAMEL CORN

EASY - DO AHEAD

ingredients: 4 cups air-popped popcorn
1/2 cup brown sugar
2 tbsp. fat-free caramel-flavored yogurt

directions: Place popcorn in large mixing bowl and lightly spray with nonfat cooking spray. Combine sugar and yogurt in a small saucepan and cook over medium heat, stirring frequently, until mixture becomes thick. Pour over popcorn and mix until popcorn is coated. Form popcorn into balls or serve in bowl.

Serves: 4

Nutrition per Serving		Exchanges
Calories	130	1 starch
Carbohydrate	32 grams	1 fruit
Cholesterol	< 1 milligram	
Dietary Fiber	< 1 gram	
Fat	< 1 gram	
Protein	1 gram	
Sodium	13 milligrams	

Shopping List: air-popped popcorn, brown sugar, fat-free caramel-flavored yogurt (Dannon).

TREMENDOUS TEENS

CRUNCHY CRISPY MIX
EASY - DO AHEAD

ingredients:
1 cup fat-free goldfish pretzel mix
1 cup melba toast, broken in half
1 cup fat-free rye crisp crackers, broken up
1 cup Chex cereal
1 1/2 tbsp. Worcestershire sauce
1 1/2 tsp. onion powder
1 1/2 tsp. garlic powder
2 tsp. sugar
4 1/2 tbsp. water

directions:
Preheat oven to 300 degrees. Line baking sheet with foil and lightly spray with nonfat cooking spray. Combine pretzel mix, melba toast, rye crackers, and cereal in a large bowl. Combine remaining ingredients in a small bowl and mix until blended; pour into large bowl and mix until ingredients are well coated. Spread onto baking sheet(s) in single layer and bake in preheated oven, 20-25 minutes until browned and crisp. Remove from oven and cool completely. Store in sealed containers.

Serves: 4

Nutrition per Serving		**Exchanges**
Calories	170	2 1/3 starch
Carbohydrate	37 grams	
Cholesterol	0 milligrams	
Dietary Fiber	3 grams	
Fat	< 1 gram	
Protein	6 grams	
Sodium	483 milligrams	

Shopping List: fat-free goldfish pretzel mix, melba toast, fat-free rye crisp crackers, Chex cereal, Worcestershire sauce, onion powder, garlic powder, sugar.

TREMENDOUS TEENS

CARROT CAKE BARS

EASY - DO AHEAD - FREEZE

ingredients:
1 1/4 cups flour
1/2 cup sugar
1/2 cup brown sugar
1/2 cup canned carrots, mashed
1/2 cup egg substitute
1 tsp. vanilla
3/4 tsp. baking powder
1/2 tsp. baking soda
1 1/2 tsp. cinnamon
1/4 tsp. nutmeg
1 packet fat-free vanilla glaze (Cake Mate)

directions:
Preheat oven to 350 degrees. Lightly spray a 9x13-inch baking dish with nonfat cooking spray. Combine sugar, brown sugar, mashed carrots, egg substitute, and vanilla in a large bowl; blend until creamy and smooth. Add flour, baking soda, baking powder, cinnamon, and nutmeg; mix until dry ingredients are moistened and blended. Spread batter into prepared pan and bake in preheated oven 25-30 minutes, until knife inserted in center comes out clean. Remove from oven and cool completely. Drizzle vanilla glaze over cake; cut and serve.

*If you cannot find packaged glaze, make your own: 1/2 cup powdered sugar, 1/2 cup skim milk and 1 teaspoon vanilla; mix well and drizzle over cake.

Serves: 16

Nutrition per Serving		Exchanges
Calories	105	1 1/3 starch
Carbohydrate	24 grams	
Cholesterol	< 1 milligram	
Dietary Fiber	< 1 gram	
Fat	< 1 gram	
Protein	2 grams	
Sodium	68 milligrams	

Shopping List: 6 ounces canned carrots, 4 ounces egg substitute, flour, sugar, brown sugar, vanilla, baking powder, (Cake Matge) baking soda, cinnamon, nutmeg, fat-free vanilla glaze (Cake Mate).

CINNAMON OATMEAL RAISIN COOKIES

EASY - DO AHEAD - FREEZE

ingredients:
1/4 cup sugar
1/2 cup brown sugar
2 tbsp. corn syrup
1/4 cup egg substitute
1 tsp. vanilla
1/4 cup cinnamon applesauce
3/4 cup flour
1/4 tsp. baking soda
3/4 tsp. cinnamon
1/8 tsp. nutmeg
1 1/4 cups quick-cooking oatmeal
1/2 cup raisins

directions:
Preheat oven to 350 degrees. Line baking sheet(s) with foil and lightly spray with nonfat cooking spray. Combine sugar, brown sugar, corn syrup, egg substitute, vanilla and applesauce in a large bowl; mix until blended and creamy and smooth. Add flour, baking soda, cinnamon, nutmeg, and oatmeal; mix until ingredients are blended. Fold in raisins. Drop dough by rounded teaspoonful; flatten cookies and bake in preheated oven, 10 to 12 minutes until lightly browned.

Serves: 24

Nutrition per Serving		Exchanges
Calories	72	1 starch
Carbohydrate	16 grams	
Cholesterol	0 milligrams	
Dietary Fiber	1 gram	
Fat	< 1 gram	
Protein	1 gram	
Sodium	15 milligrams	

Shopping List: quick-cooking oatmeal, 2 ounces cinnamon applesauce, flour, sugar, brown sugar, corn syrup, 2 ounces egg substitute, raisins, baking soda, cinnamon, nutmeg, vanilla.

CINNAMON RAISIN BARS

EASY - DO AHEAD - FREEZE

ingredients:	1/2 cup egg substitute 4 large egg whites 1/2 cup sugar 1/2 cup brown sugar 1 tsp. vanilla 1 tsp. baking powder 1 1/2 tsp. cinnamon 1 cup flour 3 cups raisins
directions:	Preheat oven to 350 degrees. Lightly spray 9x13-inch baking dish with nonfat cooking spray. Combine egg substitute, egg whites, sugar, brown sugar, and vanilla in a large mixing bowl and mix until blended. Add flour, baking powder, and cinnamon; mix until all ingredients are blended. Fold in raisins. Spread batter into prepared pan and bake in preheated oven 25-30 minutes, until knife inserted in center comes out clean. Remove from oven and cool completely. Sprinkle with cinnamon-sugar or powdered sugar, if desired. Cut into squares and serve.

Serves: 16

Nutrition per Serving
Calories	146
Carbohydrate	35 grams
Cholesterol	0 milligrams
Dietary Fiber	2 grams
Fat	< 1 gram
Protein	3 grams
Sodium	50 milligrams

Exchanges
2 starch

Shopping List: 4 ounces egg substitute, whole eggs, sugar, brown sugar, flour, vanilla, baking powder, cinnamon, raisins.

TREMENDOUS TEENS

MARSHMALLOW CREME BROWNIES

EASY - DO AHEAD - FREEZE

ingredients:
1 cup egg substitute
4 large egg whites
1/2 cup sugar
1/2 cup brown sugar
2 tbsp. vanilla
3/4 cup unsweetened cocoa powder
1 1/4 cups flour
1 1/2 tsp. baking powder
1 1/2 cups marshmallow creme
2 tbsp. reduced-fat chocolate chips
powdered sugar, for topping

directions:
Preheat oven to 350 degrees. Lightly spray a 9x13-inch baking dish with nonfat cooking spray. Combine egg substitute, egg whites, sugar, brown sugar, and vanilla in a large mixing bowl and blend until creamy and smooth. Add flour and baking powder; mix until all ingredients are blended. Fold in marshmallow creme and swirl through batter. Spread batter into prepared pan; sprinkle with chocolate chips and bake in preheated oven 20-25 minutes, until knife inserted in center comes out clean. Cool completely; sprinkle with powdered sugar, cut in squares and serve.

Serves: 16

Nutrition per Serving

		Exchanges
Calories	181	1 starch
Carbohydrate	42 grams	1 2/3 fruit
Cholesterol	0 milligrams	
Dietary Fiber	< 1 gram	
Fat	< 1 gram	
Protein	4 grams	
Sodium	79 milligrams	

Shopping List: 8 ounces egg substitute, whole eggs, sugar, brown sugar, unsweetened cocoa powder, marshmallow creme, reduced-fat chocolate chips, flour, baking powder, vanilla, powdered sugar.

M&M BROWNIES

EASY - DO AHEAD - FREEZE

ingredients:
1/4 cup egg substitute
1 cup sugar
1 cup flour
1/3 cup unsweetened cocoa powder
1/2 cup corn syrup
1 tsp. vanilla
1 tsp. baking powder
1/4 cup miniature M&M's

directions:
Preheat oven to 350 degrees. Lightly spray 9x9-inch baking dish with nonfat cooking spray. In a large bowl, combine egg substitute, sugar, corn syrup, and vanilla; mix until creamy and smooth. Add flour, cocoa powder, and baking powder; mix until all ingredients are blended. Fold in M&M's. Spread batter into prepared pan and bake in preheated oven 25-30 minutes, until knife inserted in center comes out clean. Cool completely; cut into squares and serve.

Serves: 12

Nutrition per Serving
Calories	151
Carbohydrate	36 grams
Cholesterol	0 milligrams
Dietary Fiber	< 1 gram
Fat	< 1 gram
Protein	2 grams
Sodium	46 milligrams

Exchanges
2 starch

Shopping List: 2 ounces egg substitute, sugar, unsweetened cocoa powder, flour, 4 ounces corn syrup, vanilla, baking powder, miniature M&M's.

TREMENDOUS TEENS

SCRUMPTIOUS BANANA SPLIT

EASY

ingredients: 2 large bananas, cut in half
2 cups fat-free frozen vanilla yogurt
2 cups fat-free frozen strawberry yogurt
1/2 cup lite chocolate syrup
1/4 cup Grape-Nuts
4 maraschino cherries
1 cup fat-free Cool Whip

directions: Slice bananas in quarters; arrange 2 banana pieces in each dessert dish. Place 1/2 cup vanilla and 1/2 cup strawberry yogurt in each dish; drizzle with 2 tablespoons chocolate syrup. Sprinkle 1 tablespoon Grape-Nuts over syrup; spoon on 2 tablespoons Cool Whip and top with cherries.

Quite a caloric indulgence - save for special occasions or share with a friend!

Serves: 4

Nutrition per Serving		Exchanges	
Calories	381	1 milk	
Carbohydrate	86 grams	4 3/4 fruit	
Cholesterol	0 milligrams		
Dietary Fiber	1 gram		
Fat	< 1 gram		
Protein	10 grams		
Sodium	204 milligrams		

Shopping List: 2 large bananas, 1 pint fat-free frozen vanilla yogurt, 1 pint fat-free frozen chocolate yogurt, 4 ounces lite chocolate syrup, Grape-Nuts cereal, maraschino cherries, 8 ounces fat-free Cool Whip.

Fat Free Living® Cooking with "5" Ingredients or Less

- Breakfast

- Soups and Salads

- Main Dishes

- Side Dishes

- Desserts

BLUEBERRY PANCAKES

EASY - DO AHEAD - FREEZE

ingredients:
2 cups flour
2 cups fat-free blueberry yogurt
1/2 cup egg substitute
2 tsp. baking soda
1 cup fresh blueberries

directions:
Combine flour and yogurt in a large mixing bowl and mix until blended; cover and refrigerate overnight. Add egg substitute and baking soda to flour mixture and blend well; fold in blueberries. Lightly spray large nonstick skillet with nonfat cooking spray and heat over medium heat. Using 1/4-cup measure, pour batter into hot skillet. Cook pancakes until bubbles form on top; flip pancakes and cook until lightly browned on the bottom. Remove and keep warm; repeat with remaining batter.

Serves: 6

Nutrition per Serving		Exchanges
Calories	204	1 fruit
Carbohydrate	40 grams	1 2/3 starch
Cholesterol	2 milligrams	
Dietary Fiber	2 grams	
Fat	< 1 gram	
Protein	9 grams	
Sodium	349 milligrams	

Shopping List: flour, 16 ounces fat-free blueberry yogurt, 4 ounces egg substitute, baking soda, 1/2 pint fresh blueberries.

5 INGREDIENTS OR LESS

EGG CASSEROLE

EASY - DO AHEAD

ingredients: 12 slices fat-free French bread, cut in cubes
2 cups skim milk
2 cups egg substitute
2 tsp. onion powder
1/2 tsp. dry mustard

directions: Lightly spray 9x12-inch baking dish with nonfat cooking spray. Spread bread cubes over bottom of dish. Combine remaining ingredients in blender, or whisk until blended smooth. Pour over bread cubes, cover and refrigerate overnight. Preheat oven to 400 degrees. Bake egg casserole 35-40 minutes until cooked through.

Serves: 6

Nutrition per Serving		Exchanges
Calories	236	1/2 milk
Carbohydrate	40 grams	1 meat
Cholesterol	1 milligram	2 starch
Dietary Fiber	2 grams	
Fat	< 1 gram	
Protein	16 grams	
Sodium	453 milligrams	

Shopping List: 1 pound fat-free French bread, 16 ounces skim milk, 16 ounces egg substitute, onion powder, dry mustard.

CHICKEN NOODLE SOUP

EASY - DO AHEAD - FREEZE

ingredients: 8 cups fat- free chicken broth
1/4 lb. fat-free chicken tenders, cooked and
shredded
1 1/2 cups frozen carrot slices
4 oz. vermicelli, broken into 2-inch pieces
3/4 cup frozen peas

directions: Combine chicken broth and chicken in a large
soup pot; bring to a boil over high heat. Add
vermicelli, carrots and peas; cook over medium-
high heat 8-10 minutes until pasta is tender and
vegetables are cooked through.

Serves: 6

Nutrition per Serving		Exchanges
Calories	125	1 starch
Carbohydrate	21 grams	1/2 meat
Cholesterol	12 milligrams	1 vegetable
Dietary Fiber	1 gram	
Fat	< 1 gram	
Protein	8 grams	
Sodium	1269 milligrams	

Shopping List: 64 ounces fat-free chicken broth, 1/4 pound fat-
free chicken tenders, 16 ounces frozen carrot slices,
4 ounces vermicelli, frozen peas.

GUILTLESS GAZPACHO

EASY - DO AHEAD

ingredients: 4--14 1/2 oz. cans Mexican stewed tomatoes, undrained
1 large cucumber, peeled and chopped
1 1/2 cups frozen pepper strips, thawed and chopped
2 tbsp. chopped green chilies
1 cup chopped celery

directions: Combine all ingredients in a large bowl and mix well. Cover and refrigerate several hours or overnight before serving. Serve with fat-free tortilla chips or fat-free flour tortillas.

Serves: 6

<u>**Nutrition per Serving**</u>

Calories	91
Carbohydrate	22 grams
Cholesterol	0 milligrams
Dietary Fiber	4 grams
Fat	< 1 gram
Protein	3 grams
Sodium	732 milligrams

<u>**Exchanges**</u>
4 vegetable

Shopping List: 4--14 1/2-ounce cans Mexican stewed tomatoes, 1 large cucumber, 16-ounce package frozen pepper strips, 4-ounce can chopped green chilies, celery.

BANANA-BERRY YOGURT SALAD

EASY - DO AHEAD

ingredients: 2 cups frozen mixed berries, thawed and
  drained
1 large banana, sliced
1 cup miniature marshmallows
1 cup fat-free banana yogurt*
1 tbsp. shredded coconut

directions: Combine all the ingredients except coconut in a
large glass bowl; toss gently until fruit is mixed
and coated. Sprinkle with coconut; refrigerate 1-2
hours before serving.

Serves: 6

Nutrition per Serving

		Exchanges
Calories	91	1 1/2 fruit
Carbohydrate	20 grams	
Cholesterol	1 milligram	
Dietary Fiber	2 grams	
Fat	< 1 gram	
Protein	2 grams	
Sodium	28 milligrams	

Shopping List: 16-ounce package frozen mixed berries, 1 large
banana, miniature marshmallows, *8-ounce fat-
free banana yogurt, shredded coconut.

*You can substitute 8 ounces fat-free mixed berry
or coconut yogurt.

5 INGREDIENTS OR LESS

293

BLACK BEAN SALAD

EASY - DO AHEAD

ingredients: 3--16 oz. cans fat-free black beans, rinsed and
drained
3 cups chopped red and green bell peppers
2 cups chopped tomatoes
1 cup sliced green onions
1/4 cup lemon juice

directions: Combine beans, peppers, tomatoes and green onions in a large bowl; mix well. Pour lemon juice
over top and mix well. Cover and refrigerate several hours before serving.

Serves: 6

Nutrition per Serving		Exchanges
Calories	236	2 starch
Carbohydrate	45 grams	3 vegetable
Cholesterol	0 milligrams	
Dietary Fiber	7 grams	
Fat	< 1 gram	
Protein	15 grams	
Sodium	1002 milligrams	

Shopping List: 3--16-ounce cans fat-free black beans, 2 small green
bell peppers, 2 small red bell peppers, 2 medium
tomatoes, 1 bunch green onions, 2 ounces lemon
juice.

5 INGREDIENTS OR LESS

BLT SALAD

EASY - DO AHEAD

ingredients:
6 cups shredded lettuce
6 pieces fat-free turkey bacon, cooked and
    crumbled
3 cups cherry tomatoes, halved
1 cup fat-free finely-shredded cheddar cheese
3/4 cup fat-free ranch salad dressing

directions:
In a large glass bowl, layer ingredients as follows: lettuce, 3/8 cup salad dressing (do not mix with lettuce), bacon, tomatoes, cheese and remaining dressing. Cover and refrigerate overnight. Toss just before serving.

Serves: 6

Nutrition per Serving

Calories	113
Carbohydrate	15 grams
Cholesterol	15 milligrams
Dietary Fiber	2 grams
Fat	< 1 gram
Protein	10 grams
Sodium	787 milligrams

Exchanges
3 vegetable
1 meat

Shopping List: 16-ounce package shredded lettuce, fat-free turkey bacon, 1 1/2 pints cherry tomatoes, 4 ounces fat-free finely-shredded cheddar cheese, 6 ounces fat-free ranch salad dressing.

5 INGREDIENTS OR LESS

CHICKEN SALAD

EASY - DO AHEAD

ingredients: 3/4 cup fat-free ranch salad dressing
2 tsp. dijon mustard
2 tsp. dried tarragon
1 lb. fat-free chicken tenders, cooked and cubed
3/4 cup chopped celery

directions: Combine salad dressing, mustard and tarragon in a medium bowl; mix until blended. Add chicken and celery; stir to coat. Refrigerate several hours before serving. Stuff into pita pocket, roll in tortilla, or make a sandwich with fat-free bread.

Serves: 6

Nutrition per Serving		Exchanges
Calories	109	2 meat
Carbohydrate	9 grams	2 vegetable
Cholesterol	27 milligrams	
Dietary Fiber	< 1 gram	
Fat	< 1 gram	
Protein	16 grams	
Sodium	491 milligrams	

Shopping List: 1 pound fat-free chicken tenders, 6 ounces fat-free ranch salad dressing, dijon mustard, dried tarragon, celery.

COLESLAW
EASY - DO AHEAD

ingredients:
4 cups shredded cabbage mix
1/2 cup fat-free mayonnaise
2 tbsp. white wine vinegar
1 tbsp. sugar
1/2 tsp. celery seed

directions:
Combine mayonnaise, vinegar, sugar and celery seed; mix until blended smooth. Combine cabbage mix and dressing in a large bowl; toss until coated. Cover and refrigerate several hours before serving.

Serves: 6

Nutrition per Serving		Exchanges
Calories	38	1 1/2 vegetable
Carbohydrate	9 grams	
Cholesterol	0 milligrams	
Dietary Fiber	1 gram	
Fat	< 1 gram	
Protein	1 gram	
Sodium	153 milligrams	

Shopping List: 16-ounce package cabbage mix (or 8-ounce packages broccoli slaw mix and 8-ounce package cabbage mix), 4 ounces fat-free mayonnaise, white wine vinegar, sugar, celery seed.

5 INGREDIENTS OR LESS

CRUNCHY TUNA-PINEAPPLE SALAD

EASY - DO AHEAD

ingredients: 3--7 oz. cans fat-free tuna, drained
3/4 cup chopped water chestnuts
3/4 cup crushed pineapple in juice, drained
1/2 cup chopped celery
1/2 cup fat-free mayonnaise

directions: Combine tuna, water chestnuts, pineapple and celery in a medium bowl; mix well. Gradually add mayonnaise and mix until creamy and blended. Refrigerate 1-2 hours before serving. Stuff in pita pocket, roll in tortilla, or sandwich with fat-free bread, bagel or bialy.

Serves: 6

Nutrition per Serving		Exchanges
Calories	172	2/3 fruit
Carbohydrate	10 grams	4 meat
Cholesterol	18 milligrams	
Dietary Fiber	< 1 gram	
Fat	< 1 gram	
Protein	30 grams	
Sodium	504 milligrams	

Shopping List: 3--7-ounce cans fat-free tuna, canned sliced water chestnuts, 8-ounce can crushed pineapple in juice, celery, 4 ounces fat-free mayonnaise.

CHICKEN-BROCCOLI PITA POCKET

EASY - DO AHEAD

ingredients:
6 fat-free pita pockets
3/4 lb. fat-free chicken tenders, cooked and chopped
8 oz. low-fat cream of chicken soup
1 cup frozen chopped broccoli, thawed and drained
2 tbsp. chopped green chilies

directions:
Preheat oven to 350 degrees. Line baking sheet with foil and lightly spray with nonfat cooking spray. Arrange chicken tenders on baking sheet in single layer. Bake in oven 12-15 minutes until no longer pink and cooked through; remove from oven and chop into bite-size pieces. Cut pita pockets in half; slightly separate to open, but do not cut through. Wrap pitas in foil and heat in oven 5 minutes until warmed. Combine chicken, soup, broccoli and chilies in medium saucepan; cook over medium heat until mixture begins to boil. Remove from heat; stuff into warm pita pockets and serve. Chicken and soup mixture can also be heated in microwave. Pitas can also be prepared ahead of time, refrigerated, and served cold.

Serves: 6

Nutrition per Serving		Exchanges
Calories	187	1 starch
Carbohydrate	26 grams	2 vegetable
Cholesterol	36 milligrams	1 1/2 meat
Dietary Fiber	2 grams	
Fat	< 1 gram	
Protein	17 grams	
Sodium	544 milligrams	

Shopping List: fat-free pita pockets, 3/4 pound fat-free chicken tenders, 8 ounces low-fat cream of chicken soup, frozen chopped broccoli, chopped green chilies.

5 INGREDIENTS OR LESS

CRISPY OVEN-FRIED CHICKEN

EASY - DO AHEAD - FREEZE

---

ingredients:
1/2 cup egg substitute
1 cup evaporated skim milk
3 cups cornflake crumbs
2 tbsp. Montreal chicken seasoning (Schilling)
1 1/2 lb. fat-free chicken breasts

directions:
Preheat oven to 400 degrees. Line baking sheet with foil and lightly spray with nonfat cooking spray. Combine egg substitute and milk in a shallow baking dish. Combine cornflake crumbs and seasoning in a large plastic bag; shake until blended. Dip chicken in egg mixture; place in plastic bag and shake until coated with crumbs. Arrange in single layer on baking sheet; sprinkle with remaining crumbs. Bake in preheated oven 35-40 minutes until browned and cooked through.

Serves: 6

Nutrition per Serving		Exchanges
Calories	313	2 1/2 starch
Carbohydrate	38 grams	3 1/2 meat
Cholesterol	73 milligrams	
Dietary Fiber	0 grams	
Fat	< 1 gram	
Protein	32 grams	
Sodium	1062 milligrams	

Shopping List: 4 ounces egg substitute, 8 ounces evaporated skim milk, cornflake crumbs, Montreal chicken seasoning (Schilling), 1 1/2 pound fat-free chicken breasts.

5 INGREDIENTS OR LESS

FRUIT-GLAZED
CHICKEN TENDERS

EASY - DO AHEAD

ingredients: 1 1/2 lb. fat-free chicken tenders
3/4 cup fat-free Italian salad dressing
1 tbsp. ground ginger
1 tsp. garlic powder
1/3 cup apricot preserves

directions: Combine salad dressing, ginger and garlic powder in a small bowl; mix until blended. Place
chicken tenders in shallow baking dish; pour dressing mix over chicken and toss until well coated.
Cover and refrigerate 3-6 hours. Preheat broiler on
high heat. Line baking sheet with foil and lightly
spray with nonfat cooking spray. Remove chicken
from marinade and arrange on baking sheet. Pour
1/2 cup marinade into small saucepan and bring
to a boil over high heat. Reduce heat to medium-
low; stir in preserves until melted and blended.
Brush chicken with half the sauce; broil 5 minutes.
Turn chicken, brush with remaining sauce and
broil 5-6 minutes until no longer pink. Serve over
cooked rice.

Serves: 6

Nutrition per Serving
(Does not include rice)

Calories	173
Carbohydrate	17 grams
Cholesterol	71 milligrams
Dietary Fiber	< 1 gram
Fat	< 1 gram
Protein	23 grams
Sodium	395 milligrams

Exchanges

1 fruit
3 meat

5 INGREDIENTS OR LESS

Shopping List: 1 1/2 pounds fat-free chicken tenders, 6 ounces
fat-free Italian salad dressing, apricot preserves,
ground ginger, garlic powder.

ITALIAN CHICKEN
SKILLET DINNER

EASY - DO AHEAD

ingredients: 1 pound fat-free chicken tenders, cubed
3 medium potatoes, cut in 1/2-inch cubes
1 cup frozen pepper strips
28 oz. fat-free pasta sauce with peppers and
    mushrooms
1 1/2 tsp. Italian seasoning

directions: Lightly spray large nonstick skillet with nonfat
cooking spray. Add chicken to skillet and cook 5
minutes until beginning to brown. Add potatoes
and peppers; cook 5-7 minutes, stirring frequently.
Pour pasta sauce into skillet; sprinkle Italian seasoning over sauce and stir to mix. Increase heat to
high and bring to a boil. Immediately reduce heat
to medium-low, cover, and simmer 30-35 minutes
until chicken and potatoes are tender.

Serves: 6

Nutrition per Serving		Exchanges
Calories	195	3 vegetable
Carbohydrate	28 grams	1 starch
Cholesterol	47 milligrams	1 meat
Dietary Fiber	2 grams	
Fat	< 1 gram	
Protein	18 grams	
Sodium	593 milligrams	

Shopping List: 1 1/2 pounds fat-free chicken tenders, 3 medium
potatoes, 28 ounces fat-free pasta sauce, frozen
pepper strips, Italian seasoning.

SLOPPY TURKEY JOES

EASY - DO AHEAD - FREEZE

ingredients: 1 lb. fat-free ground turkey
1 tbsp. onion powder
1 1/2 cups barbecue sauce
6 fat-free sourdough English muffins

directions: Lightly spray large nonstick skillet with nonfat cooking spray. Combine turkey and onion powder in skillet and cook over medium heat until turkey is no longer pink and is cooked through. Pour barbecue sauce into skillet and mix with turkey. Bring to a boil over medium-high heat; reduce heat to low, cover, and simmer 20 minutes. Toast English muffins; serve sloppy joes over toasted muffins.

Serves: 6

Nutrition per Serving		Exchanges
Calories	284	3 starch
Carbohydrate	49 grams	1 meat
Cholesterol	27 milligrams	
Dietary Fiber	1 gram	
Fat	< 1 gram	
Protein	15 grams	
Sodium	1716 milligrams	

Shopping List: 1 pound fat-free ground turkey, 12 ounces barbecue sauce, onion powder, fat-free sourdough English muffins.

5 INGREDIENTS OR LESS

303

SWEET AND SOUR CHICKEN

EASY

ingredients: 1 1/2 lb. fat-free chicken tenders
16 oz. package frozen pepper strips
8 oz. pineapple chunks in juice, drained
1 3/4 cups sweet and sour sauce
3 cups fat-free cooked rice

directions: Prepare rice according to package directions (for quick preparation use Minute Rice) and keep warm. Lightly spray large nonstick skillet with nonfat cooking spray and heat over medium-high heat. Add chicken to skillet; stir-fry 5 minutes until chicken begins to brown. Add peppers, pineapple and sauce to skillet. Cook over medium heat, stirring frequently, until chicken is no longer pink. Stir in rice and mix well.

Serves: 8

Nutrition per Serving

		Exchanges
Calories	233	1 fruit
Carbohydrate	37 grams	1 vegetable
Cholesterol	53 milligrams	1 starch
Dietary Fiber	2 grams	2 meat
Fat	< 1 gramFat < 1 gram	
Protein	19 grams	
Sodium	379 milligrams	

Shopping List: 1 1/2 pounds fat-free chicken tenders, 16-ounce package frozen pepper strips, 8-ounce can pineapple chunks in juice, 14 ounces sweet and sour sauce, Minute Rice.

TURKEY SCALLOPINI

EASY

---

ingredients: 1 1/2 lb. fat-free turkey cutlets
1 1/2 tbsp. lemon pepper
1 tbsp. paprika
3 tbsp. lemon juice
3/8 cup water

directions: Lightly spray large nonstick skillet with nonfat cooking spray and heat over medium-high heat. Pound turkey cutlets until flattened. Sprinkle with lemon pepper and paprika. Cook 3-4 minutes in skillet; turn cutlets over and cook 4-5 minutes until no longer pink and cooked through. Remove turkey from skillet and keep warm. Add lemon juice and water to skillet; cook over medium heat, stirring constantly, until heated through. Spoon sauce over turkey cutlets and serve.

Serves: 6

Nutrition per Serving

Calories	106	
Carbohydrate	5 grams	
Cholesterol	41 milligrams	
Dietary Fiber	0 grams	
Fat	< 1 gram	
Protein	16 grams	
Sodium	456 milligrams	

Exchanges
1/3 fruit
2 1/2 meat

Shopping List: 1 pound fat-free turkey cutlets, lemon pepper, paprika, lemon juice.

5 INGREDIENTS OR LESS

BARBECUED SHRIMP AND PEPPER KABOBS

EASY - DO AHEAD

ingredients: 1 1/2 lb. medium fat-free shrimp
1 medium green bell pepper, cut in 1-inch pieces
1 medium red bell pepper, cut in 1-inch pieces
1/2 cup barbecue sauce
1 1/2 cups basmati rice

directions: Cook rice according to package directions; set aside and keep warm. Preheat broiler on high heat. Line baking sheet with foil and lightly spray with nonfat cooking spray. Arrange shrimp and peppers on metal skewers; broil 3-4 inches from heat for 3-4 minutes. Remove from oven; brush generously with barbecue sauce and broil 3-4 minutes until shrimp turn pink and curl. Serve over rice.

Serves: 6

Nutrition per Serving		Exchanges
Calories	309	1 starch
Carbohydrate	60 grams	3 vegetable
Cholesterol	13 milligrams	1 meat
Dietary Fiber	1 gram	2 fruit
Fat	< 1 gram	
Protein	16 grams	
Sodium	923 milligrams	

Shopping List: 1 1/2 pounds medium fat-free shrimp, 1 green bell pepper, 1 red bell pepper, 4 ounces barbecue sauce, 9-ounce package basmati rice.

MEXICAN COD WITH RICE

EASY - DO AHEAD

ingredients: 1 1/2 lb. cod fillets
1 1/2 cups garden-style salsa
1/2 cup fat-free finely-shredded Mexican cheese
9 oz. Spanish rice

directions: Cook rice according to package directions (do not add butter); set aside and keep warm. Preheat oven to 425 degrees. Lightly spray shallow baking dish with nonfat cooking spray. Arrange fish fillets in dish; pour salsa over top. Cover dish with foil and bake in preheated oven 20-25 minutes, until fish flakes easily. Remove from oven; sprinkle with cheese and bake 5-10 minutes until cheese is melted and lightly browned. Serve over rice.

Serves: 6

Nutrition per Serving

Calories	258
Carbohydrate	34 grams
Cholesterol	50 milligrams
Dietary Fiber	1 gram
Fat	< 1 gram
Protein	26 grams
Sodium	765 milligrams

Exchanges

2 starch
1 vegetable
2 1/2 meat

Shopping List: 1 1/2 pounds cod fillets, 12 ounces garden-style salsa, 2 ounces fat-free finely-shredded Mexican cheese, 9-ounce package Spanish rice.

5 INGREDIENTS OR LESS

MUSHROOM RICE

EASY - DO AHEAD

ingredients: 3 cups fat-free Minute Rice, uncooked
1 cup low-fat cream of chicken soup
2 cups fat-free chicken broth
1 cup canned sliced mushrooms

directions: Combine cream of chicken soup and chicken broth in medium saucepan; bring to a boil over high heat. Add rice and mushrooms, cover, and let stand 5 minutes. Fluff with a fork and serve.

Serves: 6

Nutrition per Serving		Exchanges
Calories	191	2 starch
Carbohydrate	40 grams	1 vegetable
Cholesterol	1 milligram	
Dietary Fiber	2 grams	
Fat	< 1 gram	
Protein	4 grams	
Sodium	465 milligrams	

Shopping List: Minute Rice, 8 ounces low-fat cream of chicken soup, 16 ounces fat-free chicken broth, 8-ounce can sliced mushrooms.

5 INGREDIENTS OR LESS

ANGEL HAIR PASTA WITH ITALIAN COD FILLETS

EASY - DO AHEAD

ingredients:
1 1/2 lb. cod fillets
1 1/2 cups fat-free pasta sauce
1/3 cup fat-free Parmesan cheese
8 oz. fat-free angel hair pasta

directions:
Cook pasta according to package directions; drain well and keep warm. Preheat oven to 425 degrees. Lightly spray baking dish with nonfat cooking spray. Arrange fish in dish; pour sauce over top. Cover baking dish with foil and bake in preheated oven 20-25 minutes, until fish flake easily with a fork. Remove foil; sprinkle with cheese and bake 5-10 minutes until cheese is lightly browned. Serve over cooked pasta.

Serves: 6

Nutrition per Serving		Exchanges
Calories	229	2 vegetable
Carbohydrate	27 grams	1 starch
Cholesterol	49 milligrams	3 meat
Dietary Fiber	1 gram	
Fat	< 1 gram	
Protein	27 grams	
Sodium	283 milligrams	

Shopping List: 1 1/2 pounds cod fillets, 12-ounce jar fat-free pasta sauce, fat-free Parmesan cheese, 8 ounces fat-free angel hair pasta.

5 INGREDIENTS OR LESS

SEAFOOD PASTA

EASY

ingredients: 12 oz. fat-free angel hair pasta
12 oz. canned crabmeat, drained
8 oz. low-fat cream of celery soup
1/3 c. fat-free Parmesan cheese

directions: Cook pasta according to package directions and drain well; set aside and keep warm. Heat soup in microwave or small saucepan until heated through. Combine pasta, crabmeat and soup in large serving bowl; toss with Parmesan cheese and serve.

Serves: 6

Nutrition per Serving

Calories	236	
Carbohydrate	38 grams	
Cholesterol	70 milligrams	
Dietary Fiber	2 grams	
Fat	< 1 gram	
Protein	20 grams	
Sodium	482 milligrams	

Exchanges
2 starch
2 meat

Shopping List: 12 ounces fat-free angel hair pasta, 12 ounces canned crabmeat, 8 ounces low-fat cream of celery soup, fat-free Parmesan cheese.

RED AND WHITE MACARONI

EASY - DO AHEAD - FREEZE

ingredients:
12 oz. macaroni, cooked and drained
12 oz. fat-free pasta sauce
1 tsp. Italian seasoning
12 oz. fat-free finely-shredded mozzarella
    cheese

directions:
Cook macaroni according to package directions; drain well and keep warm. Preheat oven to 375 degrees. Lightly spray 10-inch baking dish with nonfat cooking spray. Combine pasta sauce and Italian seasoning in small saucepan or microwave-safe dish; cook until heated through. Combine pasta and sauce in baking dish; sprinkle with cheese. Bake in preheated oven 5-7 minutes, just until cheese is melted.

Serves: 6

Nutrition per Serving

Calories	322
Carbohydrate	47 grams
Cholesterol	0 milligrams
Dietary Fiber	2 grams
Fat	< 1 gram
Protein	26 grams
Sodium	586 milligrams

Exchanges
2 1/2 starch
2 vegetable
2 meat

Shopping List: 12 ounces macaroni, 12 ounces fat-free pasta sauce, 12 ounces fat-free finely-shredded mozzarella cheese, Italian seasoning.

5 INGREDIENTS OR LESS

BEAN AND CHEESE NACHOS

EASY - DO AHEAD

---

ingredients:
2 cups fat-free spicy refried beans
3/4 cup salsa
2 cups fat-free finely-shredded Mexican cheese
2 tbsp. sliced jalapeño peppers
6 oz. low-fat tortilla chips

directions:
Preheat oven to 450 degrees. Line baking sheet with foil and lightly spray with nonfat cooking spray. Arrange chips in a single layer on baking sheet. Combine beans and salsa in a medium bowl; mix well. Spread mixture over chips; top with cheese and jalapeños. Bake in preheated oven 5-10 minutes until cheese is melted and lightly browned.

Serves: 8

Nutrition per Serving		Exchanges
Calories	193	2 starch
Carbohydrate	31 grams	1 meat
Cholesterol	1 milligram	
Dietary Fiber	6 grams	
Fat	< 1 gram	
Protein	15 grams	
Sodium	708 milligrams	

Shopping List: 16 ounces fat-free spicy refried beans, 6 ounces salsa, 8 ounces fat-free finely-shredded Mexican cheese, 4-ounce can sliced jalapeño peppers, 6 ounces low-fat tortilla chips.

CHILI-CHEESE TORTILLA ROLL-UP

EASY - DO AHEAD

ingredients:
6 fat-free flour tortillas
1 1/2 cups fat-free chili with beans
1 1/2 cups finely-shredded Mexican cheese
3/4 cup salsa, optional

directions:
Preheat oven to 350 degrees. Wrap tortillas in foil; heat in oven 5-7 minutes until heated through. Place chili in small saucepan or microwave-safe dish and cook until heated through. Spoon 1/4 cup chili into center of each tortilla; sprinkle with 1/4 cup cheese. Fold and roll tortillas. Wrap chili tortillas in foil and bake in oven 5-7 minutes until cheese is melted. Serve with salsa, if desired.

Serves: 6

Nutrition per Serving		Exchanges
Calories	193	2 starch
Carbohydrate	32 grams	1 meat
Cholesterol	1 milligram	
Dietary Fiber	3 grams	
Fat	< 1 gram	
Protein	16 grams	
Sodium	655 milligrams	

Shopping List: fat-free flour tortillas, 16 ounces fat-free chili with beans, 6 ounces fat-free finely-shredded Mexican cheese, salsa.

5 INGREDIENTS OR LESS

CREAMY MASHED POTATOES

EASY

ingredients:
2 lb. baking potatoes, peeled and cubed
3/4 cup fat-free sour cream
1/3 cup skim milk, warmed
1/4 cup chopped green onions

directions:
Place potatoes in 4-quart saucepan and cover with water; bring to a boil over high heat. Reduce heat to low, cover, and simmer 12-15 minutes until potatoes are tender. Drain well. Place potatoes in large mixing bowl. Using potato masher or fork, mash potatoes until smooth. Stir in sour cream, milk and chives; mix well. Serve immediately.

Serves: 6

Nutrition per Serving
Calories	151
Carbohydrate	32 grams
Cholesterol	< 1 milligram
Fat	< 1 gram
Dietary Fiber	2 grams
Protein	5 grams
Sodium	32 milligrams

Exchanges
2 starch

Shopping List: 2 pounds baking potatoes, 6 ounces fat-free sour cream, skim milk, green onions.

HONEY-MUSTARD
POTATOES

EASY - DO AHEAD

ingredients: 6 large baking potatoes, peeled and sliced
1 cup fat-free honey dijon dressing
1/4 tsp. pepper

directions: Preheat oven to 375 degrees. Line baking sheet(s) with foil and lightly spray with nonfat cooking spray. Place potato slices in Dutch oven and cover with water; bring to a boil over medium-high heat. Cook 10-15 minutes until potatoes are tender; drain well. Return potatoes to pan; add salad dressing and pepper. Toss until potatoes are well coated. Spread potatoes on baking sheet(s) and bake in preheated oven 20-25 minutes until browned.

Serves: 6

Nutrition per Serving

		Exchanges
Calories	188	2 1/2 starch
Carbohydrate	43 grams	
Cholesterol	0 milligrams	
Dietary Fiber	4 grams	
Fat	< 1 gram	
Protein	3 grams	
Sodium	368 milligrams	

Shopping List: 6 baking potatoes, 8 ounces fat-free honey dijon salad dressing, pepper.

MEXICAN STUFFED POTATOES

EASY - DO AHEAD

ingredients: 6 large baking potatoes
1 lb. fat-free ground turkey
1 tbsp. chili/barbecue seasoning
3/4 cup fat-free salsa
1/2 cup fat-free finely-shredded Mexican cheese

directions: Preheat oven to 450 degrees. Prick potatoes with fork; bake in preheated oven 1 hour until cooked through (or microwave on High 25-30 minutes until cooked through). Cool potatoes until easy to handle; cut in half lengthwise. Scoop out potato pulp, leaving 1/4-inch around edges; mash potato pulp. Lightly spray large nonstick skillet and heat over medium-high heat. Add turkey to skillet; sprinkle with seasoning and cook over medium-high heat until turkey is no longer pink and is cooked through. Drain turkey in colander. Add turkey and salsa to mashed potato pulp and mix until blended. Line baking sheet with foil and lightly spray with nonfat cooking spray. Spoon potato mixture into potato shells; sprinkle with cheese and place on baking sheet. Bake potatoes 10-15 minutes until cheese is melted and potatoes are heated through.

Serves: 6

Nutrition per Serving		Exchanges
Calories	237	2 starch
Carbohydrate	39 grams	2 vegetable
Cholesterol	27 milligrams	1 meat
Dietary Fiber	4 grams	
Fat	< 1 gram	
Protein	17 grams	
Sodium	590 milligrams	

Shopping List: 6 large baking potatoes, 1 pound fat-free ground turkey, 6 ounces salsa, 2 ounces fat-free finely-shredded Mexican cheese, chili/barbecue seasoning (or use combination of chili powder, paprika, red pepper, brown sugar, cumin and ginger).

SIMPLE STUFFING

EASY - DO AHEAD - FREEZE

ingredients: 1 lb. fat-free French bread, cut into cubes
1 cup chopped cranberries
3 tbsp. brown sugar
3 tbsp. orange juice
1 1/4 cups fat-free chicken broth

directions: Preheat oven to 350 degrees. Lightly spray 9x13-inch baking dish with nonfat cooking spray. Combine all ingredients in large mixing bowl; toss until ingredients are moistened. Spoon into prepared dish, cover with foil and bake in preheated oven, 30-35 minutes. Remove foil and bake 5-10 minutes until stuffing is lightly browned.

Serves: 8

Nutrition per Serving		Exchanges
Calories	190	2 starch
Carbohydrate	40 grams	2/3 fruit
Cholesterol	0 milligrams	
Dietary Fiber	2 grams	
Fat	< 1 gram	
Protein	6 grams	
Sodium	402 milligrams	

Shopping List: 1 pound fat-free French bread, 8 ounces cranberries, 10 ounces fat-free chicken broth, brown sugar, orange juice.

5 INGREDIENTS OR LESS

BERRY FRUIT PARFAIT

EASY - DO AHEAD - FREEZE

ingredients: 16 oz. frozen mixed berries, thawed and drained
3 tbsp. lemon juice
1 1/2 cups fat-free Cool Whip
1 1/2 cups fat-free mixed berry yogurt
1/2 cup fat-free granola

directions: Combine berries and lemon juice in blender or food processor; process until smooth. Pour mixture into bowl and freeze. Combine Cool Whip and yogurt in large bowl; mix until blended. Spoon yogurt mixture into 6-8 cup glass bowl; spread to smooth. Sprinkle granola over yogurt mixture; pour berry blend over granola. Freeze several hours before serving. Top with additional Cool Whip and sliced strawberries for garnish, if desired.

Serves: 6

Nutrition per Serving

Calories	108
Carbohydrate	23 grams
Cholesterol	1 milligram
Dietary Fiber	2 grams
Fat	< 1 gram
Protein	3 grams
Sodium	41 milligrams

Exchanges
1/2 milk
1 fruit

Shopping List: 16 ounces frozen mixed berries, 12 ounces fat-free Cool Whip, 12 ounces fat-free mixed berry yogurt, fat-free granola, lemon juice.

5 INGREDIENTS OR LESS

318

CHOCOLATE RASPBERRY BROWNIES

EASY - DO AHEAD - FREEZE

ingredients:
18 oz. package fat-free brownie mix
3/4 cup fat-free vanilla yogurt
1/2 cup mixed berry applesauce
1/2 cup frozen raspberries
1/4 cup fat-free chocolate-raspberry sauce

directions:
Preheat oven to 350 degrees. Lightly spray 9-inch baking dish with nonfat cooking spray. In a large bowl, combine brownie mix, yogurt and applesauce; mix until blended smooth. Fold in raspberries. Spread batter into prepared pan and bake in preheated oven 30-35 minutes, until knife inserted in center comes out clean. Cool completely; cut into squares and drizzle with chocolate-raspberry sauce.

Serves: 16

Nutrition per Serving		Exchanges
Calories	140	1 starch
Carbohydrate	33 grams	1 fruit
Cholesterol	0 milligrams	
Dietary Fiber	< 1 gram	
Fat	< 1 gram	
Protein	1 gram	
Sodium	189 milligrams	

Shopping List: 18-ounce package fat-free brownie mix, 6 ounces fat-free vanilla yogurt, 4 ounces mixed berry applesauce, frozen raspberries, 4 ounces fat-free chocolate raspberry sauce.

5 INGREDIENTS OR LESS

CINNAMON-APPLE KABOBS

EASY

ingredients: 6 large Granny Smith apples, cut in chunks
1/4 cup reconstituted Butter Buds
1/4 cup sugar
1 tbsp. cinnamon

directions: Preheat oven to 400 degrees. Line baking sheet with foil and lightly spray with nonfat cooking spray. Combine sugar and cinnamon in small bowl and mix until blended. Arrange apple chunks on baking sheet; drizzle with Butter Buds and sprinkle with cinnamon-sugar mixture. Bake in prepared oven 10-15 minutes until softened. Serve over fat-free frozen yogurt, if desired.

Serves: 6

Nutrition per Serving		**Exchanges**
Calories	132	2 fruit
Carbohydrate	34 grams	
Cholesterol	0 milligrams	
Dietary Fiber	4 grams	
Protein	< 1 gram	
Fat	< 1 gram	
Sodium	170 milligrams	

Shopping List: 6 large Granny Smith apples, Butter Buds, sugar, cinnamon.

RASPBERRY-PEACH SORBET

EASY - DO AHEAD - FREEZE

ingredients: 32 oz. raspberry-flavored peach slices
                   1/4 cup lemon juice

directions: Freeze canned fruit 24 hours until frozen solid. Fill
                   bowl with very hot water; place can in water 1-2
                   minutes. Open can and pour into food processor
                   or blender; process until smooth. Add lemon juice
                   and process until completely blended. Serve im-
                   mediately, or cover and freeze.

                   Serves: 6

Nutrition per Serving   **Exchanges**
Calories   114   2 fruit
Carbohydrate   31 grams
Cholesterol   0 milligrams
Dietary Fiber   1 gram
Fat   < 1 gram
Protein   1 gram
Sodium   9 milligrams

Shopping List: 32 ounces canned fruit in syrup, 2 ounces lemon
                   juice.

5 INGREDIENTS OR LESS

YOGURT POPS

EASY - DO AHEAD - FREEZE

ingredients: 3 oz. raspberry-lemonade frozen concentrate
1 cup fat-free vanilla yogurt

directions: Combine juice concentrate and yogurt in a food processor or blender, and process until smooth. Pour into popsicle containers or paper cups (insert wooden sticks if desired) and freeze 4-6 hours until frozen solid.

Serves: 8

Nutrition per Serving		Exchanges
Calories	32	1/2 fruit
Carbohydrate	9 grams	
Cholesterol	1 milligram	
Dietary Fiber	< 1 gram	
Fat	< 1 gram	
Protein	1 gram	
Sodium	18 milligrams	

Shopping List: frozen raspberry-lemonade concentrate*, 8 ounces fat-free vanilla yogurt.

*substitute other varieties of juice concentrate and yogurt.

ROLL yourself thin

in **12** minutes...

▼ **Shape your body in 12 minutes a day**

▼ **Exercises you can do anywhere**

▼ **Jyl's fat free secrets**

▼ **Healthful hints**

by Jyl Steinback

This exercise program is intended for people in good health. If you have a medical condition, or experience problems with your neck, shoulders, back, joints, muscles or are pregnant, you should consult your physician before performing any stretching or exercises in this book.

If you have had total hip replacement regardless of your age, these exercises are NOT recommended for you.

All guidelines and warnings should be read carefully. The author and publisher cannot accept responsibility for injuries or damage arising out of a failure to check with your physician.

We believe for best results these exercises should be performed on a carpeted floor. If this is uncomfortable or if you have problems with your shoulder, neck or other muscle pains, then perform these exercises on a padded mat or foam rubber with your doctor's permission.

ROLL
yourself
thin

in twelve minutes

by
Jyl Steinback

contents

ROLL yourself thin **in twelve minutes**

Fat Free Living
Six Step Lifestyle
Program

"Give me your body for twelve minutes a day and I can assure you that you will lose pounds and inches by following the advice I've put together in this book in approximately one month."

Aerobic Exercise (swimming, walking, running, inline skating, biking, stair climbing machines, etc.)
▼ Twenty minutes three times per week. ▼ Means "with oxygen" and enhances the size and strength of muscles.
▼ Do not overdo.

Anaerobic Exercise
▼ Means "without oxygen" ▼ Weight training and band resistance ▼ Enhances the size and hardness of a muscle
▼ Twenty minutes, three times a week ▼ Listen to your body and work hard

Nutrition
▼ Limit the fat in your diet to no more than 20% of your total calories. ▼ Limit the sugar and salt in your diet.
▼ Consume more fiber (fruits & vegetables) and eat balanced meals. ▼ Drink six to eight, eight ounce glasses of water per day.

THIS PROMISE IS MADE TO YOU ON THE DAY YOU EMBRACE OUR HEALTHY LIFESTYLE PROGRAM. IT IS A SIMPLE NON DEMANDING PROGRAM WHICH CONSISTS OF THE BASIC ELEMENTS WHICH WHEN INCORPORATED INTO YOUR LIFESTYLE WILL PRODUCE A HEALTHIER YOU.

• •

Stretching

▼ Make stretching a daily habit, especially before and after exercise. ▼ Stretch slowing and hold each stretch for thirty seconds (don't bounce). ▼ Stretching reduces muscle tension, promotes circulation, and prevents injury.

Meditation

▼ Five minutes or more per day. ▼ Find a positive beautiful part of your body and be thankful for that as well as the other things in your life. ▼ Meditation is a way to recharge your energy and is "your" time.

Commitment

▼ The key to any success is commitment. ▼ Set realistic achievable goals. ▼ Listen to your body. ▼ It takes twenty-one days to make a habit and thirty days to establish a lifestyle. *You can do it!*

• •

With those ideas now a part of your life, **Roll Yourself Thin in Twelve Minutes** will tone and strengthen your body in twelve minutes a day. You will lose inches in the places your desire and a new you will emerge.

Frequently Asked Questions

Q&A *What is pelvic tilt?*

To relieve tension in your lower back, tighten your buttock muscle and place the small of the back to the floor by tilting the pelvic up and keeping the stomach muscles tight and firm. Now flatten the lower back to the floor a little more.

Q&A *When will I see results with Roll Yourself Thin in 12 Minutes A Day?*

In one month your will see wonderful results as long as you are following all of my lifestyle tips. You will lose pounds and inches. (No Cheating)

Q&A *What if I can't start out with 12 minutes a day, will I get results or shouldn't I even try doing the exercises?*

Start out slow, if you are new to exercise and you want to roll yourself thin, start out with two to five rolls per exercise and see how you feel the next day. If you have no problems or soreness than add an extra roll a day until you can do one minute of each exercise a minimum of three times per week. REMINDER: LESS IS BETTER AND SLOW IS BEST!

Q&A *What if I can't touch my hand in some of the rolls or reach my elbows to my knee?*

That is perfectly OK. Again do what you can without stress or strain to your body. It's a great stretch and it should feel good to your body so enjoy.

Q&A *What if my neck and shoulders hurt on the sitting up rolls?*

Take it slow. You may need to strengthen the shoulder and neck muscles which is why I suggest you skip these exercises and add the two additional exercises at the end which I added for people like you. Hand to Toe Roll and Elbow to Toe Roll. These two are less stressful to the neck and shoulders and can be performed until you are able to add the other two exercises to your program. Your body will tell when you overdo or when you're ready to go on, so listen closely to your body.

Q&A *I was so sore the next day. Did I do something wrong?*

You probably did too much. Remember start out slow and gradually build up to 12 minutes. To me less is better. These exercises are not intended to cause pain, so if you're experiencing pain slow down and consult your physician.

Stretching

Stretching is an invaluable tool for increasing flexibility, mobility, and preventing injury. It is important to incorporate stretching into a regular routine.

▼ Stretching should be performed in a slow and easy manner with slow controlled breathing

▼ Never bounce

▼ Concentrate on relaxing the arms, shoulders, neck and then the whole body

▼ Focus your attention on the muscles being stretched

▼ Stretching should not be stressful, but rather a means to feeling good

▼ It should be performed before and after exercise for a minimum of five minutes

▼ Stop if you feel pain and do not stretch beyond a comfortable position

A book I suggest is Stretching by Bob Anderson, 800-333-1307. It is very well written and illustrated. ***If stretching is a new exercise for you, please consult your physician before beginning.

1 ROLL & REACH

Position:
▼ Sit tall
▼ Stomach tight
▼ Legs straight in front of you
▼ Both hands behind you, hands out, elbows soft
▼ Relax shoulders

12

Action:
- ▼ Roll your body on to the right hip
- ▼ Lean on to your right arm (relax shoulders)
- ▼ Left foot rolls on top of right foot as rolling
- ▼ Left arm stretches above your head
- ▼ Left elbow close to the (ear) head
- ▼ Be sure to stretch the arm up towards the sky

- ▼ Repeat same action for the left side
- ▼ Repeat for one minute (about 25 repetitions)

Tips:
- ▼ The taller you reach the more the spine is stretched
- ▼ Be sure to hold in your stomach, pelvic tilted
- ▼ Go slow and easy

2 *PENGUIN ROLL*

Position:
▼ Sit tall
▼ Stomach tight
▼ Legs straight in front of you
▼ Both hands behind you, hands out, elbows soft
▼ Relax shoulders

14

Action:
▼ Roll your body on to the right hip
▼ Lean on to your right arm (relax shoulders)
▼ Left foot rolls on top of right foot as you roll
▼ Repeat same action for the left side
▼ Repeat for one minute (about 25 repetitions)

Tips:
▼ Roll like a penguin
▼ Nice and easy, side to side
▼ Tummy tight
▼ Be sure to roll on to your hip
▼ *This is the same rolling position as exercise 1, but without the arms

3 *KNEE ROLL*

Position:
▼ Bend knees and pull your feet close to the buttocks
▼ Both hands behind you, hands out, elbows soft
▼ Relax your shoulders
▼ Stomach tight with your pelvic tilt
▼ Keep knees closely together

Action:

▼ Slowly drop both knees to the right

▼ Return back to center

▼ Drop both knees to the left

▼ Repeat same action for the left side

▼ Repeat for one minute (about 25 repetitions)

Tips:

▼ Hold knees tightly together when rolling side to side

▼ Round the back, stomach tight

▼ Relax your shoulders and neck

4 *WIDE LEG ROLL*

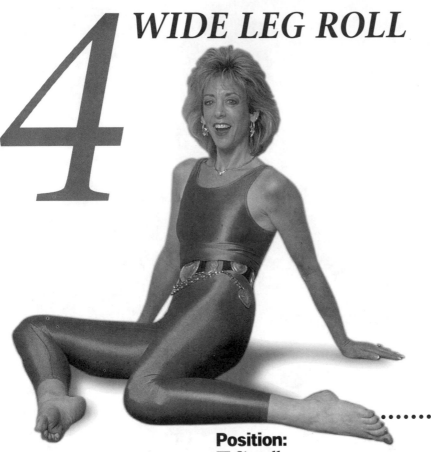

....

Position:
▼ Sit tall
▼ Bend knees pulling your
   feet close to the
   buttocks
▼ Spread your feet as wide
   as you can with your
   feet still on the floor
   (close to the buttocks
   and knees bent)
▼ Both hands behind you,
   elbows slightly bent
▼ Relax your shoulders

Action:
▼ Slowly drop both knees
    to the right
▼ Return both knees back
    to center
▼ Slowly drop both knees
    to the left
▼ Repeat for one minute
    (about 25 repetitions)

Tips:
▼ Relax your shoulders
    and neck
▼ Stomach tight with
    your pelvic tilt
▼ When knees are bent
    they are about 5-6
    inches away from
    your buttocks or a
    comfortable distance

5 KNEE TO CHEST ROLL

1

Position:
▼ Sit tall
▼ Bend knees pulling your feet close to the buttocks
▼ Lean back on both arms for support, elbows soft
▼ Relax your shoulders
▼ Knees held tightly together
▼ Slowly bring both knees to the chest

Action:
▼ Roll both knees to the right dropping to the right hip
▼ Bring both knees back to the center and into the chest, slightly lifting the knees into the chest at the same time
▼ Stomach tight and back rounded
▼ Roll both knees to the left dropping on to the left hip

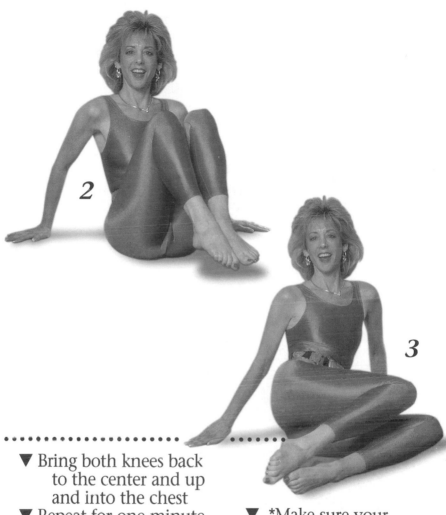

2

3

▼ Bring both knees back
to the center and up
and into the chest
▼ Repeat for one minute
(about 25 repetitions)

Tips:
▼ Knees held tight
together at all times
▼ Keep back rounded
▼ Relax the shoulders
and neck
▼ Relax your arms and keep
elbows slightly bent

▼ *Make sure your
shoulders are relaxed
and rest if your need
to
▼ This exercise is more
difficult than the others
and may require some
repetition to get used
to it
▼ Go slow and easy

6 BUTTOCKS ROLL

Position:
▼ Sit tall
▼ Legs straight in front of you
▼ Lean on your arms behind you for support
▼ Bend your arms and go down to your elbows
▼ Round your back and keep your stomach tight

Action:

▼ Roll to your right hip
▼ Left leg goes on top of the right leg
▼ Straighten left arm as you roll to the right side, elbow soft, this will help push your left side over your right hip
▼ Lean on your right arm and elbow
▼ Left foot should be on top of right foot and held closely together
▼ Return back to center

▼ Repeat same action for left side
▼ Repeat for one minute (about 25 repetitions)

Tips:

▼ Buttocks never leaves the floor
▼ Shoulders and neck are relaxed
▼ *Great for the hips, waist, stomach and legs - one of my favorites

7 *CRISS-CROSS ROLL*

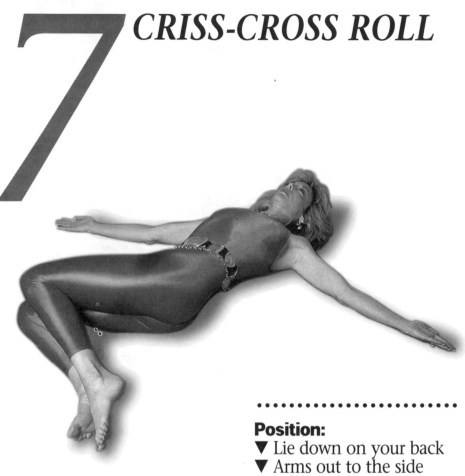

Position:
▼ Lie down on your back
▼ Arms out to the side palms facing up
▼ Arms are slightly below the shoulders
▼ Elbows are slightly bent
▼ Knees bent and close together
▼ Pull feet close to the buttocks

· ·

Action:

▼ Slowly drop both knees to the right
▼ Return both knees back to center
▼ Round the back and pelvic tilt
▼ Slowly drop both knees to the left
▼ Return both knees back to center
▼ Repeat for one minute (about 25 repetitions)

Tips:

▼ Be sure to relax the arms, neck, and shoulders
▼ Hold knees close together at all times
▼ Relax your back
▼ *Don't forget to pelvic tilt between each roll

8 WIDE LEG CRISS-CROSS ROLL

Position:
▼ Lie down on your back
▼ Arms straight out, palms facing up
▼ Arms are slightly below the shoulders
▼ Elbows are slightly bent
▼ Knees bent and feet close to the buttocks
▼ Spread your feet as wide as you can (feet still on the floor close to the buttocks)

Action:
- ▼ Slowly drop both knees to the right
- ▼ Return both knees back to center
- ▼ Pelvic tilt each time your return to center
- ▼ Slowly drop both knees to the left
- ▼ Repeat for one minute (about 25 repetitions)

Tips:
- ▼ Relax your shoulders
- ▼ *Be sure to keep your pelvic tilt each time you return to the center. This will protect your back and strengthen your stomach muscles.

9 SIDE TO SIDE ROLL

2

1

Position:
- ▼ Lie down on your back
- ▼ Arms straight out, palms facing up
- ▼ Arms are slightly below the shoulders
- ▼ Elbows are slightly bent
- ▼ Knees together and over your hips

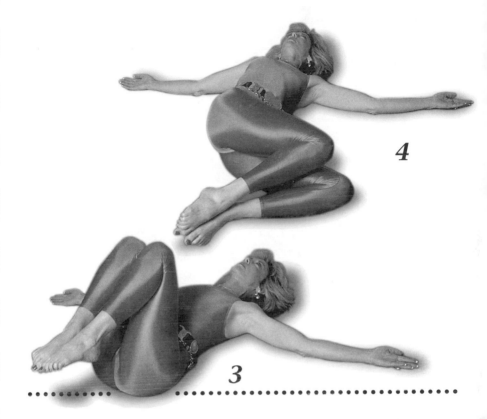

Action:

▼ Slowly drop both knees to the right holding the knees together at all times

▼ Don't touch the floor

▼ Slowly roll back to center, holding knees together

▼ Be sure to keep the small of your back on the floor

▼ Slowly drop both knees to the left

▼ Repeat for one minute (about 25 repetitions)

Tips:

▼ Be sure to keep both elbows on the floor

▼ Be sure to keep the small of your back on the floor when you are in the center and don't arch your back

10 LOVE HANDLE ROLL

2

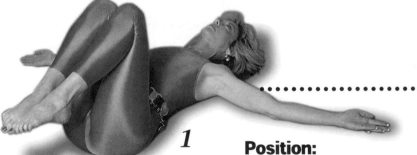

1

Position:
▼ Lie down on your back
▼ Arms straight out, palms facing up
▼ Arms are slightly below the shoulders
▼ Elbows are slightly bent
▼ Knees together and over your hips

30

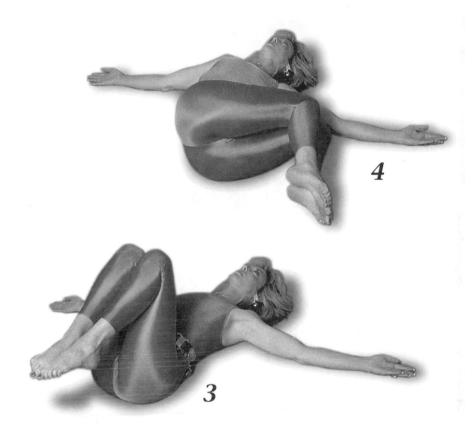

Action:
▼ Bring both knees
   together up to the
   right elbow
▼ Return back to center
   with the small of the
   back on the floor
▼ Bring both knees
   together up to the left
   elbow
▼ Return back to center

Tips:
▼ *This is a fabulous
   exercise for your love
   handles
▼ Be sure each time your
   return to center the
   small of your back is
   on the floor
▼ This will strengthen
   your lower back, and
   stomach muscles

11 *FIGURE EIGHT ROLL*

2

1

Position:
▼ Lie down on your back
▼ Arms straight out,
   palms facing up
▼ Arms are slightly below
   the shoulders
▼ Elbows are slightly bent
▼ Knees together and over
   your hips

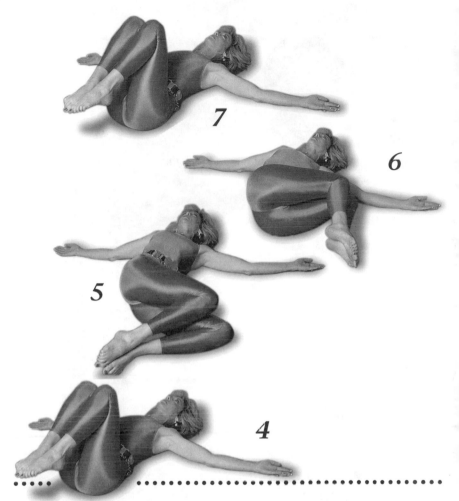

Action:
▼ Slowly drop both knees to the right at hip level
▼ Then bring both knees directly up to the right elbow
▼ Return back to center with the knees over the hips and lower the back to the floor
▼ Repeat same action for the left side

Tips:
▼ *I call this the figure 8 and it is one of my all time favorites because it works everything

12 *LOG ROLL*

Position:
▼ Lie down on your back
▼ Legs straight out
▼ Arms overhead
▼ Small of your back to
    the floor

Action:
▼ Roll your whole body on to your right hip
▼ Left foot on top of right foot
▼ Stop yourself from rolling on to your stomach with your left hand
▼ Right arm still stays over your head
▼ Roll back to center (on your back)
▼ Repeat same motion for left side
▼ Repeat for one minute (about 25 repetitions)

Tips:
▼ Be sure in between each roll to place the small of the back to the floor for a tight firm back and stomach

13 *HAND TO TOE ROLL*

Position:
▼ Lie down on your back
▼ Arms straight out, palms facing up
▼ Arms are slightly below the shoulders
▼ Elbows are slightly bent
▼ Knees bent and feet lose to the buttocks
▼ Drop both knees to the right

Action:
▼ Lift the left foot to touch the right hand
▼ Return to center with knees bent and feet back together on the floor with a pelvic tilt
▼ Repeat same action for left side
▼ Repeat for one minute (about 25 repetitions)

Tips:
▼ *Don't lift the hands off the floor
▼ Don't get discouraged if your foot won't touch your hand, it's new and may take some time to get used to this motion.

14 *ELBOW TO TOE ROLL*

1

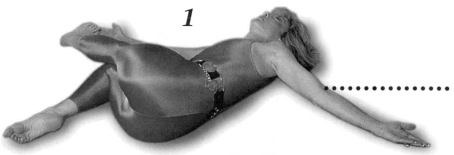

Position:
▼ Lie down on your back
▼ Arms straight out,
  palms facing up
▼ Arms are slightly below
  the shoulders
▼ Elbows are slightly bent
▼ Knees together over
  chest

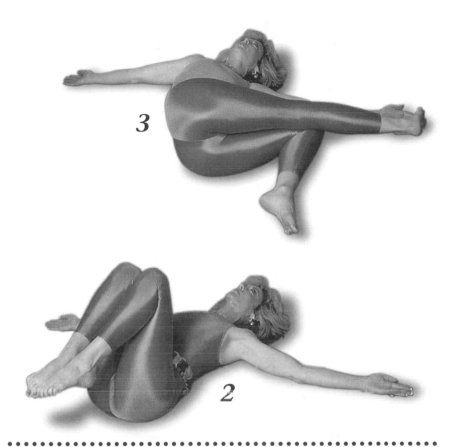

Action:

▼ Roll both knees to the right elbow and lift the left foot to the right hand

▼ Roll back to center with the back to the floor

▼ Repeat same action for left side

▼ Repeat for one minute (about 25 repetitions)

Tips:

▼ *Be sure not to lift either hands from the floor

▼ When you return to center be sure to bring the knees in and up over the chest to work the lower stomach muscles and strengthen your lower back.

The ten basic rules to healthy eating

1 Eat only when hungry.

2 Drink more water.
(six to eight glasses per day).

3 Eat five to six small meals a day.

4 Eat less fat.

5 Eat less sugar.

6 Eat more fiber.

••

7 Eat more water foods.
(fruits & vegetables)

••

8 Eat a balanced diet.

••

9 For women; make sure you
consume enough iron & calcium
(daily requirement 18mg iron & 1000mg calcium).

••

10 Eat slowly.

••

Healthful Hints

· ·

▼ Food is for fuel only. It takes 20 minutes for the mind to tell the stomach it's full, so eat slowly and learn to differentiate from being hungry to just finishing what's on your plate because it tastes good.

▼ Snack on high fiber foods; fruits, air popped popcorn, foods with bran.

▼ Eat five to six small meals per day. (this helps overeating and assists with increasing metabolism)

▼ Wear a tight belt when going out to dinner. (helps avoid overeating)

▼ When going to dinner parties, out to dinner or even to the supermarket never go hungry. Snack on healthful foods before going out.

▼ Bring a healthy dish with you when you visit someone else's home (you then always have something to eat on when you're hungry).

▼ Hug yourself.

▼ Get fat tested.

▼ Take time for yourself daily.

▼ When you feel water retention, drink more water (six to eight, eight ounce glasses per day).

▼ Aerobic exercise three times per week for a minimum of twenty minutes.

▼ Anaerobic exercise three times per week for a minimum of twenty minutes.

▼ Meditate daily.

▼ Learn to enjoy life and have fun!

• •

Jyl's 15 secrets to giving up the fat

▼ Toss cooked pasta with fat free broths instead of oil to prevent sticking

▼ Fat free substitutions to thicken sauces or dressings - Puree fat free cottage cheese or fat free ricotta cheese & substitute for part of the liquid in recipe - Blend one or more tablespoons of mashed potatoes into sauces

▼ Substitute fat free turkey, chicken, or fat free beef crumbles for ground beef in recipes

▼ To thicken soups, add bread crumbs, pureed vegetables or evaporated skim milk

▼ For lean cream sauce, heat a cup of nonfat buttermilk with a tablespoon each of corn-starch & mustard

▼ For baking breads and sweets, substitute fat and oils with apple butter, apple sauce or Lighter Bake (800-447-5218) or 1/2 baby prunes and 1/2 apple butter

▼ Marinate or baste fish or chicken with fruit, vegetable juice or teriyaki sauce to enhance tenderness and flavor

▼ Fruit juices, wine and fat free broths are great additions to steamed vegetables

▼ Steam fresh or frozen vegetables and enhance their flavor with minced garlic, crushed spices, or low sodium teriyaki sauce

▼ Use fat free salsa, fat free flavored mustards or fat free salad dressings instead of mayonnaise or cream sauces for sandwiches, salads or baked potatoes

▼ Coat chicken with fat free sour cream, fat free yogurt, or egg substitution. Roll the chicken in fat free seasoned bread crumbs or seasoned cornflakes crumbs for a simple "unfried" meal. Bake at 400 degrees.

▼ Baked casseroles can be sprinkled with fat free cheese after baking; cheese will melt on the heated food

▼ Use fat free broths (chicken, beef, oriental or vegetable) instead of oil for fried, sauteed, or stir-fried foods

▼ Always use fat free products when available

Index

METRIC CONVERSION GUIDE

U.S. UNITS	CANADIAN METRIC	AUSTRALIAN METRIC
Volume		
1/4 teaspoon	1 mL	1 ml
1/2 teaspoon	2 mL	2 ml
1 teaspoon	5 mL	5 ml
1 tablespoon	15 mL	20 ml
1/4 cup	50 mL	60 ml
1/3 cup	75 mL	80 ml
1/2 cup	125 mL	125 ml
2/3 cup	150 mL	170 ml
3/4 cup	175 mL	190 ml
1 cup	250 mL	250 ml
1 quart	1 liter	1 liter
1 1/2 quarts	1.5 liter	1.5 liter
2 quarts	2 liters	2 liters
2 1/2 quarts	2.5 liters	2.5 liters
3 quarts	3 liters	3 liters
4 quarats	4 liters	4 liters
Weight		
1 ounce	30 grams	30 grams
2 ounces	55 grams	60 grams
3 ounces	85 grams	90 grams
4 ounces (1/4 lb.)	115 grams	125 grams
8 ounces (1/2 lb.)	225 grams	225 grams
16 ounces (1 lb.)	455 grams	500 grams
1 pound	455 grams	1/2 kilogram

Measurements		**Temperatures**	
Inches	**Centimeters**	**Fahrenheit**	**Celsius**
1	2.5	32°	0°
2	5.0	212°	100°
3	7.5	250°	120°
4	10.0	275°	140°
5	12.5	300°	150°
6	15.0	325°	160°
7	17.5	350°	180°
8	20.5	375°	190°
9	23.0	400°	200°
10	25.5	425°	220°
11	28.0	450°	230°
12	30.5	475°	240°
13	33.0	500°	260°
14	35.5		
15	38.0		

Note: The recipes in this cookbook have not been developed or tested using metric measures. When converting recipes to metric, some variations in quality may be noted.

INDEX

Jyl Steinback

While I am fortunate to have a wonderful life, filled with a fabulous family and successes, there was a time in my life I did not like my body. As a result, I was depressed, angry and upset with myself all at the same time.

At that time I was twenty pounds overfat and looked in the mirror and said, "that's it, I can't go on like this. I've got to lose weight and get into shape now." First I changed my eating habits. I no longer would eat any and everything I wanted and made a conscious effort to cut down on fat by eliminating fried and fast foods. I also started counting fat grams and began aerobic exercise 5-6 days a week. The results not only improved my physical appearance, but also gave me a tremendous boost psychologically. I started liking me!

Years later after counting fat grams and doing just aerobic exercise, I came across a "Fat Finder" calculator, which calculates the percentage of fat in foods. This simple tool changed my way of thinking forever. I thought that because the piece of cheese I was buying with two grams of fat and thirty-five calories was a healthy choice, when in fact it was 50% fat. I learned that it's important to know the percentage of fat, and serving size. In other words, read labels very carefully. Preparing fat-free recipes in the home is a simple way to balance dietary habits when faced with having to eat lunches and dinners out. This simple lesson changed my life and initiated my quest to eat fat-free, and help others eat and live healthier with the FAT FREE Living Lifestyle.

This mission has resulted in the writing of six fat-free cookbooks, the development of fat-free bread and pizza crust mixes, a patent on Perfect Body Bands™, elastic exercise bands and countless radio and TV appearances, as well as talks with school kids to teach them how to make healthier food choices.

My next major revolution in my search for a healthy fit body was the incorporation of strength training. This was accomplished with a series of exercises developed over time and now titled **Roll Yourself Thin in 12 Minutes a Day**. It tones the entire body and gives you that last little touch to help fit into those tight jeans. Aerobic exercise and low-fat/fat-free nutrition reduce body fat, where strength training enhances all of your beautiful and natural curves. The first month I started **Roll Yourself Thin in 12 Minutes a Day** I lost a clothing size all over my body. It was so much fun I couldn't believe how simple it was and how little time was needed. This was such a wonderful experience I decided to share this program with all of you. It's simple, quick, and best of all it works.

Let's do it together. Let's give the next thirty days a chance to improve our mind, our body and our soul. You will love the new you for life!